AF538968

Sikhism :
Religion and Culture

Sikhism :
Religion and Culture

Edited by

RATAN SINGH

GLOBAL PUBLICATIONS

NEW DELHI-110 002 (INDIA)

GLOBAL PUBLICATIONS
4378/4B, G-4 JMD House
Murari Lal Street, Ansari Road
Daryaganj, New Delhi - 110 002
Phone : 23278062 (Off.)
e-mail : omega_publications@yahoo.com

Head Office :
79/23, Laxmi Garden
Near Satya Jyoti School,
Gurgaon (Haryana)
Mob : 9213562438

Sikhism : Religion and Culture

First Published : 2011

ISBN : 978-93-80833-21-7

PRINTED IN INDIA

Published by Ishwari Prasad Garg for Global Publications, New Delhi-110 002 and Printed at Suman Printers, Delhi

Preface

Sikhism, the youngest of the world's religions, is barely five hundred years old. Its founder, Guru Nanak, was born in 1469. Guru Nanak spread a simple message of "Ek Onkar": we are all one, created by the One Creator of all Creation. This was at a time when India was being torn apart by castism, sectarianism, religious factions and fanaticism. He aligned with no religion, and respected all religions. He expressed the reality that there is only one God with many paths that lead to Him, and that the Name of God is Truth, "SatNam".

The foundation of Sikhism was laid down by Guru Nanak Dev Ji. Guru Nanak Dev Ji rather than simply passing the Guruship of his teachings onto his own sons (as was the custom at the time) looked for someone to show up who revealed himself as the most deserving of the Guruship. Choosing his replacement he laid his hand upon him and announced him 'Angad'(part of his own body. Subsequently the light of Guruship was passing in the same manner. Passed always to the person who showed himself to be each new Nanak's replacement. The word "Guru" is derived from the root words "Gu", which means darkness or ignorance, and "Ru", which means light or knowledge. Thus, a "Guru" is one who takes a person from darkness of ignorance to the light of knowledge. The "Guru" guides us to experience the Truth (of God).

Guru Nanak's followers were Sikhs (seekers of truth). He taught them to bow only before God, and to link themselves to the Guru, the Light of Truth, who lives always in direct consciousness of God, experiencing no separation. Through words and example, the Guru demonstrates to followers how to experience God within themselves, bringing them from darkness into light. Guru Nanak was a humble bearer of this Light of Truth. He opposed superstition, injustice, and hypocrisy and inspired seekers by singing divine songs which were touched the hearts of the most callous listeners. These songs were recorded, and formed the beginnings of the Sikhs' sacred writings, later to become the "Siri Guru Granth Sahib".

The major topics dealt in this book are : *History of Sikh Gurus; Introduction to Sikhism; Sikhism and Beliefs; Guru Granth Sahib; Sikh Religion and Culture; History of Sikhism; Hinduism and Sikhism; Jainism, Islam and Sikhism; Guru Granth Sahib; Janamsakhis; Sikh and Teachings; Women in Sikhism; Sikh Ethics; etc.*

No doubt, these will serve the purpose of trainees and trainers, professional and policy planners in the field. Since the sources of information are all secondary, we express our gratitude to the scholars whose works are cited or substantially made use of. We are thankful to all those who rendered ready help and cooperation while working on this project.

We express our gratitude to various scholars, teachers and friends for their assistance and guidance. Finally, we thank our publishers for bringing out this book in very limited time.

—Editor

Contents

1

History of Sikh Gurus

The word "Sikh" is derived from the Sanskrit 'shishya' meaning disciple. Sikhs are the disciples of their ten Gurus beginning with Guru Nanak (1469 - 1539) and ending with Guru Gobind Singh (1666 -1708) and their perpetual "living" Guru, the Guru Granth Sahib. There are over 23 million Sikhs in the world today, the vast majority live in the north Indian state of Punjab. Sikhism or Sikhi is the fifth largest organised religion in the world and the youngest.

Sikh Gurus

Guru Nanak (1469-1538)

Guru Nanak, the founder of the Sikh faith, was the son of an official with a small holding of land in a village north-west of Lahore (in present day Pakistan). Guru ji had his elementary education in the local language of the village and as a member of the Khatri caste his father made sure that he was tutored in the village Gurukul in the ancient Sanskrit and knowing well the value to be gained by learning Persian his father enrolled him with a scholar of that language as well. His father intended to train him as an accountant so that he could get a job in the court of the Muslim governor of the district. But Guru Nanak turned out to be indifferent to any attempt to teach him the standard subjects of bussiness. He soon outdistanced his teachers as each found themselves unable to teach him as he had rapidly mastered the languages they had taught him. He roamed the forests around his village engaging in long discourses with holy men both

Hindu and Muslim, who frequented the surrounding jangals, traveling through on their various pilgramages. Mixing with his friends of other castes and religions he was the despair of his parents as he would not attend to family business and spent what ever money they gave him on feeding the poor. When he grew up to be a young man, they arranged a marriage for him. For a time he devoted himself to the care of his wife, and two sons.

Then his search for truth became too over powering, having gone to work for his sister's brother in the stores of a Muslim official he went out one morning to take his usual bath in a local river only to disappear. For three days his friends and his growing cadre of admirers (Sikhs they were called) feared that he had drowned. Some, jealous of his popularity, started the rumor that he had looted his employer's stores and run away. On the third day Nanak reappeared and would only repeat, 'There is no Hindu, there is no Mussulman'. By this statement he was stating that there was no difference between what the the worshippers of the two differing religions - Hinduism and Islam were worshiping, he had realized that there was only one God who was the root of each religion and that service to ones fellow men was the way of realizing their mutual goal of being reunited with God the Father , creator of them all. After arranging for the care of his wife and sons, settling his affairs and quitting his job he and his Muslim friend, a musician named Mardana set out on his first 'Udasi' (travel) preaching as they walked from village to village. Guru ji composed his sermons in ragas (musical modes) which were sung to the accompaniment of Bhai Mardana's Rabab (a simple lute style instrument) with a curved peg tuning board which could hang over Mardana's shoulder as he walked.

Wherever they stopped, Guru Ji's teachings would inspire the people and leave them singing the simple Bani in the fields as they worked. Within a few years these disciples became a homogeneous group whose faith was exclusively the teachings of Guru Nanak Dev Ji. In several trips that covered many years the young Guru traveled all over India. With a second companion a Hindu named Bhai Balla they went as far east as Assam, as far south as Sri Lanka and as far to the north as Tibet. Later Guru Ji traveled westward beyond India to Mecca and Medina in Arabia, from where they returned by foot through Al Sham (Greater Syria), Bagdad, Persia and the land we now call Afganistan. Wherever he went, they sang Guru Nanak's hymns, which told the people that if they wanted to love God they should learn first to love each other and always keep the Name of God on their lips. In a time of brutal oppression, his simple message of one loving God, the equality of men and even women (a radical thought in those days) and a life dedicated to returning to God's Kingdom, not by practising religious austerities, but by living the life of a simple house holder (Gristi Jeevan) building a family and a loving relationship with ones wife and children - to the One God, by ones hard and honest work and even sharing ones blessings with the sick and homeless.

There are countless stories of Guru Nanak Dev Ji's travels. Once Guru Ji came to a river for his morning bath only to find the water full of many Hindus who were, doing the age old Hindu morning ritual of saluting the Sun. Guru Nanak having grown up in a Hindu family knew just what they were up to. They were taking water in their clasped hands and throwing it at the rising Sun. Already well aware of what they were doing and why, the Guru knew that they had never even questioned the age old ritual. He was the sort of teacher that we all have grown up loving and admiring. The ones we all remember from our childhood, the ones that taught by example actually leading us to discover the answers for ourselves, to feel the answer in our soul, rather than using the age old pedantic method of 'do and repeat what I say'. So giving them enough 'rope with which to hang their beliefs' in such rituals (that they had never even dared to question) he asked them what they were doing. They must have thought him mad, or at the least a stranger from some strange land, who had no idea of the important work they were doing.

One person raising the tone of his voice with each word, replied almost in disgust, "we are offering water to our ancestors who have gone to live in the stars near the Sun— their throats are parched and dry from the Sun's great heat! Guru Ji replied, "That sounds like a great idea, let me try". With this Guru Nanak Dev Ji turned in the opposite direction and started tossing handfulls of water towards the west, the crowd was dumbstruck. "What are you doing Fakir Ji?" you are wasting your time, why are you throwing water in the wrong direction. "Why, I am sending water to my parched fields in the Punjab", he said, "if your water can reach the Sun surely mine can reach the Punjab which is only a few hundred miles away". With this the people realised their folly, perhaps for the first time they questioned what they had been doing their whole lives.

Another story tells us of the time that Guru Ji met a very rich and successful man. The man invited Guru Sahib to his large and luxurious home. He had accumulated a vast fortune, no doubt by deceit and foul means and he even boasted of his wealth. He asked Guru ji if there was anything he could do for his guest, such an obvious man of God. Guru Nanak saw a needle on the floor, picked it up and handed it to him, "Please give me this needle in the next world", he said. With a puzzled look on his face the man replied, "How can I do that; One comes into this world with nothing and leaves it with nothing". It was so quiet that you could hear that needle drop to the floor as the man realised that he had wasted his whole life and that none of the wealth he had amassed could be taken to the 'next life.' He fell at Guru Sahib's feet. "Forgive me " he cried.

Guru Nanak Dev Ji's crusade was against intolerance which had become, on one hand the practice of their Muslim overlords bent on converting their Hindu subjects, to earn credits (as their 'good angel' which they all believed was sitting on their right shoulder) toted up their good deeds so they could enter the Kingdom of Heaven and on the other the meaningless rituals and gross discriminations of caste (and gender) which had become an integral part of Hindu life, where in order for some men (the Brahmins) who had written the laws in the first place to have someone to be superior to they had doomed others to lives as pariahs whose shadows, they told others, would pollute those of the higher privileged casts. Innocent men and women and children who were denied any chance at an education (would actually be killed if they were caught trying to read) and forced to do the foulest of tasks with death being their only chance to enter a higher caste.

Guru ji spent the last years of his life with his family in the village he and his followers cleared on some land donated by another of his admirers. The village named Kartarpur (the village of the Creator, God's Village) grew as people heard of this new way of living, where all men and women shared in the work and ate their meals in a communal kitchen (called the Guru ka Langar) with no distinction being made to their former caste. People flocked to the village to hear him sing his hymns. Even today Guru ji is regarded as the symbol of harmony between the Muslims and the Hindus . A popular couplet describes him as:

The teacher Nanak is the King of holy men. The mentor of the Hindus, the religious leader of the Mussulmans.

Guru Nanak Dev Ji had a following of people from both Hinduism and Islam, it was left to his nine successor Gurus to mold that following into a distinct community with its own language, literature, its own religious beliefs and institutions and its own traditions and conventions.

Guru Angad Dev (1504-1552)

Bhai Lehna Ji was a devout Hindu before he met Guru Nanak Dev Ji. At the very first meeting he fell under his spell and abandoned all other worldly businesses to devote himself to the service of the Sikh community at Kartarpur. Guru Nanak Dev Ji set a number of tasks to test his devotees, in all of them Bhai Lehna came out top. In one test Guru Nanak Dev Ji asked for someone to jump into a pool of thick mud and pick out an old cauldren, all refused saying they could get Guru Ji a better one from the local shop, only Bhai Lehna Ji jumped in without regard for his safety and brought the object back.

As time for Guru Nanak Dev Ji to ascend the heavens came, Guru Ji took a journey and said harsh words to any person following him. One by one all left his side. Those remaining were pelted with stones by Guru Ji, all abandoned the Guru except Bhai Lehna Ji. " Why are are you still following me?" Guru Nanak Dev Ji said in harsh tones. "Where else have I got to go?" replied Bhai Lehna Ji "without you O, Lord I have nothing." Guru Nanak Dev Ji took Lehna Ji in his arms, he had found the most worthy person to carry on his work. His devotion convinced Guru Nanak Dev Ji that Bhai Lehna Ji, would be a better leader then his own sons.

Guru Nanak Dev Ji proclaimed "Thou art Angad, a part of my body" and had one of his chief disciples Baba Buddha Ji place the Tilak of authority on (Guru) Angads forehead proclaiming him as the second Guru. Guru Angad Dev Ji was Guru for thirteen years (1539 – 1552). In his quite way Guru Angad Ji expanded the fledgling community, opening more centres and organising a regular system fro collecting offerings. Guru Ji made copies of Guru Nanak Dev Ji's hymns and supplied them to all the centres. The Guru also took the thirty five letters of the alphabet and developed them into the new script now called gurmukhi (*from the* Guru's Mouth). This had far reaching consequences, for the Gurus compilations became the nucleus of the sacred writings of the Sikhs. It gave the Sikhs a written language distinct from those of the Hindus and Muslims.

Guru Sahib Ji was also very keen on physical fitness and instructed all his followers to take part in drills and games after morning service. Under the auspicies of Guru Angad Dev Ji, the Sikh community was growing. Guru Ji had two sons but chose a seventy three year old disciple, Amar Das Ji as his successor. He, as had his predessor, chose service to the community rather than his own sons.

Guru Amar Das (1479- 1574)

Guru Amar Das Ji succession was resented by Guru Angad Dev Ji's son Datu, who ejected Guru Amar Das Ji from Khadur. Guru Ji moved to a town called Gowindwal. Guru Amar Das Ji was a very pious and humble person, once when Datu in a rage kicked Guru Ji, with hands together Guru Amar Ji said humbly " This must have hurt your foot."

Guru Ji showed great devotion and made the langar an integral part of Sikhism insisting that anyone who wanted to see him had first to accept hospitality by eating with the disciples. Among those who came to see Guru Ji was the Emperor Akbar, who was so impressed with the way of life in Gowindwal that he offered the Guru a jagir to support the Guru ka Langar. When the Guru refused the gift the wise Emperor offered the jagir (the revenues of several villages) to Guru Ji's daughter Bhani Ji as a marriage gift. That gift, under the next Gurus grew to be the city of Amrisar with its House of God the HarMandir now called around the world as The Golden Temple.

Guru Ji increased the number of parishes or manjis to twenty two and appointed masands to organise worship and collect the offerings. Copies were made of the hymns of Guru Nanak Dev Ji and Guru Angad Dev Ji and were added to those written by Guru Amar Das Ji. Since this was written in gurmukhi it gained great popularity amongst the masses. Guru Ji also introduced new forms of ceremonies for use at births and deaths.

The Guru rejected the practises of purdha (veiling of women) and of sati (the burning of widows on the funeral pyres of their husbands). This aroused the hostility of the Brahmins who seeing the size of their flocks dwindling started persecuting the Sikhs, they also tried to turn the Emperor against the Guru, but when he refused to take action they bribed local officials to harass the Sikhs. This was the start of Sikh oppression which eventually made them take up arms and break with their Gurus' tradition of Seli or ahimsa (non-violence).

Guru Sahib Ji lived to the age of ninety five, he did not choose any of his sons to succeed him, instead he chose his son-in-law, Ram Das, a Khatri of the Sodhi family.

Guru Ram Das (1534-1581)

Guru Sahib Ji set about looking after the community and commenced the construction of a large tank. This was to be built on land that had been purchased from Emperor Akbar for the sum of 700 Rs. The town that grew up around it was destined to become the capital of the Sikhs and was known as Chak Ram Das. Like his predecessors Guru Ji composed hymns which were later incorporated in the sacred writings. Guru Ji had three sons, of whom he considered the youngest, Arjun Mal the most suited to succeed him. This caused great resentment in the eldest son Prithi Chand. Nevertheless Guru Ji had Baba Buddha Ji invest Arjun Mal as the fifth Guru of the Sikhs. As Guru Ram Das Ji saw his end on this earth coming near he remarked, "As one lamp is lit from another, so the Guru's spirit will pass into him and will dispel the darkness from this world."

Guru Arjan (1563-1606)

As soon as his investment was proclaimed his elder brother Prithi Chand turned hostile. Guru Sahib Ji was fortunate in having the support Baba Buddha Ji and Bhai Gurdas Ji in rebutting Prithi Chand's accusations and preventing a split in the community. Guru Sahib Ji's first task was to complete the building of the temple started by his father as Chak Ram Das. Guru Ji invited a Muslim saint, Said Mian Mir Ji of Lahore, to lay the foundation stone of the Harmindar Sahib, the temple of the Almighty. Instead of building the temple on a high plinth as was the Hindu custom, Guru Ji had it built on a lower level than the surrounding land , so that the worshippers would have to go down the steps to enter. Unlike Hindu temples which have only one door, the Harmindar Sahib was open on all four sides. These features were meant to be symbolic of the new faith, which required the lowest to go even lower, and unlike the Muslim mosques, its doors were open to all who wished to enter.

To raise money for the construction all Sikhs were required to donate one tenth of their income (dasvandh) in the name of the Guru, and the masands were required to collect this revenue and bring it to the Guru. The modest town now grew into a commecial city and the tank was filled with water, it was given a new name, Amritsar. What Benaras is for the Hindus, Mecca is for the Muslims and Jerusalem is for the Christians, Amritsar became for the Sikhs—their most important place of pilgrimage.

Guru Ji had another tank built about 15km from Amritsar, which he blessed as Taran Taran (the pool of salvation). It soon gained a reputation for having healing properties and also became a place of pilgrimage. From Taran Taran, Guru Ji went to the Jallundhar district and raised another town call Kartarpur. From Kartarpur Guru Ji went to Lahore and from there to the river Beas. In five years of travelling Guru Ji brought thousands of persons into the fold.

When in 1595, Guru Ji returned to Amritsar he found that Prithi Chand had not been idle. Prithi has been writing his own compositions and inserting them in with the writings of the Gurus. Guru Arjun Dev Ji realised the danger of spurious writings gaining acceptance. So Guru Ji abandoned all other pursuits in order to make an authentic compilation of the writings of his predecessors. Guru Ji persuaded Bhai Mohan, son of Guru Amar Das Ji to give the collection of the first three Gurus, these together with his father's compositions and his own; Guru Ji then set about the compilation. Guru Ji welcomed contributions from different sects of Hindus and Muslims as long as they measured up to the strict criteria the "Nanak's" had set. This task took many years to complete as Guru Sahib Ji would dictate and Bhai Gurdas Ji would write. In 1604 the mammoth task was completed and installed at Harmindar Sahib Ji.

Guru Sahib Ji was viciously tortured, he was made to sit on a large metal plate (tavi) which had a fire blazing underneath it as burning hot sand was poured over his body. Mian Mir Ji, the Guru's friend, tried to intercede but the Guru forbid him to do so, saying that one should not interfere with the will of the Almighty. Not a word of pain or a moan was uttered by Guru Ji as he bore all the suffering that his tormentors meted out. The Guru sent word to his son, Hargobind, who was eleven years old, to ask Baba Buddha Ji to instal him as the sixth Guru. Unable to break the great man, his jailers allowed his request to bathe in the nearby river. Blessing his devotees, who were said to be in the thousands, he struggled to the river's edge on his severly blistered feet. Disappearing into the water the Guru was never to be seen again. On May 30th, 1606 Guru Ji ascended to the heavens.

Guru Arjun Dev Ji was a very gifted and prolific writer. His compositions are filled with bejewelled phrases and are of a haunting melody. Guru Ji's masterpiece was the Sukhmani Sahib, in it Guru Ji says,

> **"Of all creeds, the sovereign creed is to pray to God and do goodly deeds."**

The death of Guru Arjun Dev Ji was a turning point in the history of the Sikhs. Guru Ji was the embodiment of all the things that Guru Nanak had preached and stood for. He had brought together the Hindu and Mussalman in creating a scripture where both were represented, he was a builder of cities and brought prosperity to the community.

Guru Hargobind (1595-1644)

The death of Guru Arjun Dev Ji was a profound shock to the people. The Emperor thought that this would keep the Sikhs subdued for a long time, the result was just the opposite. The Sikhs gathered around the eleven year old Hargobind, ready to take on the enemy head on.

The young Guru took his fathers seat wearing two swords : one to symbolise spiritual power and the other temporal. " My rosary shall be the sword belt and my turban I shall wear as the emblem of royalty." Guru Ji made it known to the Sikhs that from now on he would welcome offerings of arms and horses. Guru Ji trained his men and spend much time in martial exercise and hunting. Guru Ji built a fortress, Lohgarh in Amritsar. Across from the Harmindar Sahib he built the Akal Takhat, the throne of the Timeless One, where instead of chanting hymns of peace, the congregation heard ballads of feats of heroism and conquests in battle. Guru Ji sat on a throne and was known as Sucha Patshah , the true Emperor, he held court and went out with a royal umbrella over his head and was accompanied by armed guards.

Muhsin Fani, a Muslin scribe writes about Guru Ji " The Guru has eight hundred horses in his stables, three hundred troops on horse back and sixty men with firearms are always in his service."

Guru Ji travelled far and wide consolidating the community. Guru Ji travelled through the Punjab to Uttar Pardesh and northwest to Kashmir and even as far as Kabul and Kandhar in Afghanistan. On his way back Guru Ji accepted from Raja of Bilaspur a plot of land near the foothills of the Himalayas and named it Kiratpur.

With the death of Jehangir and the accession of Shah Jahan the troubles began. In 1628 when the Emperor happened to be hunting in the neighbourhood his men clashed with the Sikhs. A a result a contingent of royal soldiers were sent to arrest Guru Hargobind Sahib Ji. They found the Gurus household busy preparing for the wedding of his daughter. They could not find the Guru but plundered his property and all the confectionery prepared for the wedding was either eaten or taken by the soldiers. Guru Sahib Ji's men soon fell upon the royal guards before they had gone very far. A battle took place in which the royal soldiers were harassed all they way back to the royal courts, in the fighting the Chief Constable, Mukhlis Khan was killed.

As time went a second clash with the imperial guards took place near Lahira, the Mughals were badly mauled by the Sikhs. Guru Ji suspecting that a large force would be sent against them moved to a place outside Bhatinda. Sometime later the Mughals again tried to capture Guru Sahib Ji, this time with the renegade Painday Khan on their side, the leader of the Pathans in the employment of Guru Ji. The Guru had raised Painday Khan from a child and loved him as a son, but he had turned against Guru Ji, and now in a fit of pride had boasted that he alone would capture Guru Ji. The two sides met outside Kartarpur and a bloody battle took place in which Guru Ji's two sons Gurditta Ji and Tegh Mal Ji took part. In the battle Guru Ji himself confronted Painday Khan. As a father speaks to a son, Guru Ji offered Painday the first three assaults. After the third Guru Ji took the offensive and killed him, even then the magnanimous Guru got off his horse and took Painday in his arms and placed his head on his thigh and wiped his brow, Painday Khan realising his folly asked for forgivness and Guru Ji blessed him.

The number of Sikhs had steadily increased and the emphasis of the faith to forthrightly declare the right to defend the faith proved extremely popular. Many more community centers needed to be set up which meant more masands to administer them.

Guru ji was a loving master who responded to the prayers and loving calls of his devoted people - he went to kashmir in response to the prayers of Mai Bhag Bhari. He rode his charger to his devotees Sadha and Rupa asking them for the cool water that they had saved for him, he blessed Mata Sulakhani with seven sons in response to her loving prayers.

Within a few years Guru Sahib Ji lost five members of his family, including three of his sons, this included Baba Gurditta Ji in 1638, add to this Gurdittas eldest son Dhirmal had turned against his grandfather. Guru Ji had two remaining sons : Suraj Mal, who showed little interest in Sikh affairs and Tegh Mal, who spent most of his time in deep contemplation, Guru Ji had named him Tegh Bahadur after his exploits on the battle field at the age of thirteen, Bahadur (brave). When the time came Guru Sahib Ji chose, Baba

Gurditta Ji's second son, Har Hai Ji to succeed him as the seventh Guru.

Guru Har Rai (1630-1661)

Within a year of assuming the Guruship, Guru Har Rai Ji had to leave Kiratpur to the relative safety of a small village in Sirmoor state. The absence of the Guru from the main centres of Sikh activity, the hostility of the disappointed claimants to the guruship and a general disintegration of the masands meant that Guru Sahib Ji had to undertake a tour of all the centres and reorganise the missions and brought many into the Sikh fold.

At the end of 1658, Guru Sahib Ji returned to Kiratpur. Guru Ji became friendly with Dara Shikoh, the eldest son of the Emperor Shah Jahan. Dara Shikoh was a sufi and preferred the company of holy men. When the war of succession began Guru Ji's sympathies lay with Dara rather then the bigoted Aurangzeb. But Dara was defeated and fled northwards to the Punjab. He called on Guru Har Rai Ji for assistance. This was sufficient to arouse the wrath of the Emperor and he summoned Guru Sahib Ji to Delhi. Guru Ji sent his son Ram Rai to represent him. Ram Rai succeeded in winning the confidence of the Emperor. Aurangzeb decided to keep Ram Rai in Delhi in the belief that, with the future incumbent of the guruship in his power, he would become the arbiter of the destinies of the Sikh community. The all knowing Guru, Guru Har Rai Ji proclaimed his intention of passing the guruship to his younger son, Har Krishan Ji. Aurangzeb encouraged Ram Rai in his pretensions for the guruship but it was not to be, Har Krishan Ji at the age of five years became the eighth Guru of the Sikhs.

Guru Har Krishan 1656-1664

The passing of the Guruship to Har Krishan Sahib Ji did not suit Aurangzeb who wanted to play a decisive role in the

Sikhs. He summoned Guru Sahib Ji to Delhi with his intentions of arbitrating between Guru Ji and Ram Rai. After sometime Guru Ji arrived at Delhi and rested at the house of Mirza Raja Jai Singh in the suburb of Raisina. Aurangzeb was in no hurry to announce his arbitration (nor would the Sikhs have paid any heed to it) but he has happy to have Guru Har Krishan Ji under surveillance. Guru Ji was however stricken with smallpox. Before Guru Ji ascended the heavens he indicated that the next guru would be found in a village of Bakala.

Guru Tegh Bahadur (1621-1675)

It was quite clear that by the words "Baba Bakale" Guru Harkrishan Sahib Ji had meant his grand-uncle, Tegh Bahadur, nevertheless a whole contingent of claimants set themselves up at Bakala as the next Guru.

A sea merchant, Makhan Shah of Lubana, when set upon by a great storm at sea, had prayed to the Guru for his safe return from the seas and had promised an offering of 500 gold coins. Upon reaching Bakala he was confused at seeing all the would-be Gurus. He placed two coins in-front of each and bowed. Each blessed him. Knowing this was not the right Guru, Makan Shah moved to the next one, when he had gone through all the pretenders he felt very sad and despondent. Upon hearing of a holy person living in a ramshackle hut he decided to pay a visit. Inside Guru Tegh Bahadur Ji was in deep meditation. Placing two coins Makhan bowed. Guru Ji spoke, "You had promised 500 gold coins but you offer only two." With this Makhan Shah had found the Guru and in a fit of happiness he climbed a building and shouted out "Guru ladho ray, Guru ladho ray " – I have found the Guru , I have found the Guru.

Tegh Bahadur was a man of retiring habits who did not wish for comfrontation. But this very reluctance turned the Sikh masses in his favour. Guru Ji left Bakala for Amritsar where the doors of Harmindar Sahib were slammed shut in his face by the corrupt masands. Guru Sahib Ji moved on and bought some land about five miles outside of Kiratpur and built a small village there. He called it Anandpur (the haven of bliss). Here people flocked by the thousands to pledge allegiance to the Guru, and Guru Sahib Ji took extensive tours managing the centres.

Guru Sahib Ji left Anandpur Sahib and toured eastwards in Uttar Pardesh. Guru Ji travelled to Agra and arrived at Patna in the state of Bihar. Wherever he went he blessed the crowds that thronged to him. Here in 1666 Mata Gujri Ji gave birth to a son, Gobind Rai. Guru Sahib Ji could not spend much time with the infant as he had to return to the Punjab due to the religious persecution that Emperor Aurangzeb had embarked upon. As time went by the Hindus were being oppressed and persecuted even more, the hated jizia ("a so called protection tax, levied on non-muslims) was reinstated by the fundamentalist Aurangzeb adding to the heavy taxes they already paid. They suffered much hardship.

In 1675 a delegation of Hindus Pandits from Kashmir had come to meet with the Guru carrying grave news. The Hindus of Kashmir were to face death if they did not soon accept Islam, they needed protection and they had come to the "House of Guru Nanak". Gobind Rai, now aged nine years walked in on his father who was in deep thought. Asking what the matter was Guru Sahib Ji replied that the Hindus were in great threat and it would require a noble act of sacrifice from a very holy person to end their peril. Gobind Rai responded by saying "What greater person is there than you my father for such a task, go and protect their religion." So, Guru Tegh Bahadur sent word by the Pandits, to tell their Muslim ruler that if Aurangzeb could cause Guru Tegh Bahadur to convert to Islam then they would all convert as well. The Mughal ruler's thought had been that if the respected

Pandits of Kashmir could be converted then all the Hindus of his kingdom could be easily converted.

But now this noble man of peace, himself a Sikh, set out for Delhi with his brave companions. Hearing of the challenge the Emperor had the men arrested near Agra and carted into Delhi in chains on public view. Offered a chance to escape certain death and fearsom torture each man stood firm in his resolve.

The Sikhs that accompanied Guru Sahib Ji were first tortured and put to death. Bhai Mati Das Ji was sawed in two, Bhai Sati Das Ji was wrapped in wool and set on fire, Bhai Dayala Ji was boiled in a cauldron, such were the sacrifices that the Sikhs made. Then the tormentors turned their attention to Guru Sahib Ji. First they tortured him and then executed the Guru. There in Chandni Chawk they gave their lives not for the defense of their own religion but in defense of "the others" religious rights. This took place on November 11th, 1675 at Chandni Chawk, Delhi.

Gobind Rai at the age of nine now became the tenth Guru. Later in life Guru Gobind Singh Ji in his autobiography The Bachittar Natak, writes of this most noble of acts:

> To protect their right to wear their caste-marks and sacred threads,
>
> He did, in the age of darkness, perform the supreme sacrifice.
>
> To help the saintly he went to the utmost limit,
>
> He gave his head, but never cried in pain.
>
> He suffered martyrdom for the sake of his faith.
>
> He lost his head but revealed not his secret.
>
> He disdained to perform miracles or tricks.
>
> For such fill men of God with shame.

He burst the bonds of mortal clay.

And went to the abode of God.

No one hath ever performed an act as noble as his.

Tegh Bahadur passed, the world was stricken with sorrow.

A wail of horror rent the earth,

A victor's welcome given by the hosts of heaven. (Bachittar Natak)

Guru Gobind Singh (1666-1708)

Gobind Rai succeeded the guruship at the tender age of nine. He spent his boyhood learning Persian, Sanskrit, Braj and Urdu and learning martial skills. Guru Ji describes his mission in the following words :

> 'To uphold righteousness in every place and destroy sin and evil; that righteousness may triumph, that good may live and tyranny by uprooted from the land'.

He taught his Sikhs the morality of of the use of force when it was for the cause of truth.

> **'When all modes of righting a wrong having failed, it is righteous to draw the sword'.**

Guru Gobind Singh Ji made Sikhism into an active movement to fight the tyranny and injustice of emperor Aurangzeb. His goal was to create a nation that would be pure and strong enough to free itself from the oppression of priests and rulers alike. He had 52 poets in his court who would translate the hindu texts. Guru ji himself wrote extensively, the main theme being the gloryfication of the Almighty. When the battle of Bhangani was forced upon him by the surrounding hill chiefs , he fought them boldly and inflicted a crushing defeat upon them. But all the while Guru Ji thought of how he should shape his Sikhs in to such a force that none could withstand it.

On the day of Baisakhi 13th April 1699 a momentus event took place, the young Guru assembled his Sikhs, numbering 200,000 - 250,000, at Anandpur Sahib. Guru Ji demanded a head of a Sikh, finally a Sikh stepped forward. Guru Ji took him into a small tent and the sound of sword against flesh was heard. The blood seeped out from under the tent, the crowd looked on in stunned silence , four more times Guru Ji with fiery eyes demanded the head of a Sikh, each time a Sikh submitted his life to the will of his Guru. After a small interval Guru Ji brought out all five Sikhs, alive and well, dressed in saffron clothing.

The Panj Piyarai or five beloved ones were :

- Bhai Daya Singh, who had been a Khatri from Lahore, Punjab.
- Bhai Dharam Singh who had been a farmer from Hastinapur (Delhi)
- Bhai Himmat Singh who had been a water carrier from Puri (Orissa)
- Bhai Mukham Singh who had been a Calico printer from Dwarka (Kathiawar)
- Bhai Sahib Singh who had been a barber from Bidhar, Karnataka.

Guru Ji baptised the five with Amrit. Amrit was prepared by stirring together water, from the nearby river, and sugar, supplied by the Guru's wife, in a Sarbloh (an iron cauldron) with a Khanda (double edged sword), while reciting the five proscribed bani's or prayers. The five prayers being:

- Japji Sahib, morning prayer composed by Guru Nanak
- Jaap Sahib, morning prayer composed by Guru Gobind Singh

- Amrit Sawayia, 10 verses, composed by Guru Gobind Singh
- Bainti Chaupai, 10 verses, composed by Guru Gobind Singh
- Anand Sahib, evening prayer composed by Guru Amar Das.

The Five Beloved became the first members of the brotherhood of the Khalsa (the pure). The word Khalsa coming from the sanskrit word khaals meaning pure.

Guru Ji prepares the Amrit. Mata Sahib Devan added the patasey (suger candy).

All five men, each from different castes, drank the Amrit out of the same bowl and 'Singh' (lion), was added to their names. The Guru then in turn asked the men, now his equal brothers, to Baptist him. Thousands were so initiated that day with the name Singh for males and Kaur (Princess) for women, thus removing all caste barriers.

The significance of this cannot be underestimated. For members of different castes to drink from the same bowl would have been unheard of, yet Guru Ji in his great wisdom and forethought brought together castes and communites into the one Khalsa.

They were enjoined to observe the five K's. These five emblems of Sikhism being:

- Kesh, uncut hair, a natural gift from God that gave them a distinct identity,
- Kangha , a comb to keep the hair tidy,
- Kasha, undergarment shorts,worn by soldiers of the time but also to depict chastity and personal hygiene,
- Kara, steel bracelet, symbolic connection with God, and they were always to carry

- Kirpan or a sabre ready to uphold righteousness and defend the weak.

Guru Ji asks for a sacrifice.

Guru Ji prepares the Amrit by reciting the panj banies (five morning prayers)

Many explanations have been given for the ceremony of baptism. Apart from the profoundly spiritual nature of the communion, making people of different castes drink Amrit from the same bowl broke down some orthodox Hindu practices. Guru Ji gave the final form to the Sikh faith. He declared the institution of the Guruship at an end and ordered all Sikhs to bow down in front of the **Guru Granth Sahib** Ji, the holy scriptures of the Sikhs.

Guru Gobind Singh Ji's life was a long series of battles fought against heavy odds. Guru Ji laid the foundations of the Sikh military might by setting up a tradition of fearless valour which became a distinguished feature of Sikh soldiery. They came to believe in the triumph of their own cause as an article of faith, and like their Guru asked for no nobler end then on the battlefield. What Guru Ji succeeded in doing was to 'teach the sparrow to hunt the hawk and one man to fight a legion'.

Guru Ji was a prolific writer and a poet of rare quality, in everything he wrote or spoke there was a note of buoyant hope and the conviction then even if he lost his life, his mission would succeed.

O Lord, these boons of Thee I ask, Let me never shun a righteous task.

Let me be fearless when I go into battle, Give me faith that victory will be mine.

Give me power to sing Thy praise, And when comes the time to end my life. Let me fall in mighty strife. ●●

2

Introduction to Sikhism

Sikhism, the youngest of the world's religions, is barely five hundred years old. Its founder, Guru Nanak, was born in 1469. Guru Nanak spread a simple message of "Ek Onkar": we are all one, created by the One Creator of all Creation. This was at a time when India was being torn apart by castism, sectarianism, religious factions and fanaticism. He aligned with no religion, and respected all religions. He expressed the reality that there is only one God with many paths that lead to Him, and that the Name of God is Truth, "SatNam".

Guru Nanak's followers were Sikhs (seekers of truth). He taught them to bow only before God, and to link themselves to the Guru, the Light of Truth, who lives always in direct consciousness of God, experiencing no separation. Through words and example, the Guru demonstrates to followers how to experience God within themselves, bringing them from darkness into light. Guru Nanak was a humble bearer of this Light of Truth. He opposed superstition, injustice, and hypocrisy and inspired seekers by singing divine songs which were touched the hearts of the most callous listeners. These songs were recorded, and formed the beginnings of the Sikhs' sacred writings, later to become the "Siri Guru Granth Sahib".

Guru Nanak: Main Lessons

Nam Japna - To get up each day before sunrise, to clean the body, meditate on God's Name and recite the Guru's hymns to clean the mind and throughout the day to continuously remember God's Name with every breath.

Dharam di Kirat Karni - To work and earn by the sweat of the brow, to live a family way of life, and practice truthfulness and honesty in all dealings.

Vand Ke Chakna - To share the fruits of one's labour with others before considering oneself. Thus, to live as an inspiration and a support to the entire community.

The Golden Chain

The Ten Gurus of the Sikhs

The foundation of Sikhism was laid down by Guru Nanak Dev Ji. Guru Nanak Dev Ji rather than simply passing the Guruship of his teachings onto his own sons (as was the custom at the time) looked for someone to show up who revealed himself as the most deserving of the Guruship. Choosing his replacement he laid his hand upon him and announced him 'Angad'(part of his own body. Subsequently the light of Guruship was passing in the same manner. Passed always to the person who showed himself to be each new Nanak's replacement. The word "Guru" is derived from the root words "Gu", which means darkness or ignorance, and "Ru", which means light or knowledge. Thus, a "Guru" is one who takes a person from darkness of ignorance to the light of knowledge. The "Guru" guides us to experience the Truth (of God).

Each one of the ten Gurus represents a divine attribute:

Guru Nanak Dev Ji - Humility

Guru Angad Dev Ji - Obedience

Guru Amar Das Ji — Equality

Guru Ram Das Ji - Service

Guru Arjan Dev Ji - Self-Sacrifice

Guru Hargobind Ji - Justice

Guru Har Rai Ji - Mercy

Guru Harkrishan Ji - Purity

Guru Tegh Bahadur Ji - Tranquility

Guru Gobind Singh Ji - Courage

Guru Gobind Singh Ji, the Tenth Guru, exemplified the Sikh ideal of the 'Sant-Sipahi', which directly translates as Soldier-Saint. He was also an inspired and prolific writer, courageous warrior, and a source of Divine Wisdom to his Sikhs. "When all other means have failed," he said, "only then is it righteous to take up the sword." He was the defender of the poor, the meek, and the oppressed masses of India.

The Sri Guru Granth Sahib

The Sri Guru Granth Sahib or Adi Granth Sahib Ji, is more than just a scripture of the Sikhs. The Sikhs treat this Granth (holy book) as a living Guru.The Sri Guru Granth Sahib, or SGGS for short, is more than a holy book of the Sikh people. The Guruship of the Sikhs was passed by decreed of Guru Gobind Singh ji to the Granth, which is the eleventh - eternal Guru of the Sikhs. The Shri Guru Granth Sahib is held in the highest regard by the Sikhs and is treated just as their living Gurus were with the same decorum and loving traditions shown to the 10 living Gurus. The SGGS forms the central part of the Sikh 'house' of worship called a gurdwara. The Holy Scripture is placed on the dominant platform (a throne with beautiful and colourful fabric) in the main hall of the gurdwara during the day. The respect held for the Holy Granth is illustrated best at the Harmandir Sahib or as it is better known around the world the Golden Temple. Early each morning with the sound of a regal trumpet announcing the coming of The Holy Granth which is lovingly carried in a Silver and gold Palki from its place of rest at night in the Akal Takhat to the Harmandir Sahib itself to the Darbar

Sahib (The Court of the Lord). Along the way a Sikh volunteer waves a Chaur Sahib over the Granth in the same manner accorded the living human Gurus. Inside the Sanctum the Guru Granth Sahib's Manji (throne) is placed so that the Granth is seated higher than any other seat in the Darbar. The process is repeated each evening in reverse. The Chaur Seva is just one of those core traditions that the Sikhs practise to honour their Guru with the high regard and respect that Gurbani deserves.

A striking video of the Granth's procession to its place of rest in the Akal Takht can be viewed on Youtube at . If you haven't been to a Gurdwara, let alone the Harmandir Sahib, this short video will let you see firsthand the reverence recorded the Shri Guru Granth Sahib.

The Sikhs do not 'worship' the SGGS for that is forbidden – Only the One Almighty God is to be worshipped, for He is the Creator of everything that can be perceived and also those things that cannot be perceived.

During the time of the first ten Gurus, the congregation (Sangat) and Sevadar (volunteers) who came from afar to see the Gurus, wanted to be close to the Gurus and listen to their advice and guidance (Shabad). So they would sit near Guru ji and listen to the words of wisdom from the Guru and do Chaur Seva for the Guru. This seva was done turn by turn by many members of the congregation (Sangat) to be as close to their Guru as possible.

Making of the Khalsa

Guru Gobind Singh was the last Guru of the Sikhs in human form. He created the Khalsa, a spiritual brotherhood and sisterhood devoted to purity of thought and action. He gave the Khalsa a distinctive external form to remind them of their commitment, and to help them maintain an elevated state of consciousness. Every Sikh baptized as Khalsa vows to wear the Five "K's":

Kesh - uncut hair (from **head** to **toe**) and beard, as given by God, to sustain him or her in higher consciousness; and a turban, the crown of spirituality and a symbol ordained by the Guru so that they would stand out to be recognised, in a crowd or lonely pathway as a becon of help, one who anyone, in danger or need could easily identify and turn to for help.

Kangha - a wooden comb to properly groom the hair as a symbol of cleanliness.

Katchera - specially made cotton underwear as a reminder of the commitment to purity.

Kara - a steel circle, worn on the wrist, signifying bondage to Truth and freedom from every other entanglement.

Kirpan - the sword, with which the Khalsa is committed to righteously defend the fine line of the Truth.

Khalsa also vows to refrain from any sexual relationships outside of marriage, and to refrain from taking tobacco, alcohol, bhang and all other intoxicants. Furthermore, some Khalsa are against the consumption of any food containing meat or eggs.

Then Guru Gobind Singh infused his own being into the Khalsa, declaring that the Khalsa was now the Guru in all temporal matters. For spiritual matters, the Guruship was given to the "Siri Guru Granth Sahib", a compilation of sacred writings by those who have experienced Truth. For Sikhs, "Siri Guru Granth Sahib" is the living embodiment of the Guru, and is regarded with the utmost reverence and respect wherever it is found. Sikhs all over the world look to the "Siri Guru Granth Sahib" as their living Guru, as the source of spiritual instruction and guidance.

Sikh Religious Philosophy

The Sikh Religious Philosophy can be divided into 5 Sections:

Primary Beliefs and Principles

1. **"Ek Onkaar" - One God:** There is only one God, who has infinite qualities and names; She or he (see note below regarding sex neutrality) is the same for all religions.Thou have no sex, but is present within all things and all places.

2. **Earn One's Living Righteously:** One must work hard and honestly and never live off of others, but give to others from the fruits of one's own labour.

3. **Rise Early and Meditate:** The early morning hours, before the rising of the sun are used for meditation and experiencing union with God.

4. **Share With Others:** One's home is always open to all. All are served and all are welcomed. The fruits of one's labours are always shared with others.

5. **Remember God:** Love God, but hold the awe of her or him as well.

6. **Re-incarnation, Karma & Salvation:** All creatures have souls that pass to other bodies upon death until liberation is achieved.

7. **Humanhood:** All human beings are equal. We are sons and daughters of Waheguru, the Almighty.

8. **Personal Sacrifice:** Be prepared to give your life for all supreme principles – see the life of Guru Teg Bahadur.

9. **Uphold Moral Values:** Defend, safeguard, and fight for the rights of all creatures, and in particular your fellow beings.

10. **Many Paths lead to God:** The Sikhs believe that Salvation can be obtained by non-Sikhs as well.
11. **No Special Worship Days:** Sikhs do not believe that any particular day is holier than any other.
12. **Conquer the 5 Thieves:** It is every Sikh's duty to defeat these 5 thieves: ego, anger, greed, attachment, and lust.
13. **Positive Attitude to Life:** "Chardi Kala" – Always have a positive, optimistic, buoyant view of life.
14. **Disciplined Life:** Upon baptism, Sikhs must wear the 5Ks, strictly recite the 5 prayers (Banis), etc.
15. **Attack with 5 Weapons:** Compassion (Daya), Truth (Sat), Contentment (Santokh), Humility (Nimrata) and Love (Pyar).

Underlying Values

The Sikhs must believe in the following Values:

1. **Equality:** All humans are equal before God.
2. **Actions Count:** Salvation is obtained by one's actions – Good deeds, remembrance of God, etc.
3. **Living a Family Life:** Must live as a family unit (householder) to provide and nurture children.
4. **God's Spirit:** All Creatures have God's spirits and must be properly respected.
5. **Personal Right:** Every person has a right to life but this right is restricted.
6. **Sharing:** It is encouraged to share and give to charity 10 percent of one's net earnings.
7. **Accept God's Will:** Develop your personality so that you recognise happy events and miserable events as one.

8. **The 4 Fruits of Life:** Truth, Contentment, Contemplation and Naam, (in the Name of God).

Prohibited Behaviour

1. **Non-Logical Behaviour:** Superstitions and rituals not meaningful to Sikhs (pilgrimages, fasting and bathing in rivers; circumcision; worship of graves, idols, pictures; compulsory wearing of the veil for women; etc;)

2. **Sacrifice of Creatures:** Sati – widows throwing themselves in the funeral pyre of their husbands; lamb and calf slaughter to celebrate holy occasions; etc are forbidden.

3. **Material Obsession:** ("Maya") Accumulation of materials have no meaning in Sikhism. Wealth, Gold, Portfolio, Stocks, Commodities, properties will all be left here on Earth when you depart. Do not get attached to them.

4. **Non-Family Oriented Living:** A Sikh is not allowed to live as a recluse, beggar, yogi, monk, nun, or celibate.

5. **Intoxication:** Drinking alcohol, using drugs, smoking tobacco, and consumption of other intoxicants are not permitted.

6. **Worthless Talk:** Bragging, gossip, lying, etc are not permitted.

7. **No Priestly Class:** Sikhs do not have to depend on a priest for performing any religious functions.

Technique and Methods

1. **Naam Japo:** - Free Service Sewa, Meditation & Prayer Simran, Sacred Music Kirtan

2. **Wand kay Shako:** - Share your food with others in need, Free Food langar, Donation 10% of income Dasvandh, etc.

3. **Kirat Karni:** - Honest, Earnings, labour, etc while remembering the Lord

Other Observations

1. **Not Son of God:** The Gurus were not in the Christian sense "Sons of God". Sikhism says we are all the children of God and by deduction, God is our mother/ father.

2. **Multi-Level Approach:** Sikhism recognises the concept of a multi-level approach to achieving your target as a disciple of the faith. For example, "Sahajdhari" (slow adopters) are Sikhs who have not donned the full 5Ks but are still Sikhs nevertheless.

3. **All Welcome:** Members of all religions can visit Sikh temples (Gurdwaras) but must observe certain rules – cover your head, remove shoes, no smoking or drinking intoxicants.

PRIMARY BELIEFS AND PRINCIPLES

The Sikh religion has various established beliefs and values that are inherent in the basic philosophy of the faith. A Sikh's primary belief is in only one supreme God – This sole God is the same for all the peoples of the Universe. Guru Arjan, the fifth Sikh Guru highlights this point by saying in the Sikh holy text called the Guru Granth Sahib, *"There is only the One Supreme Lord God; there is no other at all"* (SGGS p 45); this belief is the starting point of the Sikh faith.

Next, God is considered gender neutral in Sikhism. So when a Sikh refers to "God", this God can be refered to as masculine or feminine; so God can be called 'He' or 'She'.

Guru Arjan reinforces this concept by saying: *"You are my Father and You are my Mother..... You are my Protector everywhere...."* (SGGS p 103).

Further, this one God is the same God of the Sikhs, Hindus, Muslims, Christians, Jews, etc – of all the peoples of the world; everyone in this world belongs to that same one God! Guru Ram Das, the fourth Sikh Guru explains: *"All living beings are Yours - You are the Giver of all souls"* (SGGS p 10).

The Sikhs believe that God is formless but realisable; He is fearless, without enemies, self-created, without birth or otherwise subjected to time, etc. The Sikh holy scripture, given the full name of Sri Guru Granth Sahib explains the various facets of God in substantial detail. This principle of one God leads to the next primary concept for the Sikhs: The concept of equality of all the human races, sects, gender, social classes, etc. The adherents of Sikhism believe that all peoples of the world are equal in the eyes of God; man is equal to woman; a rich person is equal to a poor man; a black person enjoys the same rights in God's domain as a white person and so on.

From this follows the next recognised belief in Sikhi that people of all faiths can reunite with God provided they follow the **true path** of their **own religion**. So the Sikh does not believe that they have a monopoly on God or are the 'chosen' people of the Lord. Anyone can get favours from God depending only on His or her actions and thoughts. God does not see ones colour or gender or social status when passing judgement!

Further, the Sikhs believe in the evolution of the Soul and the principle of reincarnation. The soul is believed to be a tiny spark of God's light detached from the Almighty. This spark is separated from God and wants to become pure so that it can reunite with God. For this to happen, the Soul has to evolve and purify itself so that this reunification with the Supreme Soul can take place.

The law of Karma is another concept central to this faith. Ones actions in this life will have a direct influence on the type of life in your next existence! So to adhere to these principles, the dedicated follower must lead a disciplined personal life and must uphold the moral and ethnical rights of all the peoples of the world. So it is a must to lead a spiritually correct life at all times and to be ready to be subjected to personal sacrifices if the liberty of any weak person(s) is at stake.

Another central tenet of Sikhism is the concept of 'Chardi kala' – Positive attitude to life at all times. Graciously and with humility to accept the will of God at all times. Always to lead ones life unattached and untangled with the material world. Not to come under the influence of Maya – the illusionary and transient world around us. To remain detached from this world but to recognise ones duties to God and his creation.

One God

There is only ONE God who has infinite qualities and names; S/He* is the same for all religions; God is Creator & Sustainer -All that you see around you is God's Creation; S/He* is everywhere, and in everything; S/He is fearless and with no Enemies; Only God is without birth or death and S/He* has and will exist forever.

Below are quotations from Guru Granth Sahib (SGGS) which reinforce the summaries outlined above:

(a) There is One God: from SGGS page 45:

paarbarahm parabh ayk hai doojaa naahee ko-ay.

There is only the One Supreme Lord God; there is no other.

jee-o pind sabh tis kaa jo tis bhaavai so ho-ay.

Soul and body are all Yours; whatever pleases You, shall happen.

gur poorai pooraa bha-i-aa jap naanak sachaa so-ay.

Through the Perfect Guru, one becomes perfect; O Nanak, meditate on the True One.

(b) God the creator ? from page 1036:

"He formed the planets, solar systems and nether regions, and brought what was hidden to manifestation

When He so willed, He created the world.

Without any supporting power, He sustained the universe."

Brotherhood of Mankind

Sikhs believe that all human beings are equal. "We are sons and daughters of Waheguru, the Almighty". Sikhs have to treat all peoples of the world on an equal footing. No gender, racial, social, etc discrimination is allowed. This is the message of Guru Nanak as taught by the 10 Sikh Masters during the period 1469 to 1708.

Guru Angad stood for a caste-less and class-less society, in which no one was superior to the other and no one, through greed or selfishness, could be allowed to encroach upon the rights of others. In short, he visualized a society in which members lived like a family, helping and supporting one another. He not only preached equality but practised it. To promote the acceptance of human equality, Guru established a community kitchen where all sat together in a row, regardless of caste or status, and ate the same food.

Guru Angad said, *"He Himself creates, O Nanak; He establishes the various creatures. How can anyone be called bad?.*

There is One Lord and Master of all; He watches over all, and assigns all to their tasks. Some have less, and some have more; no one is allowed to leave empty." – Guru Angad Dev

Furthermore, the guru stressed the importance of adopting a uniform way of praising God and the utility of a social organisation based on equality. He established a holy congregation, or Sangat, where people of different beliefs and varying social status sat together to hear the Master's singing of hymns and to be inspired to lead a noble life.

The following lines from SGGS explain about the importance of treating every person as an equal:

> "They look upon all with equality, and recognize the Supreme Soul, the Lord, pervading among all. Those who sing the Praises of the Lord, Har, Har, obtain the supreme status; they are the most exalted and acclaimed people. ((2))" SGGS Page 446

> "He is within - see Him outside as well; there is no one, other than Him. As Gurmukh, look upon all with the single eye of equality; in each and every heart, the Divine Light is contained. ((2))" SGGS Page 599

> "There is only one breath; all are made of the same clay; the light within all is the same. The One Light pervades all the many and various beings. This Light intermingles with them, but it is not diluted or obscured. By Guru's Grace, I have come to see the One. I am a sacrifice to the True Guru. ((3))" SGGS Page 96

Uphold Personal Rights of All

The Sikh Gurus have defended, safeguarded, fought and sacrificed to uphold the rights of others no matter what their religion, caste, gender or race. The message promoted by the Guru is to allow all to live freely without undue interference and restrictions. No one is to be forced into a different belief system under threat of force. This philosophy was vigorously defended by all the Sikh Gurus]] but came into sharp focus when the ninth Sikh master, Guru Teg Bahadur choose to sacrifice his life for the defence of the Kashmiri pandits who were being persecuted by the Mughal government during that time.

Personal Sacrifice

The Gurus have left a legacy for the Sikhs to follow. To uphold high moral standards and to undertake personal sacrifice to protect and guard these high principles. The prime candidates in understanding this principle is realised by examining the lives of Guru Arjan Dev (5th Guru), Guru Tegh Bahadur (9th Guru) and Guru Gobind Singh (10th Guru).

Guru Tegh Bahadur sacrificed his life to save the Kashmiri Pundits from persecution by the Mughal rulers of the time. When these Pundits came to ask for help from the Guru, the Guru did not flinch from his responsibility to protect the weak and in so doing, paid the ultimate price. The tyrant Emperor Aurangzeb beheaded the Guru for not converting to Islam. But this sacrifice, the Guru's determination and sacrifice showed the rulers the solid resolve of the masses and thus the persecution of the masses subsided.

By carrying out this ultimate sacrifice, the leader of the Sikhs showed them the way to challenge oppression. Oppression and Tyranny had to tackled with a strong and unwavering resolve. Many other examples like this can be found in the History of the Sikhs.

On page 1377 of SGGS the Guru tells us:

"Kabeer, if you desire to play the game of love with the Lord, then cut off your head, and make it into a ball. Lose yourself in the play of it, and then whatever will be, will be. ||239|| Kabeer, if you desire to play the game of love with the Lord, play it with someone with commitment. Pressing the unripe mustard seeds produces neither oil nor flour. ||240||"

So can play this game of love with commitment and sacrifice.

Many Paths Lead to God

The Sikh Gurus tell us that salvation can be obtained by following various spiritual paths. Therefore, Sikhs do not have a monopoly on Salvation – "Many Spiritual paths lead to God" – Sikhs do not therefore consider themselves as having a monopoly on God or a "superior" right to salvation. The Sikhs do not consider themselves as the "chosen people of God". However, the Sikh scripture is probably the only known holy book that advances this message of "religious equality" and offers advise for Muslims to be better Muslims and for Hindus to be better Hindus. Christian, Hindus, Muslim, Jews, etc all have the same right to liberty as a Sikhs.

Positive Attitude to Life

Chardi Kala This term is an important expression used in Sikhism for a mind frame that a Sikh has to accept and practise. It loosely means a "positive, buoyant and optimistic" attitude to life and the future. Always be – in "high spirits", "ever progressive", "always cheerful", etc are some other terms used to describe this phrase.

Sikhism dictates that Sikhs believes in the Will of God and that God is without enemies and is always merciful. Hence acceptance of his Will is in the interest of and for the benefit of His Creation, even if at times one suffers severe hardship.

This attitude of "Chardi Kala" is to allow one to sail through the ups and downs of life with as little harm as possible to the individual.

To join and help others in their hour of need is part of this "Chardi Kala" spirit.

Must not Engage in Meaningless Rituals

The Sikh faith condemns empty rituals and superstitions. The practice of blind rituals, worshiping of idols and inanimate objects, participating in religious fasts, pilgrimage to holy places, offering of food to sadhus (religious leaders), or believing in any other such rituals, superstitions or fads, will not bring one closer to God or make one a better human being. In all societies round the world, through fear and uncertainty, members undertake in ritualistic and worthless behaviour at times of worry, uncertainty or trouble. These poor people, wrongly believe that undertaking these empty customs and penances will bring them special assistance from Waheguru or some other higher power.

The reliance on these blind customs appears to increase at time of stress in human existence. For example, In 1989, Susan Starr Sered conducted fieldwork among women who has just had a baby on the maternity ward of a Jerusalem hospital. The women who she interviewed reported having performed close to two hundred different religious and secular rituals during pregnancy, birth, and the immediate post-partum period. So, it is clear that ritualism has not faded but may be on the increase.

Superstition is an irrational belief arising from ignorance or doubt. Many people all around the world are gripped by various superstitions and they live their lives in fear and uncertainty. Most of these fears are irrational and superfluous but they still cannot unbind themselves from these evil and false notions. Some common and well-known examples of superstitions are:

- *"When a black cat crosses one's path, something will happen if one crosses the line where the cat passed. To "undo" either wait for someone who didn't know about the black cat to cross the path or think of another route."*

- *"If you wash your hair on the first day of the month you will have a short life."*
- *"13 in the western world is considered an unlucky number. This double-digit represents* Judas, *who was the guest at the Last Supper who betrayed* Jesus. *As a result it is also thought to be unlucky to have a dinner party with 13 guests. Many hotels are missing a thirteenth floor or have omitted the number from their room doors. Friday the 13th of any month is said to be an unlucky day."*

But the SGGS says *"The mind is diseased with doubt, superstition and duality."* (SGGS p416) and also *"High and low, social class and status - the world wanders lost in superstition."* (SGGS p1243). Superstition is like a disease for the mind it brings confusion and fear and takes you away from reality. ●●

3

Sikhism and Beliefs

Sikhism (Sikhi in Panjabi) is one of the major world religions, primarily developed in 16th and 17th century India. *"Sikhi"* comes from the word *"Sikh"*, and the word "Sikh" comes from the Sanskrit root "œisya" which means "disciple" or "learner". Guru Nanak was the founder of Sikhi. He was born in 1469 in the village of Nankana Sahib, near Lahore in present-day Pakistan. The faith system is based on the teachings of Guru Nanak Dev and ten successive Sikh Gurus (the last one being the sacred text Guru Granth Sahib) and is the fifth-largest organised religion in the world. This system of religious philosophy and expression has been traditionally known as the Gurmat (literally the counsel of the gurus) or the Sikh Dharma.

The principal belief of Sikhism is faith in waheguru—represented using the sacred symbol of ik ôaEkâr, the Universal God. Sikhism advocates the pursuit of salvation through disciplined, personal meditation on the name and message of God. A key distinctive feature of Sikhism is a non-anthropomorphic concept of God, to the extent that one can interpret God as the Universe itself.

The followers of **Sikhism** are ordained to follow the teachings of the ten Sikh Gurus, or enlightened leaders, as well as the holy scripture entitled the Gurû Granth Sâhib, which, along with the writings of six of the ten Sikh Gurus, includes selected works of many devotees from diverse socio-economic and religious backgrounds. The text was decreed by

Guru Gobind Singh, the tenth guru, as the final guru of the Khalsa Panth.

Sikhism's traditions and teachings are distinctively associated with the history, society and culture of the Punjab. Adherents of Sikhism are known as Sikhs (students or disciples) and number over 23 million across the world. Most Sikhs live in Punjab in India and, until India's partition, millions of Sikhs lived in what is now Pakistani Punjab.

Sikhism is also called Sikhi or Gurmat or Sikh Matt or Aad-Matt.

Core Beliefs

The core beliefs of Sikhism are:

Belief in one God

The belief in one pantheistic God. The opening sentence of the Sikh scriptures is only two words long, and reflects the base belief of all who adhere to the teachings of the religion: *Ek Onkar "Ek"* is One and *"Onkar"* is God - *"There is only one God."*

The Teachings of the Sikh Gurus

The teachings of the Ten Sikh Gurus (as well as other selected Muslim and Hindu saints and scholars) are enshrined in the Guru Granth Sahib. These teachings propagate the following values:

- to see God in everyone; understand and practice equality among all races irrespective of caste, religion, colour, status, age, gender, etc;
- to remember God at all times; to always engage in Simran or "remembrance of God", the primal being; virtuous, merciful, bountiful, fearless and Creator of everything; be always aware of His persona and behave accordingly;

- to value and respect positive ideals like truth, compassion, contentment, humility, love, etc; (a reflection of God-like features)
- to suppression of inner evils lust, anger/rage, greed, material attachment, ego, etc; (a reflection of anti-God features)
- to aspire and engage in useful, productive, honest and peaceful life of a householder; to work diligently while holding the image of God within you; (Kirit Karni)
- to engage in selfless service (Sewa) and help build a loving community life; to be a contributor to society whenever possible; (Wand kay shakna)
- to be ready to protect and stand for the rights of the weak among us; to fight for justice and fairness for all;
- to always accept the Will of God, (Hukam) and stay focused and in "Positive Spirits" (Chardikala), etc.

History of Sikhism

Guru Nanak Dev (1469-1538), the founder of Sikhism, was born in the village of Talwandi, now called Nankana Sahib, near Lahore in present-day Pakistan. His father, Mehta Kalu was a Patwari- an accountant of land revenue in the government. Guru's mother was Mata Tripta and he had one older sister, Bibi Nanki. From the very childhood, Bibi Nanki saw in him the Light of God but she did not reveal this secret to anyone. She is known as the first disciple of Guru Nanak. Even as a boy, Nanak was fascinated by religion, and his desire to explore the mysteries of life eventually led him to leave home. He wandered all over India in the manner of Hindu saints. It was during this period that Nanak met Kabir (1441-1518), a saint revered by both Hindus and Muslims. He made four distinct major journeys, which are called Udasis spanning many thousands of miles.

In 1538, Guru Nanak chose Bhai Lehna, his disciple as a successor to the Guruship rather than his son. Bhai Lehna was renamed Guru Angad and became the second guru of the Sikhs. He continued the work started by Guru Nanak. Guru Amar Das became the third Sikh guru in 1552 at the age of 73. Goindwal became an important centre for Sikhism during the Guruship of Guru Amar Das. He continued to preach the principle of equality for women, the prohibition of Sati and the practise of Langar. In 1567, Emperor Akbar sat with the ordinary and poor people of Punjab to have Langar. Guru Amar Das also trained 140 apostles of which 52 were women to manage the rapid expansion of the religion. Before he died in 1574 aged 95, he appointed his son-in-law, Jetha as the fourth Sikh Guru.

Jetha became Guru Ram Das and vigorously undertook his duties as the new guru. He is responsible for the establishment of the city of Ramdaspur later to be named Amritsar. In 1581, Guru Arjan- youngest son of fourth guru - became the Fifth Guru of the Sikhs. In addition to being responsible for the construction of the Golden Temple, he prepared the Sikh Sacred text and his personal addition of some 2,000 plus hymns in the Guru Granth Sahib. In 1604 he installed the Adi Granth for the first time as the Holy Book of the Sikhs. In 1606, he was arrested and fined an enormous sum, by the newly installed Mughal Emperor Jahangir, which he refused to pay. His followers and a highly respected friend the Sufi Sant Hazrat Mian Mir attempted to intercede on his behalf, but believing he had done nothing to warrant the fine he told them he wanted no one to interfere with the workings of Waheguru. He was also asked to change some wording of the former Gurus which he had collected in the Adi Granth—this he refused to do. He was tortured severely and finally allowed to bath in the nearby river. His followers and admirers watched as he walked on his badly burned and blistered feet to the river's edge, waded in and then disappeared under the water never to be seen again, becoming the first Martyr of the Sikhs.

Guru Hargobind, became the sixth guru of the Sikhs. He carried two swords; one for Spiritual reasons and one for temporal (worldly) reasons. From this point onward, the Sikhs became a military force and always had a trained fighting force to defend their independence. In 1644, Guru Har Rai became Guru followed by Guru Har Krishan, the boy Guru in 1661. Guru Teg Bahadur became Guru in 1665 and led the Sikhs until 1675, when he sacrificed his life in defense the Kashmiri Hindus who had come to him for help.

In 1675, Aurangzeb ordered the public execution of the ninth Sikh Guru, Guru Tegh Bahadur. Sikh mythos (above) says that Guru Tegh Bahadur sacrificed himself to save Hindus, after Kashmiri pandits came to him for help when the Emperor condemned them for failing to convert to Islam. This marked a turning point for Sikhism. His successor, his son Guru Gobind Rai further militarised his followers (see Khalsa). After the treachery of his neighboring Hill chieftains (Katri Rajputs who he had expected to join him in expelling or at least putting an end to the Mughal tyranny and forced conversions of Hindus) who took the side of the Mughals and tricked him and the Sikhs, under a guarantee of safe passage, into abandoning Anandpur, many of his Sikhs including his four sons and his mother, Gobind Singh on reaching safety sent Aurangzeb a letter known as the Zafarnama (*Epistle of Victory*).

Shortly before passing away Guru Gobind ordered that Guru Granth Sahib, the Sikh Holy Scripture, would replace the line of human Gurus and become the spiritual authority for the Sikhs and placed the temporal authority with the Khalsa Panth; the Sikhs themselves.

The first Sikh Holy Scripture was compiled and edited by the Fifth Guru, Guru Arjan in 1604, although some of the earlier gurus are also known to have documented their revelations. This is one of the few scriptures in the world that has been compiled by the founders of a faith during their own life time. The Guru Granth Sahib is particularly unique among sacred texts in that it is written in Gurmukhi script but contains many languages including Punjabi, Hindi-Urdu, Sanskrit, Bhojpuri and Persian. Sikhs consider the Guru Granth Sahib the last, perpetual living guru.

The Gurus of Sikhism

The Ten Gurus of Sikhism

Sikhism was established by ten Gurus; teachers or masters; over the period 1469 to 1708. These teachers were enlightened souls whose main purpose in life was the spiritual and moral well-being of the masses. Each master added to and reinforced the message taught by the previous, resulting to the creation of the religion of Sikhism. Guru Nanak was the first Guru and Guru Gobind Singh the final Guru in human form. When Guru Gobind Singh left this world, he made the Sri Guru Granth Sahib the ultimate and final Sikh Guru.

The Sri Guru Granth Sahib

The Guru Granth Sahib is a sacred text considered by Sikhs to be their eleventh and final Guru. Sikhism was influenced by reform movements in Hinduism (e.g. Bhakti, monism, Vedic metaphysics, guru ideal, and bhajans) as well as Sufi Islam. It departs from some of the social traditions and structure of Hinduism and Islam (such as the caste system and purdah, respectively). Sikh philosophy is characterised by logic, comprehensiveness, and a "without frills" approach to both spiritual and material concerns. Its theology is marked by simplicity. In Sikh ethics there is no conflict between an individual's duty to oneself and that towards society.

The Guru Granth Sahib is the eleventh and final Guru of the Sikhs, is held in the highest regard by the Sikhs and is treated as the Eternal Guru, as instructed by Guru Gobind Singh.

It is perhaps the only scripture of its kind which not only contains the teachings of its own religious founders but also writings of people from other faiths. Besides the Banis of the Gurus, it also contains the writings of saints like Kabir, Namdev, Ravidas, Sheikh Farid, Trilochan, Dhanna, Beni, Sheikh Bhikan, Jaidev, Surdas, Parmanad, Pipa and Ramanand.

The Granth forms the central part of the Sikh place of worship called a gurdwara. The Holy Scripture is placed on the dominant platform in the main hall of the gurdwara during the day. It is placed with great respect and dignity upon a throne with beautiful and colourful fabric.

Sikh Religious Philosophy

The Sikh religious philosophy can be divided into the following five sections:

Primary Beliefs and Principles

Sikhism advocates the belief in one pantheistic God (Ek Onkar) who is omnipresent and has infinite qualities. Sikhs do not have a gender for God nor do they believe God takes a human form. All human beings are considered equal regardless of their religion, sex or race. All are sons and daughters of Waheguru, the Almighty.

Followers of Sikhism are encouraged to wake in the early morning hours, before the sun has risen, and meditate on God's name. They must work hard and honestly and never live off of others, but give to others from the fruits of one's own labour. A Sikh's home should always be open to all.

Sikhs believe in the concept of reincarnation. All creatures are believed to have souls that pass to other bodies upon death until liberation is achieved. Sikhs should defend, safeguard, and fight for the rights of all creatures, and in particular fellow human beings. They are encouraged to have a "Chardi Kala" or positive, optimistic and buoyant view of life.

The Sikh religion is not considered the only way to salvation - people of other religions may also achieve salvation. This concept is shared with other religions.

Upon baptism, Sikhs must wear the 5Ks, strictly recite the 5 prayers. Sikhs do not believe that any particular day is holier than any other and general adopt the religous day of the country within which they reside.

It is every Sikh's duty to defeat these five vices: ego, anger, greed, attachment, and lust in his/her being with contentment, charity, kindness, positive attitude and humility.

Underlying Values

The Sikhs must believe in the following values:

1. **Equality:** All humans are equal before God.
2. **God's spirit:** All creatures have God's spirits and must be properly respected.
3. **Actions count:** Salvation is obtained by one's actions, including good deeds, remembrance of God, etc.
4. **Personal right:** Every person has a right to life but this right is restricted.
5. **Living a family life:** Must live as a family unit to provide and nurture children.
6. **Accept God's will:** Develop your personality so that you recognize happy events and miserable events as one.

7. **Sharing:** It is encouraged to share and give to charity 10 percent of one's net earnings.

8. **The four fruits of life:** Truth, contentment, contemplation and Naam, (in the name of God).

Prohibited Behaviour

1. **Non-logical behaviour:** Superstitions and rituals are not meaningful to Sikhs (pilgrimages, fasting, bathing in rivers, circumcision, worship of graves, idols or pictures, compulsory wearing of the veil for women, etc.).

2. **Sacrifice of creatures:** (Sati). Widows throwing themselves in the funeral pyre of their husbands, lamb and calf slaughter to celebrate holy occasions, etc. are forbidden.

3. **Material obsession:** ("Maya") Accumulation of materials has no meaning in Sikhism. Wealth such as gold, portfolio, stocks, commodities, and properties will all be left here on Earth when you depart. Do not get attached to them.

4. **Non-family oriented living:** A Sikh is not allowed to live as a recluse, beggar, yogi, monk, nun, or celibate.

5. **Intoxication:** Alcohol, drugs, tobacco, and consumption of other intoxicants is not permitted.

6. **Worthless talk:** Bragging, gossip, lying, etc. are not permitted.

7. **Priestly class:** Sikhs do not have to depend on a priest for performing any religious functions. They are not supposed to follow a class/caste system where the priestly class reigns highest. Everyone is equal.

Technique and Methods

1. **Naam Japo:** - Free service (Sewa), meditation and prayer (Simran), sacred music (Kirtan).
2. **Kirat Karni:** - Honest earnings, labour, etc. while remembering the Lord.
3. **Wand kay Shako:** - Share with others in need, free food (langar), donate 10% of income Daasvand, etc.

Other Observations

1. **Not son of God:** The Gurus were not in the Christian sense "Sons of God". Sikhism says all humans are the children of God and by deduction, God is mother/ father.
2. **All are welcome:** Members of all religions may visit Sikh temples (Gurdwaras), but must observe certain rules: cover the head, remove shoes, no smoking or drinking intoxicants inside, and visitors must not be under the influence of any drugs, especially alcohol.
3. **Multi-level approach:** Sikhism recognises the concept of a multi-level approach to achieving one's target as a disciple of the faith. For example, "Sahajdhari" (slow adopters) are Sikhs who have not donned the full 5Ks but are still Sikhs nevertheless.

Sikhs Today

Today, Sikhs can be found all over India and elsewhere in the world. Sikh men as well as some Sikh women can be identified by their practice of always wearing a turban to cover their long hair. The turban is quite different from the ones worn by the Muslim clergy and should not be confused with them. The surname or more usually the middle name Singh[1] (meaning lion) is very common for males, and Kaur (meaning princess) for women. Of course, not all people named Singh or Kaur are necessarily Sikhs, the Sikhs adopted the name Singh in 1699 during the Birth of the Khalsa. The name Singh is closely linked to the martial antiquities of North India dating back to at least the Eighth Century CE.

The Five Ks

Practicing Sikhs are bound to wear five items, known as The Five Ks, at all times. It is done either out of respect for the tenth Sikh Guru, Guru Gobind Singh, or out of sense of duty or from understanding of their function and purpose and relevance in daily life. It is important to note that The Five Ks are not merely present for symbolic purposes. The tenth Guru, Guru Gobind Singh, ordered these Five Ks to be worn so that a Sikh could actively use them to make a difference to their own spirituality and to others' spirituality.

The 5 items are: Kesh (uncut hair), Kanga (small comb), Kara (circular bracelet), Kirpan (small sword) and Kacha (shorts).

Sikhs Around the World

A Sikh known as Yogi Bhajan brought the Sikh way of life to many young people in the Western hemisphere. In addition to Indian-born Sikhs, there are now thousands of individuals of Western origin who were not born as Sikhs, but have embraced the Sikh way of life and live and teach all over the world.

In the late 1970s and 1980s a limited political separatist movement arose in India with the mission to create a separate Sikh state, called Khalistan, in the Punjab area of India and Pakistan.

Currently, there are about 23 million Sikhs in the world, making it the fifth largest world religion. Approximately 19 million Sikhs live in India with the majority living in the state of Punjab ('greater Punjab' extends across the India-Pakistan border but few Sikhs remained in Pakistan due to persecution during the split of India in 1947). Large populations of Sikhs can be found in the United Kingdom, Canada, and USA. They also comprise a significant minority in Malaysia and Singapore, where they are sometimes made fun of for their distinctive appearance, but are respected for their drive and high education standards, as they dominate the legal profession.

Following the Indian general election, 2004, Dr Manmohan Singh has become the first Sikh Prime Minister of India. He is also the first non-Hindu Prime Minister of India.

Sikhs comprise 10% of the Indian Armed Forces. In 2005, the first Sikh General of the Indian Army was designated. Also they have a major presence in the Transport Industry in India.

Observations

The founder of Sikhism, Guru Nanak, was born in 1469 to a Khatri family in central Punjab (in what is present day Pakistan). After four epic journeys (north to Tibet, south to Sri Lanka, east to Bengal and west to Mecca and Baghdad) Guru Nanak preached to Hindus, Muslims and others, and in the process attracted a following of Sikhs or disciples. Religion, he taught, was a way to unite people, but in practice he found that it set men against one another. He particularly regretted the antagonism between Hindus and Muslims as well as certain ritualistic practices that distracted people from focusing on God. He wanted to go beyond what was being practised by either religion and hence a well-known saying of Guru Nanak is, "There is no Hindu, there is no Muslim." Guru Gobind Singh reinforced these words by saying, "Regard the whole human race as equal".

Guru Nanak was opposed to the caste system. His followers referred to him as the guru (teacher). Before his death he designated a new Guru to be his successor and to lead the Sikh community. This procedure was continued, and the tenth and last Guru, Guru Gobind (AD 1666–1708) initiated the Sikh ceremony in AD 1699 ; and thus gave a distinctive identity to the Sikhs. The five baptised Sikhs were named Panj Pyare (Five Beloved Ones), who in turn baptised the Guru at his request.

Guru Nanak's doctrinal position is clear, despite the appearance that it is a blend of insights originating from two very different faiths. Sikhism's coherence is attributable to its single central concept – the sovereignty of the One God, the Creator. Guru Nanak called God the "True Name" because he wanted to avoid any limiting terms for God. He taught that the True Name, although manifest in many ways, many places and known by many names, is eternally One, the Sovereign and omnipotent God (the Truth of Love).

Guru Nanak's ascribed to the concept of *maya,* regarding material objects and realities as expressions of the creator's eternal truth, which tended to erect "a wall of falsehood" around those who live totally in the mundane world of material desires. This materialism prevents them from seeing the ultimate reality, as God created matter as a veil, so that only spiritual minds, free of desire, can penetrate it by the grace of the Guru (Gurprasad).

The world is immediately real in the sense that it is made manifest to the senses as maya, but is ultimately unreal in the sense that God alone is ultimate reality. Retaining the Hindu doctrine of the transmigration of souls, together with its corollary, the law of *karma,* Guru Nanak advised his followers to end the cycle of reincarnation by living a disciplined life – that is, by moderating egoism and sensuous delights, to live in a balanced worldly manner, and by accepting ultimate reality. Thus, by the grace of Guru (Gurprasad) the cycle of re-incarnation can be broken, and the Sikh can remain in the abode of the Love of God.

A Sikh should balance work, worship and charity - and meditate by repeating God's name, *Nam japna* (to enhance spiritual development). Salvation, Guru Nanak said, does not mean entering paradise after a last judgment, but a union and absorption into God, the true name. Sikhs believe in neither heaven nor hell. They strive for the grace of the Guru during the human journey of the soul.

Political pressure from surrounding Muslim nations forced the Sikhs to defend themselves and by the mid-nineteenth century, the Punjab area straddling modern-day India and Pakistan, Afghanistan and Kashmir was ruled by them. The Sikh's Khalsa Army defeated the invading British army and signed treaties with China.

All are Welcome

Members of all religions may visit Sikh temples (gurdwaras = the Guru's door) but are asked to observe the following rules out of respect for sikh sensibilities:

- To cover one's head (there will be bandana-like rumaals available there)
- To take off one's shoes
- To not smoke or indulge in the consumption of alcoholic or tobacco-related materials (even in the vicinity of the gurdwara)
- Not to bring or possess any alcoholic or tobacco-related items, or be under their effects when entering the gurdwara.

Multi-Level Approach

Sikhism recognises the concept of a multi-level approach to achieving your target as a disciple of the faith. For example, Sahajdhari (slow adopters) are **Sikhs** who have not donned the full Five Ks but are still Sikhs nonetheless.

The Khalsa

A baptised Sikh becomes a member of the Khalsa or the "Pure Ones". When a Sikh joins the Khalsa, he/she is supposed to have devoted their life to the Guru, and is expected not to desist from sacrificing anything and everything in a struggle for a just and righteous cause.

The word "Khalsa" has two literal meanings. It comes from Persian. One literal meaning is "Pure" and the other meaning is "belonging to the king". When the word "Khalsa" is used for a Sikh, it implies belonging to the King, where the King is God himself. To become a Khalsa, a Sikh must surrender themselves completely to the supreme King or God and obey God's will without question or delay.

Sikhs and Punjabis

Since Sikhism originated in the region of Punjab, most Sikhs trace their roots to that region (though in recent times, with the spread both of Sikhism and Sikhs, one might encounter Sikhs belonging to other geographical locations across the world). With the revisions of the state boundaries in 1966, 65% of the population in Punjab is now made up of Sikhs, whereas Sikhs comprise only 2% of the population in India as a whole. Consequently, and also because the Guru Granth Sahib is written in Gurmukhi, a script of the Punjabi language, most Sikhs are able to speak, read or write the language, or are at least familiar with it.

Followers of Sikhism

A Sikh is a follower of Sikhism. The word Sikh is derived from the Sanskrit word *shishya* which means disciple or student. In the Punjabi language the word Sikh also means humble follower. So a Sikh is a disciple of the Ten Gurus and a follower of the teachings in Sikhism's holy scriptures who they regard as a living guru, the Guru Granth Sahib.

●●

4
Guru Granth Sahib

Guru Granth Sahib or Adi Sri Granth Sahib Ji or Adi Granth or Adi Guru Darbar, is more than just a scripture of the Sikhs. The Sikhs treat this Granth (*holy book*) as a living Guru. The holy text spans 1430 pages and contains the actual words spoken by the founders of the Sikh religion (the Ten Gurus of Sikhism) and the words of various other Saints from other religions including Hinduism and Islam.

Guru Granth Sahib was given the Guruship by the last of the living Sikh Masters, Guru Gobind Singh Ji in 1708. Guru Gobind Singh said before his demise that the Sikhs were to treat the Granth Sahib as their next Guru. Guru Ji said – "Sab Sikhan ko hokam hai Guru Manyo Granth" meaning "All Sikhs are commanded to take the Granth as Guru" So today if asked, the Sikhs will tell you that they have a total of 11 Gurus. (10 in human form and the SGGS).

When one visits a Gurdwara (a Sikh temple) , the Guru Granth Sahib forms the main part of the Darbar Sahib or Main Hall. The holy book is placed on a dominant platform and covered in a very beautiful and attractively coloured fine cloth. The platform is always covered by a canopy, which is also decorated in expensive and very attractive coloured materials. The text in which the Granth is written is a script called Gurmukhi (literally "From the Guru's mouth"), which is considered a modern development of the ancient language called Sanskrit.

Composition of Guru Granth Sahib

Guru Nanak brought the "Word of God" to manifest upon Earth. Through his Hymns and Prayers (Shabads), he inspired and uplifted humankind to live a life of truth, righteousness and spirituality. These enlightening words were sung by his companions, Bala and Mardana, and by the Sangats (congregations) which grew up around Guru Nanak. In his later years at Kartarpur, it became customary for the members of the Sikh community to sing certain hymns on a daily basis: Japji in the morning; So Dar and So Purakh, the beginnings of Rehiras, in the evenings.

Guru Angad, Guru Amar Das and Guru Ram Das all composed Shabads (hymns), and the Sikhs began to collect these in books called Pothis (small books). Chanting these Shabads, the Sikhs became vehicles for the vibrations of the "Word of God", and they achieved a state of higher consciousness, a transcendent meditative union with God and Guru.

Standardisation of Shabads

Even early in Sikh history, however, there were mal-quotations, and pretenders to the Throne of Spirituality. The elder brother of Guru Arjun, Prithia, composed his own hymns and passed them off as writings of Guru Nanak. Although pothis existed of authentic Gurbani, there were many different collections of Shabads, and many differing versions of the same Shabads.

Guru Arjun realized that a standardized, authenticated collection of the Guru's Bani (called Gurbani) was needed to preserve the integrity of the Shabad.

The most complete collection of Shabads of Guru Nanak, Guru Angad and Guru Amar Das was in the possession of Mohan, a son of Guru Amar Das.

Retrieving the Pothi from Mohan

Guru Arjun sent Bhai Gurdas to Mohan's home in Goindwal, to request this collection of Shabads. Mohan felt slighted at having been passed over for Guruship – his father, Guru Amar Das, had seen the Divine Light in Guru Ram Das, and had bestowed the Guruship upon him. Mohan refused to answer the door when Bhai Gurdas knocked, and Bhai Gurdas returned to Guru Arjun empty-handed.

Guru Arjun then sent Baba Buddha to Mohan's house. Baba Buddha was by then a very old and respected man in the Sikh community, having been a disciple of all the Gurus, from Guru Nanak through Guru Arjun. When Mohan did not answer Baba Buddha's knock, he entered the house anyway. Inside, he found Mohan in a deep meditative trance. Mohan's younger brother convinced Baba Buddha not to disturb him, and Baba Buddha also returned to Guru Arjun empty-handed.

So it was that in 1603, Guru Arjun found it necessary to go to Mohan's house himself, to retrieve the Shabads himself. When Guru Arjun approached his house, he called out in a sweet voice, but there was no response. The Guru sat upon his doorstep and began to sing these lines,

"Oh, Mohan, your mansion is so lofty, there is no other place like yours.

Oh, Mohan, even the Saints adorn the door of your temple.

Show compassion and kindness, Oh Kind Lord—be merciful to the poor.

Says Nanak, I am thirsting for the Blessed Vision of Your Darshan Grant me this gift, and I shall be happy."

Mohan is a name of God, calling upon Him as the Beloved. When Guru Arjun sang this Hymn, he was singing the Praises of God, in the form of a song to win Mohan's heart. Mohan threw open the window and called out to Guru Arjun, "You stole the Guruship from my family, and now you come to steal what remains of my heritage!"

Guru Arjun responded with sweet words,

> "Oh Mohan, your words are like no others, and your behaviour is exemplary.
>
> Oh Mohan, you believe in the One God and treat all others as garbage.
>
> Says Nanak, please preserve my honor - all your servants seek Your Sanctuary."

Mohan grumbled and protested, muttering about his claim to the Shabads. But finally, he came down and sat by Guru Arjun, as the Guru continued to sing,

> "Oh Mohan, the Sadh Sangat, the Company of the Holy, meditates upon You, and yearns to obtain the Blessed Vision of Your Darshan.
>
> Oh Mohan, at the very last moment of life, death shall not approach You.
>
> All who worship You in thought, word and deed shall obtain Your Gifts.
>
> Even the impure, the stupid and the foolish obtain Divine Knowledge upon seeing You.
>
> Says Nanak, Oh God, You are present within all,
>
> You are above all."

Gazing upon Guru Arjun's enlightened face, feeling the love and radiance emanating from him, hearing the sweet words of love and humility, Mohan's heart was softened, and opened at last. He acknowledged Guru Arjun's true place upon the throne of Guru Nanak, and gave all of the Shabads in his possession to Guru Arjun.

Work begins to Compile the Aad Granth

Guru Arjun then set to compile the Shabads into a single volume, the Adi Granth. He sifted through the Shabads which had been passed down from the first four Gurus, and filtered out those which had been added by imposters. Bhai Gurdas was the scribe who recorded the words of Guru Arjun. When he asked Guru Arjun how he could distinguish between the true and the false Shabads, Guru Arjun replied, "Even in a great herd of cows and calves, the mother cow will recognize the cry of her calf, above all others. Just so, the True Shabad resonates truly, and is easily distinguished from the false."

Guru Arjun added a great many of his own Shabads to those of Guru Nanak, Guru Angad, Guru Amar Das and Guru Ram Das. He also added Shabads of thirty-six Hindu and Muslim Saints, among them Kabir, Ravi Das, Naam Dev, Trilochan and Sheikh Farid. This was the first time any religion incorporated the works of sincere devotees of other religions into its own scripture; it reflects the universality of thought which underlies the Sikh belief in One God, and the one family of humanity as children of God.

Guru Arjun left some blank pages in the Granth. When Bhai Gur Das asked the purpose of this, he answered that one of the Gurus to follow him would add the Shabads in their proper place at the proper time. In time the shabads of Guru Teg Bahadur, the ninth Manifestation of the Guru's Light, were added by Guru Gobind Singh and thus the Siri Guru Granth Sahib was complete.

Guru Gobind Singh Recreates Holy Granth

Guru Gobind Singh proceeded to dictate it to Bhai Mani Singh, who recorded it on paper. While some have questioned the authenticity of this story, it is well for us to remember that, of course, Guru Gobind Singh was no ordinary person at all. And, in the old days of bards and story-tellers, it was not unusual for them to recite from memory entire epic poems. Hajis, for example can recite the entire Qur'an and many Hindus priests could recite the Mahabarata. In a time when many people could not read or write, oral traditions were very important. The Sri Guru Granth Sahib is like the Qur'an and the Gita and is set in the form of music and rhythm making them much easier to remember.

Guru Gobind Singh included the Shabads of his father, Guru Teg Bahadur, but he did not include his own Shabads; instead, he placed them in a separate Granth, the Dasam Granth. The Dasam Granth is not revered as Guru, however. The great task of re-writing the entire Guru was finally completed in 1705. The "Damdama Sahib Bir" as it is now called was then taken to Nanded where it was installed.

First Installation of the Holy Granth

The Adi Granth was completed in 1604, and installed in the Golden Temple; Baba Buddha was appointed Guru's Granthi. Guru Arjun told his Sikhs that the Adi Granth was the embodiment of the Guru, and should be treated in the same fashion as they respect him. When Guru Arjun first completed the Adi Granth, he placed it upon his own bed and slept on the floor. Its words were written without any spaces or breaks, which nowadays is hard for most people to follow.

Guru Gobind Singh, the tenth and last of the Sikh Gurus to take human form, dictated the entire Granth Sahib at Talwandi Sabo now called Damdama Sahib. Dhir Mal, the son of Baba Gurditta and grandson of Guru Hargobind, had taken possession of the Adi Granth; he refused to give it to Guru Gobind Singh when the Guru asked for it. Dhir Mal taunted the Guru, "If you are a Guru, then prepare your own."

Installation as Perpetual Sikh Guru

Guru Gobind Singh installed this expanded version of the Adi Granth as Guru on October 20, 1708. This day is celebrated today as Guru Gadi Divas (Enthronement Day). At the time of his death, he declared that the Word of God embodied in the Siri Guru Granth Sahib was to be Guru for all time. He said, "O Beloved Khalsa, let any who desire to behold me, behold the Guru Granth. Obey the Granth Sahib, for it is the visible body of the Guru. Let any who desire to meet me, diligently search its Bani." Thus the Word of God, which has manifested as Guru in Nanak, and had passed through the ten incarnations of Guru, was now returned to its form as the Word, the Bani, the Shabad.

Structure of the Guru Granth Sahib

Within it's 1430 pages, the shabads (hymns) of the Sri Guru Granth Sahib are arranged in thirty-one Ragas, the traditional Indian musical measures and scales. Within the Ragas, they are arranged by order of the Sikh Gurus, with the shabads of the Hindu and Muslim Saints following. The shabads are written in various meters and rhythms, and are organised accordingly. For instance, Ashtapadi - eight steps, or Panch-padi - five steps. The Sri Guru Granth Sahib is written in Gurmukhi script, but the shabads were written in many different languages including Punjabi, Sanskrit and Persian.

The original bir of Guru Granth Sahib did not contain an index. However, this is provided in some modern print of the bir to make it easy to find the location of some of the common banis. For example, from the index, (see main article here) it can be seen that the Japji Sahib starts at page 1 and ends at page 8; Sukhmani Sahib is located from pages 262 to 296; the Bara Maha bani can is found at pages 133 to 136; The bani called Anand Sahib(Bliss) can be found at pages 917 to 922, etc.

The Beginning

The **Guru Granth Sahib** begins with the word "Ek Onkar" – *The All Pervading Being*. From this Word to the tenth Word "Gur-parshad" is called the Mool Mantra. After this is the rest of the composition called the Japji composed by Guru Nanak Dev. This comprises 38 Pauris or stanzas, a Prologue and an Epilogue. This is one of the morning prayer of the Sikhs.

The next composition has two parts - (1) "So Dar" and (2) "So Purkh". The Bani, "So Dar" contains 5 Shabads and "So Purkh" contains 4 Shabads. This form most of the evening prayer of the Sikhs and is called the Rehras. After this is the Bani called Sohila (full name, Kirtan Sohila), which contains 5 Shabads and is the bed-time prayer.

The 31 Ragas

The Adi Granth starts with the a non-raga section which begins with Japji as the first entry followed by Rehras and ending with Kirtan Sohila. Then begins the main section consisting of 31 Ragas or chapters. A raga is a musical structure or set of rules of how to build a melody. It specifies a scale, as well as rules for movements up and down the scale; which notes should figure more and which notes should be used more sparingly; etc. The result is a framework that can be used to compose or improvise melodies in, so that melodies in a certain raga will always be recognisable yet allowing endless variation.

Just as a raga has emotional overtone, so each chapter has spiritual implication. The thirty-one ragas appear in the following serial order: Sri raga, Manjh, Gauri, Asa, Gujri, Devagandhari, Bihagara, Wadahans, Sorath, Dhanasri, Jaitsri, Todi, Bairari, Tilang, Suhi, Bilaval, Gond (Gaund), Ramkali, Nut-Narayan, Mali-Gaura, Maru, Tukhar, Kedara, Bhairav (Bhairo), Basant, Sarang, Malar, Kanra, Kalyan, Prabhati and Jaijawanti.

Within the 1430 pages are found Saloks of Bhagat Kabir, Sheikh Farid, Guru Tegh Bahadur, etc.

The Closing Section

The Main section which consists of 31 chapters forming the the Raga section is followed by a brief closing section. This is composed of the Mundavani (The Closing Seal), a salok by Guru Arjan and the final composition of the SGGS, which is the Ragamala

Historical Volumes of the Siri Guru Granth Sahib

- **Kartarpur Vaali Bir:** As described above, Guru Arjun dictated the Adi Granth to Bhai Gur Das. This first volume, or Bir, was made in Amritsar and later transferred to Kartarpur, where it remains today. The opening lines are in the hand of Guru Arjun, and it bears the signature of Guru Hargobind at the end. There are several blank pages, left by Guru Arjun to hold the writings of Guru Teg Bahadur.Apart frommany handwritten copies of Sri Guru Granth Sahib possessed by various persons and found in some gurdwaras the most important is the Bir recension at Kartarpur, near Jullundur in the custody of Sodhi Amarjit Singh, a descendant of Dhirmal

- **Bhai Banno Vaali Bir:** After completing the Adi Granth, Guru Arjun asked one of his Sikhs, Bhai Banno, to take the manuscript to Lahore to have it bound. During this journey, Bhai Banno had a copy made for his own use. He inserted a few Shabads of his own choosing, however. This version remains with his descendents.Hand written Manuscript of Bhai Banno wali Bir is said to be available at Gurdwara Banno Sahib in Kanpur city in India.

- **Damdama Vaali Bir:** This is the volume dictated by Guru Gobind Singh at Damdama Sahib to Mani

Singh. In it, Guru Gobind Singh included the Shabads of Guru Teg Bahadur. The volumes of the Siri Guru Granth Sahib which preside over our Gurdwaras now are copies of this edition.

Using the Gurmukhi Bir and the English Translation

In the West, it has become common to use the English translation of the Siri Guru Granth Sahib in Gurdwara programmes and Akhand Paaths, because many of the Western Sikhs are not fluent in Gurmukhi. This has served to bring many to the Feet of the Guru who otherwise may not have had the opportunity to experience the Shabad Guru. It should be noted, however, that it is ideal to install the full Gurmukhi Bir in the Gurdwara in order to fully experience and develop a relationship with the Guru. The English translation can be installed on a separate Palki on the side and serve to illuminate the sangat in the meaning of the Words of the Guru. The English translation may be used during an Akhand Paath in which the participants are not fluent in Gurmukhi. Howev er, if a special Gurdwara programme is being planned, the English Akhand Paath days can be accomodated so that the full Gurmukhi Bir of Siri Guru Granth Sahib presides.

A Sikh is encouraged (but not a must) to learn to read Gurmukhi so as to deepen his or her experience of Gurbani and so that the full body of the Guru may be installed in the Gurdwara.

Note: English and other translations of the Sre Guru Granth Sahib Ji should be considered as just another "style" (language) of talking/deitating/praising the guru. Trying to force a person to learn punjabi/gurmukhi is highly undesirable.

Comments on Sri Guru Granth Sahib by Non-Sikhs

This is what Max Arthur Macauliffe wrote about the authenticity of the Guru's teaching

- The Sikh religion differs as regards the authenticity of its dogmas from most other theological systems. Many of the great teachers the world has known, have not left a line of their own composition and we only know what they taught through tradition or second-hand information. If Pythagoras wrote of his tenets, his writings have not descended to us. We know the teachings of Socrates only through the writings of Plato and Xenophanes. Buddha has left no written memorial of his teaching. Kungfu-tze, known to Europeans as Contuscius, left no documents in which he detailed the principles of his moral and social system. The founder of Christianity did not reduce his doctrines to writing and for them we are obliged to trust to the gospels according to Matthew, Mark, Luke and John. The Arabian Prophet did not himself reduce to writing the chapters of the Quran. They were written or compiled by his adherents and followers. But the compositions of the Sikh Gurus are preserved and we know at first hand what they taught.

- .... "**Guru Granth Sahib** enshrines the message of universal brotherhood and good of all mankind." said **Dalai Lama**,The Spiritual Leader Of Tibetian Buddhism .

- ... "I am very much impressed about Sikhism and the bravery of it's followers.I have felt and rightly too that in the welfare of this religion lies the welfare of India." said **Col.Phin Mubukant - Minister Of Religious Affairs in Thailand in 1963**.

Miss Pearl S. Buck, a Nobel laureate, gives the following comment on receiving the First English translation of the **Guru Granth Sahib** (The Sikh Holy Book):

- .... I have studied the scriptures of the great religions, but I do not find elsewhere the same power of appeal to the heart and mind as I find here in these volumes. They are compact in spite of their length, and are a revelation of the vast reach of the human heart, varying from the most noble concept of God, to the recognition and indeed the insistence upon the practical needs of the human body. There is something strangely modern about these scriptures and this puzzles me until I learned that they are in fact comparatively modern, compiled as late as the 16th century, when explorers were beginning to discover that the globe upon which we all live is a single entity divided only by arbitrary lines of our own making. Perhaps this sense of unity is the source of power I find in these volumes. **They speak to a person of any religion or of none***. They speak for the human heart and the searching mind. ...

Message of Guru Granth Sahib

The **Guru Granth Sahib** provides unique and unequalled guidance and advice to the whole of the human race. It is the torch that will lead humanity out of Kaljug, (the dark era) to a life in peace, tranquillity and spiritual enlightenment for all the nations of the World. The main message can be summaried as:

1 All Peoples of the World are Equal

2 Women as Equals

3 One God for All

4 Speak and Live Truthfully

5 Control the Five Vices

6 Live in God's Hukam

7 Practise Humility, Kindness, Compassion, Love, etc.

Care and Protocol to be Observed

Personal Behaviour

Any person carrying out any *Service or Sewa* for SGGS MUST observe the following:

- Head must be covered at all times.
- observe basic standards of personal hygiene.
- Shoes must be removed outside the Guru's room.
- If you have to visit the toilet, have a shower and change your clothing before serving the Guru again.
- No eating or drinking while in service.
- When reading from the Guru, you must cover your mouth...
- No small talk while in Guru's service.

While in the vicinity of SGGS, everyone should observe the following:

- Head must be covered at all times.
- Shoes must be removed, especially if indoors.
- When Guru Granth Sahib passes past one must show reverence and respect for the Guru.

Environment

- Guru Granth Sahib should always be placed in an independent, well-ventilated and separate room.
- The floor, walls and ceilings should be cleaned or washed as appropriate and suitably decorated.
- A canopy, of suitably material should always be placed over the Guru just below the ceiling.

- Maharaj has to be placed on a Manji Sahib. The dimension of the Manji Sahib must be at least 12 inches high, 36 inches wide and 18 inches deep.

- Guru's Attire: Clothing appropriate to the season is to be placed upon the throne of the Guru. In the summer, thin clothing and in winter, warm clothing i.e. a thick blanket/duvet must be used.

- A Chaur Sahib should be provided besides the Guru with a small platform to house the Kar Parshad and other implements.

- The Plain white sheet that is placed under the Manji Sahib is to be of better quality, and separate, to that of the Granthi Singh.

On The Move

Whilst the Guru is on the move the following should be observed:

- Five Singhs (Minimum of three) are to accompany the Guru at all times when travelling

- These Singhs are to remain bare-footed.

- One Singh is to do Chaur Sahib Seva

- One Singh is to go ahead of Satguru and sprinkle water or wet flower petals.

- The Main Singh carrying the Guru must put a clean Rumalla on his Turban before carefully and with respect placing the Guru on this Rumalla. At all times, the Guru should be covered with a small Rumalla so that the Guru's Sarop is always fully "covered".

- The other two Singh walk besides the Main Singh – one on his left and the other on his right.

- In order to make the Sangat aware that the Guru is coming in their direction, gongs or other appropriate instruments are to be played or recitation of "Waheguru" at all times.
- When travelling by car, etc, if possible carry the Guru on the head or the lap. In each case a clean Rumalla must be place below the Guru.

RELIGIOUS PHILOSOPHY

The Sikh Religious Philosophy can .be divided into 5 Sections:

Primary Beliefs & Principles:

1. **One God:** - There is only ONE God who has infinite qualities and names; He is the same for all religions;
2. **Re-incarnation, Karma & Salvation:** – Every creature has a Soul; on death, the Soul is passed from one body to another until Liberation.
3. **Remember God:** Love God but have fear of Him* as well.
4. **"Humanhood" (Brotherhood*):** All human beings are equal. We are sons and daughters of Waheguru, the Almighty.
5. **Personal Sacrifice:** Be prepared to give your life for all supreme principles – see the life of Guru Teg Bahadur.
6. **Uphold Moral Values:** Defend, safeguard and fight for the rights of all creatures and in particular your fellow beings.
7. **Many Paths lead to God:** – Sikhs are not Special: The Sikhs are not the chosen people of God – By just calling yourself a Sikh does not bring you salvation.

8. **Disciplined Life:** Upon baptism, must wear the 5Ks; strict recital of the 5 prayers Banis, etc.

9. **Positive Attitude to Life:** "Chardi Kala" – Always have a positive and obtemistic view of life.

10. **No Special Worship Days:** Sikhs do not believe that any particular day is holier than any other.

11. **Attack with 5 Weapons:** Compassion (Daya), Truth (Sat), Contentment (Santokh), Humility (Nimrata) and Love (Pyar)

12. **Conquer the 5 Thieves:** It every Sikhs duty to defeat these 5 thieves

Underlying Values:

The Sikhs must believe in the following Values:

1. **Equality:** All humans are equal before God – No discrimination is allowed on the basis of Caste, Race, Sex, Creed, Origin, colour, education, status, wealth, etc.

2. **Personal Right:** Every person has a right to life but this right is restricted and has attached certain duties – Simple Living is essential.

3. **God's Spirit:** All Creatures have God's spirits and must be properly respected. Show love for all living things. Mistreatment of any living creature is tabooed and forbidden.

4. **Actions Count:** Salvation is obtained by one's actions – Good deeds, remembrance of God – Naam Simran, Kirtan, etc

5. **Sharing:** It is encouraged to share and give to charity 10 percent of one's net earnings.

6. **Living a Family Life:** Must live as a family unit (householder) to provide and nurture children for the perpetual benefit of creation.
7. **Accept God's Will:** Develop your personality so that you recognise happy event and miserable events as one – the Will of God causes them.
8. **The 4 Fruits of Life:** Truth, Contentment, Contemplation and Naam, (in the Name of God)

Prohibited Behaviour:

1. **Non-Logical Behaviour:** Superstitions; rituals, which have no meaning, pilgrimages, fasting and bathing in rivers; gambling; circumcision; worship of graves, idols, pictures; compulsory wearing of the veil for women; etc;
2. **Sacrifice of Creatures:** Sati – widows throwing themselves in the funeral pyre of their husbands; lamb and calf slaughter to celebrate holy occasions; etc
3. **Material Obsession:** ("Maya") Accumulation of materials have no meaning in Sikhism. Wealth, Gold, Portfolio, Stocks, Commodities, properties will all be left here on Earth when you depart. Do not get attached to them.
4. **Worthless Talk:** bragging, gossip, lying, etc are not permitted.
5. **Non-Family Oriented Living:** A sikh is not allowed to live a recluse, beggar, yogi, monk, Nun, celibacy, etc
6. **Intoxication:** Drinking alcohol; Drugs; Smoking tobacco; consumption of other intoxicants; etc
7. **No priestly Class:** Sikhs do not have to depend on a priest fro any of the functions that need to be performed.

Technique and Methods:

1. **Naam:** Japo – Meditation & Prayer, Free Service Sewa, Simran, Sacred Music Kirtan

2. **Kirat Karni:** - Honest, Earnings, labour, etc while remembering the Lord

3. **Wand kay Shako:** - Share with Others who are deserving, Free Food langar, 10% Donation Daasvand, etc

Other Observations:

1. **Not Son of God:** The Gurus were not in the Christian sense "Sons of God". Sikhism says we are all Gods kids and S/He* is our Father/Mother.

2. **All Welcomed:** Members of All religions can visit Sikh temples ("Gurdwaras") but please observe the local rules – Cover Head, No shoes, No Smoking when going in to the Main Hall.

3. **Multi-Level Approach:** Sikhism recognises the concept of a Multi-level approach to achieving your target as a disciple of the faith. For example, "Sahajdhari" (slow adopters) are Sikhs who have not donned the full 5Ks but are still Sikhs nevertheless.

●●

5

Sikh Religion and Culture

Sikhism is a monistic religion founded in fifteenth century Punjab on the teachings of Guru Nanak Dev and ten successive Sikh Gurus (the last one being the sacred text Guru Granth Sahib). It is the fifth-largest organised religion in the world. This system of religious philosophy and expression has been traditionally known as the Gurmat (literally *the counsel of the gurus*) or the Sikh Dharma. *Sikhism* originated from the word *Sikh*.

The principal belief of Sikhism is faith in *waheguru*—represented using the sacred symbol of *ik MaEkâr*, the Universal God. Sikhism advocates the pursuit of salvation through disciplined, personal meditation on the name and message of God. A key distinctive feature of Sikhism is a non-anthropomorphic concept of God, to the extent that one can interpret God as the Universe itself. The followers of Sikhism are ordained to follow the teachings of the ten Sikh gurus, or enlightened leaders, as well as the holy scripture entitled the *Gurû Granth Sâhib*, which, along with the writings of six of the ten Sikh Gurus, includes selected works of many devotees from diverse socio-economic and religious backgrounds. The text was decreed by Guru Gobind Singh, the tenth guru, as the final guru of the Khalsa Panth. Sikhism's traditions and teachings are distinctively associated with the history, society and culture of the Punjab. Adherents of Sikhism are known as Sikhs (*students* or *disciples*) and number over 26 million across the world. Most Sikhs live in Punjab in India and, until India's partition, millions of Sikhs lived in what is now Pakistani Punjab.

Philosophy and Teachings

The origins of Sikhism lie in the teachings of Guru Nanak and his successors. The essence of Sikh teaching is summed up by Nanak in these words: "Realisation of Truth is higher than all else. Higher still is truthful living". Sikh teaching emphasizes the principle of equality of all humans and rejects discrimination on the basis of caste, creed, and gender. Sikh principles do not attach any importance to asceticism as a means to attain salvation, but stresses on the need of leading life as a householder.

Sikhism is a monotheistic religion. In Sikhism, God—termed *Vâhigurû*—is shapeless, timeless, and sightless: *niraEkâr, akâl,* and *alakh*. The beginning of the first composition of Sikh scripture is the figure "1"—signifying the universality of God. It states that God is omnipresent and infinite, and is signified by the term *çk ôaEkâr*. Sikhs believe that before creation, all that existed was God and Its *hukam* (will or order). When God willed, the entire cosmos was created. From these beginnings, God nurtured "enticement and attachment" to *mâyâ,* or the human perception of reality.

While a full understanding of God is beyond human beings, Nanak described God as not wholly unknowable. God is omnipresent (*sarav viâpak*) in all creation and visible everywhere to the spiritually awakened. Nanak stressed that God must be seen from "the inward eye", or the "heart", of a human being: devotees must meditate to progress towards enlightenment. Guru Nanak Dev emphasized the revelation through meditation, as its rigorous application permits the existence of communication between God and human beings. God has no gender in Sikhism, (though translations may incorrectly present a male God); indeed Sikhism teaches that God is "Nirankar" [Niran meaning "without" and kar meaning "form", hence "without form"]. In addition, Nanak wrote that there are many worlds on which God has created life.

Pursuing Salvation and Khalsa

Nanak's teachings are founded not on a final destination of heaven or hell, but on a spiritual union with God which results in salvation. The chief obstacles to the attainment of salvation are social conflicts and an attachment to worldly pursuits, which commit men and women to an endless cycle of birth—a concept known as *reincarnation*.

Mâyâ—defined as illusion or "unreality"—is one of the core deviations from the pursuit of God and salvation: people are distracted from devotion by worldly attractions which give only illusive satisfaction. However, Nanak emphasised mâyâ as not a reference to the unreality of the world, but of its values. In Sikhism, the influences of ego, anger, greed, attachment, and lust—known as the *Five Evils*—are believed to be particularly pernicious. The fate of people vulnerable to the Five Evils is separation from God, and the situation may be remedied only after intensive and relentless devotion.

Nanak described God's revelation—the path to salvation—with terms such as *nâm* (the divine *Name*) and *œabad* (the divine Word) to emphasise the totality of the revelation. Nanak designated the word *guru* (meaning *teacher*) as the voice of God and the source and guide for knowledge and salvation. Salvation can be reached only through rigorous and disciplined devotion to God. Nanak distinctly emphasised the irrelevance of outward observations such as rites, pilgrimages, or asceticism. He stressed that devotion must take place through the heart, with the spirit and the soul.

A key practice to be pursued is *nm*: remembrance of the divine Name. The verbal repetition of the name of God or a sacred syllable is an established practice in religious traditions in India, but Nanak's interpretation emphasized inward, personal observance. Nanak's ideal is the total exposure of one's being to the divine Name and a total conforming to Dharma or the "Divine Order". Nanak described the result of the disciplined application of *nm simran* as a "growing towards and into God" through a gradual process of five stages. The last of these is *sac khan*

(*The Realm of Truth*)—the final union of the spirit with God.

Nanak stressed now *kirat karô*: that a Sikh should balance work, worship, and charity, and should defend the rights of all creatures, and in particular, fellow human beings. They are encouraged to have a *cha[dî kalâ*, or *optimistic*, view of life. Sikh teachings also stress the concept of sharing—*van*

chakkô—through the distribution of free food at Sikh gurdwaras (*laegar*), giving charitable donations, and working for the good of the community and others (*sçvâ*).

The Ten Gurus and Religious Authority

The term guru comes from the Sanskrit *gurû*, meaning teacher, guide, or mentor. The traditions and philosophy of Sikhism were established by ten specific gurus from 1499 to 1708. Each guru added to and reinforced the message taught by the previous, resulting in the creation of the Sikh religion. Nanak was the first guru and appointed a disciple as successor. Gobind Singh was the final guru in human form. Before his death, Gobind Singh decreed that the Gurû Granth Sâhib would be the final and perpetual guru of the Sikhs. The Sikhs believe that the spirit of Nanak was passed from one guru to the next, " just as the light of one lamp, which lights another and does not diminish", and is also mentioned in their holy book.

After Nanak's passing, the most important phase in the development of Sikhism came with the third successor, Amar Das. Nanak's teachings emphasised the pursuit of salvation; Amar Das began building a cohesive community of followers with initiatives such as sanctioning distinctive ceremonies for birth, marriage, and death. Amar Das also established the *manji* (comparable to a diocese) system of clerical supervision.

Amar Das's successor and son-in-law Ram Das founded the city of Amritsar, which is home of the Harimandir Sahib and regarded widely as the holiest city for all Sikhs. When Ram Das's youngest son Arjan succeeded him, the line of male gurus from the *Sodhi Khatri* family was established: all succeeding gurus were direct descendants of this line. Guru Arjan Sahib was captured by Mughal authorities who were suspicious and hostile to the religious order he was developing. His persecution and death inspired his successors to promote a military and political organisation of Sikh communities to defend themselves against the attacks of Mughal forces.

The Sikh gurus established a mechanism which allowed the Sikh religion to react as a community to changing circumstances. The sixth guru, Har Gobind, was responsible for the creation of the concept of Akal Takht (*throne of the timeless one*), which serves as the supreme decision-making centre of Sikhdom and sits opposite the Darbar Sahib. The *Sarbat 4–âlsâ* (a representative portion of the Khalsa Panth) historically gathers at the Akal Takht on special festivals such as Vaisakhi or Diwali and when there is a need to discuss matters that affect the entire Sikh nation. A *gurmatâ* (literally, *guru's intention*) is an order passed by the Sarbat 4–âlsâ in the presence of the Gurû Granth Sâhib. A gurmatâ may only be passed on a subject that affects the fundamental principles of Sikh religion; it is binding upon all Sikhs. The term *hukamnâmâ* (literally, *edict* or *royal order*) is often used interchangeably with the term gurmatâ. However, a hukamnâmâ formally refers to a hymn from the Gurû Granth Sâhib which is given as an order to Sikhs.

History

Nanak (1469–1538), the founder of Sikhism, was born in the village of *Râi Bhôi dî Talwandî*, now called Nankana Sahib (in present-day Pakistan). His father, Mehta Kalu was a Patwari, an accountant of land revenue in the employment of Rai Bular Bhatti, the area landlord. Nanak's mother was Tripta Devi and he had one older sister, Nanaki. His parents were Khatri Hindus of the Bedi clan. As a boy, Nanak was fascinated by religion, and his desire to explore the mysteries of life eventually led him to leave home and take missionary journeys.

In his early teens, Nanak caught the attention of the local landlord Rai Bular Bhatti, who was moved by his intellect and divine qualities. Rai Bular was witness to many incidents in which Nanak enchanted him and as a result Rai Bular and Nanak's sister Bibi Nanki, became the first persons to recognise the divine qualities in Nanak. Both of them then encouraged and supported Nanak to study and travel. Sikh tradition states that at the age of thirty, Nanak went missing and was presumed to have drowned after going for one of his morning baths to a local stream called the *Kali Bein*. One day, he declared: "There is no Hindu, there is no Muslim" (in Punjabi, *"nâ kôi hindû nâ kôi musalmân"*). It was from this moment that Nanak would begin to spread the teachings of what was then the beginning of Sikhism. Although the exact account of his itinerary is disputed, he is widely acknowledged to have made four major journeys, spanning thousands of miles, the first tour being east towards Bengal and Assam, the second south towards Tamil Nadu, the third north towards Kashmir, Ladakh, and Tibet, and the final tour west towards Baghdad and Mecca.

Nanak was married to Sulakhni, the daughter of Moolchand Chona, a rice trader from the town of Bakala. They had two sons. The elder son, Sri Chand, was an ascetic, and he came to have a considerable following of his own, known as the Udasis. The younger son, Lakshmi Das, on the other hand, was totally immersed in worldly life. To Nanak, who believed in the ideal of *rj maia jôg* (detachment in civic life), both his sons were unfit to carry on the Guruship.

Growth of the Sikh Community

In 1538, Nanak chose his disciple *LahiGâ*, a Khatri of the Trehan clan, as a successor to the guruship rather than either of his sons. LahiGâ was named Angad Dev and became the second guru of the Sikhs. Nanak conferred his choice at the town of Kartarpur on the banks of the river Ravi, where Nanak had finally settled down after his travels. Though Sri Chand was not an ambitious man, the Udasis believed that the Guruship should have gone to him, since he was a man of pious habits in addition to being Nanak's son. They refused to accept Angad's succession. On Nanak's advice, Angad shifted from Kartarpur to Khadur, where his wife Khivi and children were living, until he was able to bridge the divide between his followers and the Udasis. Angad continued the work started by Nanak and is widely credited for standardising the Gurmukhî script as used in the sacred scripture of the Sikhs.

Amar Das, a Khatri of the Bhalla clan, became the third Sikh guru in 1552 at the age of 73. Goindval became an important centre for Sikhism during the guruship of Amar Das. He preached the principle of equality for women by prohibiting purdah and sati. Amar Das also encouraged the practice of langar and made all those who visited him attend laEgar before they could speak to him. In 1567, Emperor Akbar sat with the ordinary and poor people of Punjab to have laEgar. Amar Das also trained 146 apostles of which 52 were women, to manage the rapid expansion of the religion. Before he died in 1574 aged 95, he appointed his son-in-law J–mhâ, a Khatri of the Sodhi clan, as the fourth Sikh guru.

J–mhâ became Ram Das and vigorously undertook his duties as the new guru. He is responsible for the establishment of the city of Ramdaspur later to be named Amritsar. Before Ramdaspur, Amritsar was known as Guru Da Chakk. In 1581, Arjan Dev—youngest son of the fourth guru—became the fifth guru of the Sikhs. In addition to being responsible for building the Darbar/Harimandir Sahib (called the Golden Temple), he prepared the Sikh sacred text known as the Âdi Granth (literally *the first book*) and included the writings of the first five gurus and other enlightened Hindu and Muslim saints. In 1606, for refusing to make changes to the Granth and for supporting an unsuccessful contender to the throne, he was tortured and killed by the Mughal Emperor, Jahangir.

Political Advancement

Hargobind, became the sixth guru of the Sikhs. He carried two swords—one for spiritual and the other for temporal reasons (known as *mîrî* and *pîrî* in Sikhism). Sikhs grew as an organised community and under the 10th Guru the Sikhs developed a trained fighting force to defend their independence. In 1644, Har Rai became guru followed by Harkrishan, the boy guru, in 1661. No hymns composed by these three gurus are included in the Sikh holy book.

Tegh Bahadur became guru in 1665 and led the Sikhs until 1675. Teg Bahadur was executed by Aurangzeb for helping to protect Hindus, after a delegation of Kashmiri Pandits came to him for help when the Emperor condemned them to death for failing to convert to Islam. He was succeeded by his son, Gobind Rai who was just nine years old at the time of his father's death. Gobind Rai further militarised his followers, and was baptised by the *Pañj Pir*– when he formed the Khalsa on 13 April 1699. From here on in he was known as Gobind Singh.

From the time of Nanak, when it was a loose collection of followers who focused entirely on the attainment of salvation and God, the Sikh community had significantly transformed. Even though the core Sikh religious philosophy was never affected, the followers now began to develop a political identity. Conflict with Mughal authorities escalated during the lifetime of Teg Bahadur and Gobind Singh. The latter founded the Khalsa in 1699. The Khalsa is a disciplined community that combines its religious purpose and goals with political and military duties. After Aurangzeb killed four of his sons, Gobind Singh sent Aurangzeb the Zafarnamah (*Notification/Epistle of Victory*).

Shortly before his death, Gobind Singh ordered that the Gurû Granth Sâhib (the Sikh Holy Scripture), would be the ultimate spiritual authority for the Sikhs and temporal authority would be vested in the Khalsa Panth—the Sikh Nation/Community. The first scripture was compiled and edited by the fifth guru, Arjan Dev, in 1604.

A former ascetic was charged by Gobind Singh with the duty of punishing those who had persecuted the Sikhs. After the guru's death, Baba Banda Singh Bahadur became the leader of the Sikh army and was responsible for several attacks on the Mughal empire. He was executed by the emperor Jahandar Shah after refusing the offer of a pardon if he converted to Islam.

The Sikh community's embrace of military and political organisation made it a considerable regional force in medieval India and it continued to evolve after the demise of the gurus. After the death of Baba Banda Singh Bahadur, a Sikh Confederacy of Sikh warrior bands known as *misls* formed. With the decline of the Mughal empire, a Sikh Empire arose in the Punjab under Maharaja Ranjit Singh, with its capital in Lahore and limits reaching the Khyber Pass and the borders of China. The order, traditions and discipline developed over centuries culminated at the time of Ranjit Singh to give rise to the common religious and social identity that the term "Sikhism" describes.

After the death of Ranjit Singh, the Sikh Empire fell into disorder and was eventually annexed by the United Kingdom after the hard-fought Anglo-Sikh Wars. This brought the Punjab under the British Raj. Sikhs formed the Shiromani Gurdwara Prabandhak Committee and the Shiromani Akali Dal to preserve Sikhs' religious and political organisation a quarter of a century later. With the partition of India in 1947, thousands of Sikhs were killed in violence and millions were forced to leave their ancestral homes in West Punjab. Sikhs faced initial opposition from the Government in forming a linguistic state that other states in India were afforded.

The Akali Dal started a non-violence movement for Sikh and Punjabi rights. Jarnail Singh Bhindranwale emerged as a leader of the Bhindran-Mehta Jatha—which assumed the name of Damdami Taksal in 1977 to promote a peaceful solution of the problem. In June 1984, Indian Prime Minister Indira Gandhi ordered the Indian army to launch Operation Blue Star to remove Bhindranwale and his followers from the Darbar Sahib. Bhindranwale, and a large number of innocent pilgrims were killed during the army's operations.

In October, Indira Gandhi was assassinated by two of her Sikh bodyguards. The assassination was followed by the 1984 Anti-Sikh riots massacre and Hindu-Sikh conflicts in Punjab, as a reaction to the assassination and Operation Blue Star.

Scripture

There are two primary sources of scripture for the Sikhs: the Gurû Granth Sâhib and the Dasam Granth. The Gurû Granth Sâhib may be referred to as the Âdi Granth—literally, *The First Volume*—and the two terms are often used synonymously. Here, however, the Âdi Granth refers to the version of the scripture created by Arjan Dev in 1604. The Gurû Granth Sâhib refers to the final version of the scripture created by Gobind Singh.

Adi Granth

The Âdi Granth was compiled primarily by Bhai Gurdas under the supervision of Arjan Dev between the years 1603 and 1604. It is written in the Gurmukhî script, which is a descendant of the Lan

â script used in the Punjab at that time. The Gurmukhî script was standardised by Angad Dev, the second guru of the Sikhs, for use in the Sikh scriptures and is thought to have been influenced by the Úâradâ and Devanâgarî scripts. An authoritative scripture was created to protect the integrity of hymns and teachings of the Sikh gurus and selected bhagats. At the time, Arjan Sahib tried to prevent undue influence from the followers of Prithi Chand, the guru's older brother and rival.

The original version of the Âdi Granth is known as the *kartrpur b+[* and is claimed to be held by the Sodhi family of Kartarpur. (In fact the original volume was burned by Ahmad Shah Durrani's army in 1757 when they burned the whole town of Kartarpur.)

Janamsakhis

The Janamsâkhîs (literally *birth stories*), are writings which profess to be biographies of Nanak. Although not scripture in the strictest sense, they provide an interesting look at Nanak's life and the early start of Sikhism. There are several—often contradictory and sometimes unreliable—Janamsâkhîs and they are not held in the same regard as other sources of scriptural knowledge.

Dasam Granth

The Dasam Granth (formally *dasvçA pâtúâh kî granth* or *The Book of the Tenth Master*) is an eighteenth-century collection of poems by Gobind Singh. It was compiled in the shape of a book (granth) by Bhai Mani Singh some 13 to 26 years after Guru Gobind Singh Ji left this world for his heavenly abode.

From 1895 to 1897, different scholars and theologians assembled at the Akal Takht, Amritsar, to study the 32 printed Dasam Granths and prepare the authoritative version. They met at the Akal Takhat at Amritsar, and held formal discussions in a series of meetings between 13 June 1895 and 16 February 1896. A preliminary report entitled Report Sodhak (revision) Committee Dasam Patshah de Granth Sahib Di was sent to Sikh scholars and institutions, inviting their opinion. A second document, Report Dasam Granth di Sudhai Di was brought out on 11 February 1898. Basing its conclusions on a study of the old handwritten copies of the Dasam Granth preserved at Sri Takht Sahib at Patna and in other Sikh gurudwaras, this report affirmed that the Holy Volume was compiled at Anandpur Sahib in 1698 . Further re-examinations and reviews took place in 1931, under the aegis of the Darbar Sahib Committee of the Shiromani Gurdwara Prabhandak Committee. They, too, vindicated the earlier conclusion (agreeing that it was indeed the work of the Guru) and its findings have since been published.

Observances

Observant Sikhs adhere to long-standing practices and traditions to strengthen and express their faith. The daily recitation from memory of specific passages from the Gurû Granth Sâhib, especially the *Japu* (or *Japjî*, literally *chant*) hymns is recommended immediately after rising and bathing. Family customs include both reading passages from the scripture and attending the gurdwara (also *gurduârâ*, meaning *the doorway to God*; sometimes transliterated as *gurudwara*). There are many gurdwaras prominently constructed and maintained across India, as well as in almost every nation where Sikhs reside. Gurdwaras are open to all, regardless of religion, background, caste, or race.

Worship in a gurdwara consists chiefly of singing of passages from the scripture. Sikhs will commonly enter the temple, touch the ground before the holy scripture with their foreheads, and make an offering. The recitation of the eighteenth century *ardâs* is also customary for attending Sikhs. The ardâs recalls past sufferings and glories of the community, invoking divine grace for all humanity.

The most sacred shrine is the Harimandir Sahib in Amritsar, famously known as the *Golden Temple*. Groups of Sikhs regularly visit and congregate at the Harimandir Sahib. On specific occasions, groups of Sikhs are permitted to undertake a pilgrimage to Sikh shrines in the province of Punjab in Pakistan, especially at Nankana Sahib and other Gurdwaras. Other places of interest to Sikhism in Pakistan includes the *samâdhî* (place of cremation) of Maharaja Ranjit Singh in Lahore.

Sikh Festivals

Festivals in Sikhism mostly centre around the lives of the Gurus and Sikh martyrs. The SGPC, the Sikh organisation in charge of upkeep of the gurdwaras, organises celebrations based on the new Nanakshahi calendar. This calendar is highly controversial among Sikhs and is not universally accepted. Several festivals (Hola Mohalla, Diwali, and Nanak's birthday) continue to be celebrated using the Hindu calendar. Sikh festivals include the following:

- Gurpurabs are celebrations or commemorations based on the lives of the Sikh gurus. They tend to be either birthdays or celebrations of Sikh martyrdom. All ten Gurus have Gurpurabs on the Nanakshahi calendar, but it is Guru Nanak Dev and Guru Gobind Singh who have a gurpurab that is widely celebrated in Gurdwaras and Sikh homes. The martyrdoms are also known as a shaheedi Gurpurab, which mark the martyrdom anniversary of Guru Arjan Dev and Guru Tegh Bahadur.

- Vaisakhi or Baisakhi normally occurs on 13 April and marks the beginning of the new spring year and the end of the harvest. Sikhs celebrate it because on Vaisakhi in 1699, the tenth guru, Gobind Singh, laid down the Foundation of the Khalsa an Independent Sikh Identity.
- Bandi Chhor Divas or Diwali celebrates Guru Hargobind's release from the Gwalior Fort, with several innocent Hindu kings who were also imprisoned by Jahangir, on 26 October 1619.
- Hola Mohalla occurs the day after Holi and is when the Khalsa Panth gather at Anandpur and display their warrior skills, including fighting and riding.

Baptism and the Khalsa

Khalsa (meaning "pure") is the name given by Gobind Singh to all Sikhs who have been baptised or initiated by taking *ammrit* in a ceremony called *ammrit sañcâr*. The first time that this ceremony took place was on Vaisakhi, which fell on 29 March 1698/1699 at Anandpur Sahib in Punjab. It was on that occasion that Gobind Singh baptised the Pañj Piârç who in turn baptised Gobind Singh himself.

Baptised Sikhs are bound to wear the Five Ks (in Punjabi known as *pañj kakkç* or *pañj kakâr*), or articles of faith, at all times. The tenth guru, Gobind Singh, ordered these Five Ks to be worn so that a Sikh could actively use them to make a difference to their own and to others' spirituality. The 5 items are: *kçs* (uncut hair), *kaeghâ* (small comb), *ka[â* (circular iron bracelet), *kirpân* (dagger), and *kacchâ* (special undergarment). The Five Ks have both practical and symbolic purposes.

Ceremonies and Customs

Nanak taught that rituals, religious ceremonies, or idol worship is of little use and Sikhs are discouraged from fasting or going on pilgrimages. However, during the period of the later gurus, and owing to increased institutionalisation of the Sikh religion, many ceremonies and rituals did arise. In fact, nowadays Sikhism is divided into many sects and casts like Jat, Ramdasia, Ahluwalia etc. Converts to Sikhism are welcomed. The morning and evening prayers take about two hours a day, starting in the very early morning hours. The first morning prayer is Guru Nanak's *Jap Ji*. Jap, meaning "recitation", refers to the use of sound, as the best way of approaching the divine. Like combing hair, hearing and reciting the sacred word is used as a way to comb all negative thoughts out of the mind. The second morning prayer is Guru Gobind Singh's universal Jaap Sahib. The Guru addresses God as having no form, no country, and no religion but as the seed of seeds, sun of suns, and the song of songs. The Jaap Sahib asserts that God is the cause of conflict as well as peace, and of destruction as well as creation. Devotees learn that there is nothing outside of God's presence, nothing outside of God's control. Devout Sikhs are encouraged to begin the day with private meditations on the name of God.

Upon a child's birth, the Guru Granth Sahib is opened at a random point and the child is named using the first letter on the top left hand corner of the left page. All boys are given the middle name Singh, and all girls are given the middle name Kaur. Sikhs are joined in wedlock through the *anand kâraj* ceremony. Sikhs are required to marry when they are of a sufficient age (child marriage is taboo), and without regard for the future spouse's caste or descent. But nowadays the caste of the spouse plays an important role in marriages. The marriage ceremony is performed in the company of the Guru Granth Sahib; around which the couple circles four times. After the ceremony is complete, the husband and wife are considered "a single soul in two bodies."

According to Sikh religious rites, neither husband nor wife is permitted to divorce. A Sikh couple that wishes to divorce may be able to do so in a civil court but this is not condoned. Upon death, the body of a Sikh is usually cremated. If this is not possible, any means of disposing the body may be employed. The *kîrtan sôhilâ* and *ardâs* prayers are performed during the funeral ceremony (known as *antim sanskâr*).

Sikh People

Worldwide, there are 25.8 million Sikhs and approximately 75% of Sikhs live in the Indian state of Punjab, where they constitute about 60% of the state's population. Even though there are a large number of Sikhs in the world, certain countries have not recognised Sikhism as a major religion. Large communities of Sikhs live in the neighboring states, and large communities of Sikhs can be found across India. However, Sikhs only make up about 2% of the Indian population.

In addition to social divisions, there is a misperception that there are a number of Sikh sectarian groups, such as Namdharis and Nirankaris. Nihangs tend to have little difference in practice and are considered the army of Sikhism. There is also a sect known as Udasi, founded by Sri Chand who were initially part of Sikhism but later developed into a monastic order.

Sikh Migration beginning from the 19th century led to the creation of significant communities in Canada (predominantly in Brampton, along with Malton in Ontario and Abbotsford, Mission, Lower Mainland, Surrey in British Columbia), East Africa, the Middle East, Southeast Asia, the United Kingdom and more recently, Australia,Greece, New Zealand, the United States and Western Europe. Smaller populations of Sikhs are found in Mauritius, Malaysia, Fiji, Nepal, China, Pakistan, Afganistan, Iraq, Singapore and many other countries.

SIKH PHILOSOPHY

The **philosophy of Sikhism** is covered in great detail in the Sri Guru Granth Sahib, the Sikh holy text. Detailed guidance is given to followers on how to conduct their lives so that peace and salvation can be obtained. The holy text outlines the positive actions that one must take to make progress in the evolution of the person. One must remember the Creator at all times – it reminds the follower that the "soul is on loan from God, who is ever merciful", and that the follower must dedicate their life to all good causes - to help make this life more worthwhile.

The sections below give more details of the underlying message of this faith. It is easiest to discuss the topic if the details are divided into the following sections:

Underlying Values

The Sikhs must believe in the following values:

1. **Equality:** All humans are equal before God – No discrimination is allowed on the basis of caste, race, gender, creed, origin, color, education, status, wealth, et cetera. The principles of universal equality and brotherhood are important pillars of Sikhism.

2. **Actions count:** Salvation is obtained by one's actions – good deeds, remembrance of God – Naam Simran, Kirtan.

3. **Personal right:** Every person has a right to life but this right is restricted and has attached certain duties – simple living is essential. A Sikh is expected to rise early, meditate and pray, consume simple food, perform an honest day's work, carry out duties for his or her family, enjoy life and always be positive, be charitable and support the needy, et cetera.

4. **Living a family life:** Encouraged to live as a family unit to provide and nurture children for the perpetual benefit of creation. (as opposed to living as a wild hermit, which was, and remains, a common spiritual practice in India.)
5. **Accept God's will:** Develop your personality so that you recognise happy event and miserable events as one – the will of God causes them.
6. **Sharing:** It is encouraged to share and give to charity 10 percent of one's net earnings.
7. **The four fruits of life:** Truth, contentment, contemplation and Naam, (in the name of God).

Prohibited Behaviour

1. **Non-logical behaviour:** Superstitions, or rituals which have no meaning, such as pilgrimages, fasting and bathing in rivers, gambling, worship of graves, idols or pictures, and compulsory wearing of the veil for women, are prohibited.
2. **Sacrifice of creatures:** Sati – Widows throwing themselves in the funeral pyre of their husbands, the act of slaughtering lambs and calves to celebrate holy occasions
3. **Material obsession:** ("Maya") Accumulation of materials has no meaning in Sikhism. Wealth such as gold, portfolio, stocks, commodities, properties, et cetera, will all be left here on Earth when you depart. Do not get attached to them.
4. **Non-family oriented living:** A sikh is encouraged not to live as a recluse, beggar, monk, Nun, celibate, or in any similar vein.
5. **Intoxication:** The consumption of alcohol, drugs, tobacco, or other intoxicants is prohibited.

6. **Worthless talk:** Bragging, gossip, and lying are not permitted.

7. **No priestly class:** Sikhs do not have to depend on a priest for any of the functions that need to be performed.

8. **Eating meat killed in a ritualistic manner (Kutha meat):** Sikhs are strictly prohibited from eating meat killed in a ritualistic manner (such as halal or kosher, known as Kutha meat), or any meat where langar is served. In some small Sikh Sects, ie Akhand Kirtani Jatha eating any meat is believed to be forbidden, but this is not a universally held belief. The meat eaten by Sikhs is known as Jhatka meat.

9. **Having premarital or extramarital sexual relations**

Technique and Method

1. **Naam:** Meditate upon God's name (Waheguru in the Sikh religion) through verba the mind is stilled and cleansed in order to become one with God. The technique taught by the Guru Granth Sahib is "Urd Uhrd". This means to inhale with the "Wahe" syllable and exhale on the "Guru" syllable. This is the most important part of the religion.

2. **Kirat Karni:** - Earning an honest living while remembering the Lord.

3. **Wand kay Chakhna:** - Share with others who are deserving, as during langar

Other Observations

1. **One God:** - There is only one God who has infinite qualities and names. God is Creator and Sustainer - all that you see around you is His creation. He is everywhere, in everything. He is without birth or

death, and has existed before Creation and will exist forever. Sikhism does not acknowledge an anthropomorphic God. This is true to the extent than one can interpret Him as the Universe Itself. Sikhism also does not acknowledge the belief of a Personal God, as does Christianity. Instead, God is usually interpreted as being unfathomable, yet not unknowable.

2. **Reincarnation, karma and salvation:** – Every creature has a soul. Upon death, the soul is passed from one body to another until liberation. The journey of the soul is governed by the deeds and actions that we perform during our lives.

3. **Humanity (brotherhood):** All human beings are equal. We are sons and daughters of Waheguru, the Almighty.

4. **Remember God:** Love God. Only by keeping the Creator in your mind at all times will you make progress in your spiritual evolution.

5. **Uphold moral values:** Defend, protect and fight for the rights of all creatures, in particular your fellow human beings.

6. **Many paths lead to God:** – Sikhs are not special; they are not the chosen people of God. Simply calling yourself a Sikh does not bring you salvation. Members of all religions have the same right to liberty as Sikhs.

7. **Personal sacrifice:** Be prepared to give your life for all supreme principles. See the life of Guru Teg Bahadur.

8. **Positive attitude toward life:** "Chardi Kala" – Always have a positive, optimistic and buoyant view of life. God is there – He will be your help.

9. **No special worship days:** Sikhs do not believe that any particular day is holier than any other.

10. **Disciplined life:** Upon baptism, a Sikh must wear the 5Ks and perform strict recital of the five prayers Banis.

11. **Conquer the five thieves:** It is every Sikh's duty to defeat these five thieves: Pride (a'Hankar), Anger (Kr'odh), Greed (Lob'H), Attachment (Mo'H), and Lust (K'haam). Known collectively as P.A.G.A.L.

12. **Having premarital sexual or extramarital relations:** Sikhs are encouraged to be faithful to their spouse. All forms of adultery are discouraged.

13. **Attack with Five Weapons:** Contentment (Santokh), Charity (Dan), Kindness (Daya), Positive Energy (Chardi Kala), Humility (Nimarta).

14. **Not son of God:** The Gurus were not, in the Christian sense, "Sons of God". Sikhism says we are all God's children.

15. **Multi-level approach:** Sikhism recognizes the concept of a multi-level approach to achieving your target as a disciple of the faith. For example, "Sahajdhari" (slow adopters) are Sikhs who have not donned the full 5Ks but are still Sikhs regardless.

16. **All are welcome:** Members of all religions can visit Sikh temples ("Gurdwaras"), but please observe the local rules: cover head, no shoes, no smoking when going in to the main hall.

SIKH BELIEFS

- **Simran and Sewa**: These are the **Foundation of Sikhism**. It is the duty of every Sikh to practice Naam Simran daily and engage in Seva whenever there is a possibility- in Gurdwara; in community centre; old people's homes; care centres; major world disasters, etc.

- **The Holy trinity of Sikhism**: Guru Nanak formalised these three important aspects of Sikhism:
- **Naam Japna**: – A Sikh is to engage in a daily practice of meditation and Nitnem by reciting and chanting of God's Name.
- **Kirat Karni**: - To live honestly and earn by ones physical and mental effort while accepting God's gifts and blessings. A Sikh has to live as a householder carrying out his or her duties and responsibilities to the full.
- **Vand Chakna**: - The Sikhs are asked to share their wealth within the community and outside by giving Dasvand and practising charity (Daan). To "Share and consume together".
- **Kill the Five Thieves**: The Sikh Gurus tell us that our mind and spirit are constantly being attacked by the Five Evils – Kam (Lust), Krodh (Rage), Lobh (Greed), Moh (Attachment) and Ahankar (Ego). A Sikh needs to constantly attack and overcome these five vices.
- **Positive Human Qualities**: The Sikh Gurus taught the Sikhs to develop and harness positive human qualities which lead the soul closer to God and away from evil. These are: Sat (Truth); Daya (Compassion); Santokh (Contentment); Nimrata (Humility); and Pyare (Love).

PROHIBITIONS IN SIKHISM

There are a number of **religious prohibitions** in Sikhism

1. **Cutting Hair:** Cutting hair is strictly forbidden in Sikhism. Sikhs are required to keep unshorn hair.

2. **Intoxication:** Consumption of alcohol, drugs, tobacco, and other intoxicants is not allowed. Intoxicants are strictly forbidden for a Sikh.

3. **Blind spirituality** Superstitions and rituals should not be observed or followed, including pilgrimages, fasting and ritual purification; circumcision; idols, grave worship; compulsory wearing of the veil for women; etc.

4. **Adultery:** In Sikhism, the spouses must be physically faithful to one another.

5. **Material obsession :** Accumulation of material wealth is not encouraged in Sikhism.

6. **Non-family-oriented living:** A Sikh is encouraged not to live as a recluse, beggar, yogi, monastic (monk/nun) or celibate.

7. **Sacrifice of creatures:** The practice of sati (widows throwing themselves on the funeral pyre of their husbands), ritual animal sacrifice to celebrate holy occasions, etc. are forbidden.

8. **Worthless talk:** Bragging, gossip, lying, slander, "back-stabbing", etc. are not permitted. The Guru Granth Sahib tells the Sikh, "Your mouth has not stopped slandering and gossiping about others. Your service is useless and fruitless."

9. **Eating meat killed in a ritualistic manner (Kutha meat):** Sikhs are strictly prohibited from eating meat killed in a ritualistic manner (such as halal or kosher, known as Kutha meat), or any meat where langar is served. In some small Sikh Sects, ie Akhand Kirtani Jatha eating any meat is believed to be forbidden, but this is not a universally held belief. The meat eaten by Sikhs is known as Jhatka meat.

10. **No Priestly class:** Sikhism does not have priests, that were abolished by Guru Gobind Singh *(the 10th Guru of Sikhism)*. The only position he left was a Granthi to look after the Guru Granth Sahib, any Sikh is free to become Granthi or read from the Guru Granth Sahib.

11. **Having premarital or extramarital sexual relations**

Violation of Prohibitions

Not all people calling themselves Sikh subscribe to these prohibitions. Some young Sikhs are now cutting their hair to the dismay of spiritual leaders. According to the Sikh clergy, "the fad among youth to shed the pagri" is being observed more commonly among the Sikh youth in Punjab than Sikhs in other Indian states.

Nihang Sikhs of Punjab, who are defenders of historic Sikh shrines are an exception and consume an intoxicant called *bhang* (cannabis) to help in meditation , saying that it's *puratan maryada* (Punjabi for "old tradition"). Bhang is common in India; according to a legend, even the Hindu God Shiva was fond of bhang (cannabis) and it became his favourite food. In 2001, Baba Santa Singh, the Jathedar of Budha Dal, along with 20 chiefs of Nihang sects refused to accept the ban on consumption of *bhang* by the apex Sikh clergy. Baba Santa Singh was excommunicated and replaced with Baba Balbir Singh, who agreed to shun the consumption of *bhang*.

The Udasis, who consider themselves as denomination of Sikhism, lay emphasis on being ascetic, thus violating the "Non-family-oriented living" principle. Shrichand, the ascetic son of Guru Nanak, was the founder of the Udasi Sikh order, and is respected among Sikhs.

●●

6

History of Sikhism

The history of Sikhism is closely associated with the history of Punjab and the socio-political situation in medieval India. Essentially Sikh history, with respect to Sikhism as a distinct political body, can be said to have begun with the martyrdom of the fifth Sikh Guru, Guru Arjan Dev in 1606. Sikh distinction was further enhanced by the establishment of the Khalsa, by Guru Gobind Singh in 1699. The evolution of Sikhism began with the emergence of Guru Nanak as a religious leader and a social reformer during the fifteenth century in Punjab. The religious practice was formalized by Guru Gobind Singh on March 30, 1699. The latter baptised five persons from different social backgrounds to form Khalsa. The first five, Pure Ones, then baptized Gobind Singh into the Khalsa fold. This gives the Sikhism, as an organised grouping, a religious history of around 400 years.

Generally Sikhism has had amicable relations with other religions. However, during the Mughal rule of India (1556–1707), emerging religion had strained relation with the ruling Mughals. Prominent Sikh Gurus were martyred by Mughals for opposing some Mughal emperors' persecution of minority religious communities. Subsequently, Sikhism militarized to oppose Mughal hegemony. The emergence of the Sikh Empire under reign of the Maharajah Ranjit Singh was characterized by religious tolerance and pluralism with Christians, Muslims and Hindus in positions of power. The establishment of the Sikh Empire is commonly considered the zenith of Sikhism at political level, during this time the Sikh Empire came to include Kashmir, Ladakh, and Peshawar. Hari Singh Nalwa, the Commander-in-chief of the Sikh army along the North West Frontier, took the boundary of the Sikh Empire to the very mouth of the Khyber Pass. The Empire's secular administration integrated innovative military, economic and governmental reforms.

The months leading up to the partition of India in 1947, saw heavy conflict in the Punjab between Sikh and Muslims, which saw the effective religious migration of Punjabi Sikhs and Hindus from West Punjab which mirrored a similar religious migration of Punjabi Muslims in East Punjab.

Guru Nanak

Guru Nanak Dev (1469–1538), founder of Sikhism, was born to Kalu Mehta and Mata Tripta, wherein the Bedi Khatri clan of a Hindu family in the village of Talwandi, now called Nankana Sahib, near Lahore. His father, a Hindu named Mehta Kalu, was a Patwari, an accountant of land revenue in the government. Nanak's mother was Mata Tripta, and he had one older sister, Bibi Nanki.

From an early age Guru Nanak seemed to have acquired a questioning and enquiring mind and refused as a child to wear the ritualistic "sacred" thread called a Janeu and instead said that he would wear the true name of God in his heart as protection, as the thread which could be broken, be soiled, burnt or lost could not offer any security at all. From early childhood, Bibi Nanki saw in her brother the Light of God but she did not reveal this secret to anyone. She is known as the first disciple of Guru Nanak.

Even as a boy, Nanak was fascinated by religion, and his desire to explore the mysteries of life eventually led him to leave home. It was during this period that Nanak was said to have met Kabir (1440–1518), a saint revered by many. Nanak married Sulakhni, daughter of Moolchand Chona, a trader from Batala, and they had two sons, Sri Chand and Lakshmi Das.

His brother-in-law, Jai Ram, the husband of his sister Nanki, obtained a job for him in Sultanpur as the manager of the government granary. One morning, when he was twenty-eight, Guru Nanak Dev went as usual down to the river to bathe and meditate. It was said that he was gone for three days. When he reappeared, it is said he was "filled with the spirit of God". His first words after his re-emergence were: "there is no Hindu, there is no Muslim". With this secular principle he began his missionary work. He made four distinct major journeys, in the four different directions, which are called Udasis, spanning many thousands of kilometres, preaching the message of God.

Guru Nanak spent the final years of his life in Kartarpur where Langar (free blessed food) was available. The food would be partaken of by Hindus, rich, poor, high or/and so called low castes. Guru Nanak worked in the fields and earned his livelihood. After appointing Bhai Lehna as the new Sikh Guru, on 22 September 1539, aged 70, Guru Nanak met with his demise.

Guru Angad

In 1538, Guru Nanak chose Lehna, his disciple, as a successor to the Guruship rather than one of his sons. Bhai Lehna was named Guru Angad and became the successor of Guru Nanak. Bhai Lehna was born in the village of Harike in Ferozepur district in Punjab, on March 31, 1504. He was the son of a small trader named Pheru. His mother's name was Mata Ramo (also known as Mata Sabhirai, Mansa Devi, Daya Kaur). Baba Narayan Das Trehan was his grand father, whose ancestral house was at Matte-di-Sarai near Mukatsar.

Under the influence of his mother Bhai Lehna began to worship Durga (A Hindu Goddess). He used to lead a group of Hindu worshippers to Jawalamukhi Temple every year. He married Mata Khivi in January 1520 and had two sons, (Dasu and Datu), and two daughters (Amro and Anokhi). The whole Pheru family had to leave their ancestral village because of the ransacking by the Mughal and Baloch military who had come with Emperor Babur. After this the family settled at the village of Khadur Sahib by the River Beas, near Tarn Taran Sahib, a small town about 25 km. from Amritsar city.

One day, Bhai Lehna heard the recitation of a hymn of Guru Nanak from Bhai Jodha (a Sikh of Guru Nanak Sahib) who was in Khadur Sahib. He was thrilled and decided to proceed to Kartarpur to have an audience (darshan) with Guru Nanak. So while on the annual pilgrimage to Jwalamukhi Temple, Bhai Lehna left his journey to visit Kartarpur and see Baba Nanak. His very first meeting with Guru Nanak completely transformed him. He renounced the worship of the Hindu Goddess, dedicated himself to the service of Guru Nanak and so became his disciple, (his Sikh), and began to live in Kartarpur.

His devotion and service (Sewa) to Guru Nanak and his holy mission was so great that he was instated as the Second Nanak on September 7, 1539 by Guru Nanak. Earlier Guru Nanak tested him in various ways and found an embodiment of obedience and service in him. He spent six or seven years in the service of Guru Nanak at Kartarpur.

After the death of Guru Nanak on September 22, 1539, Guru Angad left Kartarpur for the village of Khadur Sahib (near Goindwal Sahib). He carried forward the principles of Guru Nanak both in letter and spirit. Yogis and Saints of different sects visited him and held detailed discussions about Sikhism with him.

Guru Angad introduced a new alphabet known as Gurmukhi Script, modifying the old Punjabi script's characters. Soon, this script became very popular and started to be used by the people in general. He took great interest in the education of children by opening many schools for their instruction and thus increased the number of literate people. For the youth he started the tradition of Mall Akhara, where physical as well as spiritual exercises were held. He collected the facts about Guru Nanak's life from Bhai Bala and wrote the first biography of Guru Nanak. He also wrote 63 Saloks (stanzas), which are included in the Guru Granth Sahib. He popularised and expanded the institution of **Guru ka Langar** that had been started by Guru Nanak.

Guru Angad travelled widely and visited all important religious places and centres established by Guru Nanak for the preaching of Sikhism. He also established hundreds of new Centres of Sikhism (Sikh religious Institutions) and thus strengthened the base of Sikhism. The period of his Guruship was the most crucial one. The Sikh community had moved from having a founder to a succession of Gurus and the infrastructure of Sikh society was strengthened and crystallized – from being an infant, Sikhism had moved to being a young child and ready to face the dangers that were around. During this phase, Sikhism established its own separate spiritual path.

Guru Angad, following the example set by Guru Nanak, nominated Sri Amar Das as his successor (the Third Nanak) before his death. He presented all the holy scripts, including those he received from Guru Nanak, to Guru Amar Das. He breathed his last on March 29, 1552 at the age of forty-eight. It is said that he started to build a new town, at Goindwal near Khadur Sahib and Guru Amar Das Sahib was appointed to supervise its construction. It is also said that Humayun, when defeated by Sher Shah Suri, came to obtain the blessings of Guru Angad in regaining the throne of Delhi.

Guru Amar Das

Guru Amar Das became the third Sikh guru in 1552 at the age of 73. Goindwal became an important centre for

Sikhism during the Guruship of Guru Amar Das. He continued to preach the principle of equality for women, the prohibition of Sati and the practise of Langar. In 1567, Emperor Akbar sat with the ordinary and poor people of Punjab to have Langar. Guru Amar Das also trained 140 apostles, of which 52 were women, to manage the rapid expansion of the religion. Before he died in 1574 aged 95, he appointed his son-in-law Jetha as the fourth Sikh Guru.

It is recorded that before becoming a Sikh, Bhai Amar Das, as he was known at the time, was a very religious Vaishanavite Hindu who spent most of his life performing all of the ritual pilgrimages and fasts of a devout Hindu. One day, Bhai Amar Das heard some hymns of Guru Nanak being sung by Bibi Amro Ji, the daughter of Guru Angad, the second Sikh Guru. Bibi Amro was married to Bhai Sahib's brother, Bhai Manak Chand's son who was called Bhai Jasso. Bhai Sahib was so impressed and moved by these Shabads that he immediately decided to go to see Guru Angad at Khadur Sahib. It is recorded that this event took place when Bhai Sahib was 61 years old.

In 1635, upon meeting Guru Angad, Bhai Sahib was so touched by the Guru's message that he became a devout Sikh. Soon he became involved in Sewa (Service) to the Guru and the Community. Under the impact of Guru Angad and the teachings of the Gurus, Bhai Amar Das became a devout Sikh. He adopted Guru as his spiritual guide (Guru). Bhai Sahib began to live at Khadur Sahib, where he used to rise early in the morning and bring water from the Beas River for the Guru's bath; he would wash the Guru's clothes and fetch wood from the jungle for 'Guru ka Langar'. He was so dedicated to Sewa and the Guru and had completely extinguished pride and was totally lost in this commitment that he was considered an old man who had no interest in life; he was dubbed Amru, and generally forsaken.

However, as a result of Bhai Sahib's commitment to Sikhi principles, dedicated service and devotion to the Sikh cause, Guru Angad Sahib appointed Guru Amar Das Sahib as third Nanak in March 1552 at the age of 73. He established his headquarters at the newly built town of Goindwal, which Guru Angad had established.

Soon large numbers of Sikhs started flocking to Goindwal to see the new Guru. Here, Guru Amar Das propagated the Sikh faith in a vigorous, systematic and planned manner. He divided the Sikh Sangat area into 22 preaching centres or Manjis, each under the charge of a devout Sikh. He himself visited and sent Sikh missionaries to different parts of India to spread Sikhism.

Guru Amar Das was impressed with Bhai Gurdas' thorough knowledge of Hindi and Sanskrit and the Hindu scriptures. Following the tradition of sending out Masands across the country, Guru Amar Das deputed Bhai Gurdas to Agra to spread the gospel of Sikhism. Before leaving, Guru Amar Das prescribed the following routine for Sikhs:

> "He who calls himself a Sikh of the True Guru, He must get up in the morning and say his prayers. He must rise in the early hours and bathe in the holy tank. He must meditate on God as advised by the Guru. And rid him of the afflictions of sins and evil. As the day dawns, he should recite scriptures, and repeat God's name in every activity. He to whom the Guru takes kindly is shown the path. Nanak! I seek the dust of the feet of the Guru's Sikh who himself remembers God and makes others remember Him. (Gauri)"

Guru Ji strengthened the tradition of 'Guru ka Langar' and made it compulsory for the visitor to the Guru to eat first, saying that 'Pehle Pangat Phir Sangat' (first visit the Langar then go to the Guru). Once the emperor Akbar came to see

Guru Sahib and he had to eat the coarse rice in the Langar before he could have an interview with Guru Sahib. He was so much impressed with this system that he expressed his desire to grant some royal property for 'Guru ka Langar', but Guru Sahib declined it with respect.

He introduced new birth, marriage and death ceremonies. Thus he raised the status of women and protected the rights of female infants who were killed without question as they were deemed to have no status. These teachings met with stiff resistance from the Orthodox Hindus. He fixed three Gurpurbs for Sikh celebrations: Diwali, Vaisakhi and Maghi.

Guru Amar Das not only preached the equality of people irrespective of their caste but he also fostered the idea of women's equality. He preaching strongly against the practice of Sati (a Hindu wife burning on her husband's funeral pyre). Guru Amar Das also disapproved of a young widow remaining unmarried for the rest of her life.

Guru Amar Das constructed "Baoli" at Goindwal Sahib having eighty-four steps and made it a Sikh pilgrimage centre for the first time in the history of Sikhism. He reproduced more copies of the hymns of Guru Nanak and Guru Angad. He also composed 869 (according to some chronicles these were 709) verses (stanzas) including Anand Sahib, and then later on Guru Arjan (fifth Guru) made all the Shabads part of Guru Granth Sahib.

When it came time for the Guru's younger daughter Bibi Bhani to marry, he selected a pious and diligent young follower of his called Jetha from Lahore. Jetha had come to visit the Guru with a party of pilgrims from Lahore and had become so enchanted by the Guru's teachings that he had decided to settle in Goindwal. Here he earned a living selling wheat and would regularly attend the services of Guru Amar Das in his spare time.

Guru Amar Das did not consider anyone of his sons fit for Guruship and chose instead his son-in law (Guru) Ram Das to succeed him. Guru Amar Das Sahib at the age of 95 died on September 1, 1574 at Goindwal in District Amritsar, after giving responsibility of Guruship to the Fourth Nanak, Guru Ram Das.

Guru Ram Das

Guru Ram Das (Born in Lahore, Punjab, Pakistan on 24 September 1534 – 1 September 1581, Amritsar, Punjab, India) was the fourth of the Ten Gurus of Sikhism, and he became Guru on 30 August 1574, following in the footsteps of Guru Amar Das. He was born in Lahore to a Sodhi family of the Khatri clan. His father was Hari Das and mother Anup Devi, and his name was Jetha, meaning 'first born'. His wife was Bibi Bhani, the younger daughter of Guru Amar Das, the third guru of the Sikhs. They had three sons: Prithi Chand Mahadev and Arjan Dev. As a Guru one of his main contributions to Sikhism was organizing the structure of Sikh society. Additionally, he was the author of Laava, the hymns of the Marriage Rites, the designer of the Harmandir Sahib, and the planner and creator of the township of Ramdaspur (later Amritsar). A hymn by Guru Ram Das from page 305 of the Guru Granth Sahib: "One who calls himself a Sikh of the True Guru shall get up early morning and meditate on the Lord's Name. Make effort regularly to cleanse, bathe and dip in the ambrosial pool. Upon Guru's instructions, chant Har, Har singing which, all misdeeds, sins and pains shall go away." Guru Ram Das nominated Guru Arjan Dev his youngest son, as the next Guru of the Sikhs.

Guru Arjan

In 1581, Guru Arjan — the youngest son of the fourth guru — became the Fifth Guru of the Sikhs. In addition to being responsible for building the Golden Temple, he prepared the Sikh Sacred text and his personal addition of some 2,000 plus hymns in the Gurû Granth Sâhib.

In 1604 he installed the Âdi Granth for the first time as the Holy Book of the Sikhs. In 1606, for refusing to make changes to the Gurû Granth Sâhib, he was tortured and killed by the Mughal rulers of the time.

Guru Har Gobind

Guru Har Gobind became the sixth guru of the Sikhs. He carried two swords — one for Spiritual reasons and one for temporal (worldly) reasons. From this point onward, the Sikhs became a military force and always had a trained fighting force to defend their independence.

Guru Har Rai

Guru Har Rai (26 February 1630 - 6 October 1661) was the seventh of the ten Gurus of Sikhism, becoming Guru on 8 March 1644, following in the footsteps of his grandfather, Guru Har Gobind, who was the sixth guru. Before he died, he nominated Guru Har Krishan, his youngest son, as the next Guru of the Sikhs.

As a very young child he was disturbed by the suffering of a flower damaged by his robe in passing. Though such feelings are common with children, Guru Har Rai would throughout his life be noted for his compassion for life and living things. His grandfather, who was famed as an avid hunter, is said to have saved the Moghul Emperor Jahangir's life during a tiger's attack. Guru Har Rai continued the hunting tradition of his grandfather, but he would allow no animals to be killed on his grand Shikars. The Guru instead captured the animal and added it to his zoo. He made several tours to the Malwa and Doaba regions of the Punjab.

His son, Ram Rai, seeking to assuage concerns of Aurangzeb over one line in Guru Nanak's verse (Mitti

Mussalmam ki pede pai kumhar) suggested that the word Mussalmam was a mistake on the copyist's part, therefore distorting Bani. The Guru refused to meet with him again. The Guru is believed to have said, "Ram Rai, you have disobeyed my order and sinned. I will never see you again on account of your infidelity." It was also reported to the Guru that Ram Rai had also worked miracles in the Mughal's court against his father's direct instructions. Sikhs are constrained by their Gurus to not believe in magic and myth or miracles. Just before his death at age, 31, Guru Har Rai passed the Gaddi of Nanak on to his younger son, the five year old – Guru Har Krishan.

Guru Har Rai was the son of Baba Gurdita and Mata Nihal Kaur (also known as Mata Ananti Ji). Baba Gurdita was the son of the sixth Guru, Guru Hargobind. Guru Har Rai married Mata Kishan Kaur (sometimes also referred to as Sulakhni), daughter of Sri Daya Ram of Anoopshahr (Bulandshahr) in Uttar Pradesh on Har Sudi 3, Samvat 1697. Guru Har Rai had two sons: Baba Ram Rai and Sri Har Krishan.

Although, Guru Har Rai was a man of peace, he never disbanded the armed Sikh Warriors (Saint Soldiers), who earlier were maintained by his grandfather, Guru Hargobind. He always boosted the military spirit of the Sikhs, but he never himself indulged in any direct political and armed controversy with the contemporary Mughal Empire. Once, Dara Shikoh (the eldest son of emperor Shah Jahan), came to Guru Har Rai asking for help in the war of succession with his brother, the murderous Aurangzeb. The Guru had promised his grandfather to use the Sikh Cavalry only in defence. Nevertheless, he helped him to escape safely from the bloody hands of Aurangzeb's armed forces by having his Sikh warriors hide all the ferry boats at the river crossing used by Dara Shikoh in his escape.

Guru Har Krishan

Guru Har Krishan borne in Kirat Pur, Ropar (7 July 1656 - 30 March 1664) was the eighth of the Ten Gurus of Sikhism, becoming the Guru on 7 October 1661, following in the footsteps of his father, Guru Har Rai. Before Har Krishan died of complications of Smallpox, he nominated his granduncle, Guru Teg Bahadur, as the next Guru of the Sikhs. The following is a summary of the main highlights of his short life:

> "Sri Guru Harkrishan Ji was the epitome of sensibility, generosity and courage. There is a famous incident from his early age. Once on the way to Delhi from Punjab he met an arrogant Brahmin Pundit called Lal Chand in Panjokhara town. The Pundit asked him to recite Salokas from the Geeta since his name was similar to that of Lord Krishna. Guru Ji invited a mute person called Chhajju Mehra and placed his stick on his head. He immediately started interpreting salokas from the Geeta. Everybody around was dumbstruck. Lal Chand's arrogance too was shattered and he asked for Guru Ji's forgiveness."

When Har Krishan stayed in Delhi there was a smallpox epidemic and many people were dying. According to Sikh history at Har Krishan's blessing, the lake at Bangla Sahib provided cure for thousands. Gurdwara Bangla Sahib was constructed in the Guru's memory. This is where he stayed during his visit to Delhi. Gurdwara Bala Sahib was built in south Delhi besides the bank of the river Yamuna, where Har Krishan was cremated at the age of about 7 years and 8 months. Guru Har Krishan was the youngest Guru at only 7 years of age. He did not make any contributions to Gurbani.

Guru Tegh Bahadur

Guru Tegh Bahadur is the ninth of the Sikh Gurus. Guru Tegh Bahadur sacrificed himself to protect Hindus. He was asked by Aurungzeb, the Mughal emperor, under coercion by Naqshbandi Islamists, to convert to Islam or to sacrifice himself. The exact place where he attained martyrdom is in front of the Red Fort in Delhi (Lal Qila) and the gurdwara is called Sisganj. This marked a turning point for Sikhism. His successor, Guru Gobind Singh further militarised his followers.

Guru Gobind Singh Ji

Guru Gobind Singh Ji was the tenth guru of Sikhs. He was born in 1666 at Patna (Capital of Bihar, India). In 1675 Pundits from Kashmir in India came to Anandpur Sahib pleading to Guru Teg Bhadur Ji (Father of Guru Gobind Singh Ji) about Aurangzeb forcing them to convert to Islam. Guru Teg Bahadur told them that martyrdom of a great man was needed. His son, Guru Gobind Singh Ji said "Who could be greater than you", to his father. Guru Teg Bahadur Ji told pundits to tell Aurangzeb's men that if Guru Teg Bahadur Ji will become Muslim, they all will. Guru Teg Bahadur Ji was then martyred in Delhi, but before that he assigned Guru Gobind Singh Ji as 10th Guru at age of 9. After becoming Guru he commanded Sikhs to be armed. He fought many battles with Aurangzeb and some other Kings of that time, but always winner.

In 1699 he created the Khalsa *panth*, by giving *amrit* to sikhs. In 1704 he fought the great battle with collective forces of Aurangzeb, Wazir Khan (Chief of Sarhind), and other kings. He left Anandpur and went to Chamkaur with only 40 sikhs. There he fought the Battle of Chamkaur with 40 sikhs, vastly outnumbered by the Mughal soldiers. His two elder sons (at ages 17, 15) were martyred there. Wazir Khan killed other two (ages 9, 6). Guru Ji sent Aurangzeb the Zafarnamah (*Notification of Victory*). Then he went to Nanded (Maharashtra, India). From there he made Baba Gurbakhash Singh, also aliased as Baba Banda Singh Bahadur, as his general and sent him to Punjab.

On the evening of the day when Baba Gurbakhash Singh left for Punjab, Guru Gobind Singh was visited by two Muslim soldiers. One of them was commissioned by Wazir Khan, Subedar of Sirhind, to assassinate Guru Gobind Singh. One of the assailants, Bashal Beg, kept a vigil outside the Guru's tent while Jamshed Khan, a hired assassin, stabbed the Guru twice. Khan was killed in one stroke by the Guru, while those outside, alerted by the tumult, killed Beg. Although the wound was sewn up the following day, the Guru died in Nanded, Maharashtra, India in 1708.

Shortly before passing away Guru Gobind Singh Ji ordered that the Guru Granth Sahib (the Sikh Holy Scripture), would be the ultimate spiritual authority for the Sikhs and temporal authority would be vested in the Khalsa Panth – the Sikh Nation. The first Sikh Holy Scripture was compiled and edited by the Fifth Guru, Guru Arjan in AD 1604, although some of the earlier gurus are also known to have documented their revelations. This is one of the few scriptures in the world that has been compiled by the founders of a faith during their own life time. The Guru Granth Sahib is particularly unique among sacred texts in that it is written in Gurmukhi script but contains many languages including Punjabi, Hindi-Urdu, Sanskrit, Bhojpuri, Assamese and Persian. Sikhs consider the Guru Granth Sahib the last, perpetual living guru.

Sikh Empire

History

Ranjit Singh was crowned on April 12, 1801 (to coincide with Baisakhi). Sahib Singh Bedi, a descendant of Guru Nanak Dev, conducted the coronation . Gujranwala served as his capital from 1799. In 1802 he shifted his capital to Lahore & Amritsar. Ranjit Singh rose to power in a very short period, from a leader of a single Sikh misl to finally becoming the Maharaja (Emperor) of Punjab.

There was strong collaboration in defense against foreign incursions such as those initiated by Ahmed Shah Abdali and Nadir Shah. The city of Amritsar was attacked numerous times. Yet the time is remembered by Sikh historians as the "Heroic Century". This is mainly to describe the rise of Sikhs to political power against large odds. The circumstances were hostile religious environment against Sikhs, a tiny Sikh population compared to other religious and political powers, which were much larger in the region than the Sikhs.

Before the Empire

The period from 1716 to 1799 was a highly turbulent time politically and militarily in the Punjab. This was caused by the overall decline of the Mughal Empire. This left a power vacuum that was eventually filled by the Sikhs in the late 18th century, after fighting off local Mughal remnants and allied Rajput leaders, Afghans, and occasionally hostile Punjabi Muslims who sided with other Muslim forces. Sikh warlords eventually formed their own independent Sikh administrative regions (misls), which were united in large part by Ranjit Singh.

Formation

The Sikh Empire (from 1801–1849) was formed on the foundations of the Punjabi Army by Maharaja Ranjit Singh. The Empire extended from Khyber Pass in the west, to Kashmir in the north, to Sindh in the south, and Tibet in the east. The main geographical footprint of the empire was the Punjab. The religious demography of the Sikh Empire was Muslim (80%), Sikh (10%), Hindu (10%),.

The foundations of the Sikh Empire, during the Punjab Army, could be defined as early as 1707, starting from the death of Aurangzeb and the downfall of the Mughal Empire. The fall of the Mughal Empire provided opportunities for the army, known as the Dal Khalsa, to lead expeditions against the Mughals and Afghans. This led to a growth of the army, which was split into different Punjabi Armies and then semi-independent misls. Each of these component armies were known as a misl, each controlling different areas and cities. However, in the period from 1762-1799 Sikh rulers of their misls appeared to be coming into their own. The formal start of the Sikh Empire began with the disbandment of the Punjab Army by the time of Coronation of Maharaja Ranjit Singh in 1801, creating the one unified political Empire. All the misldars who were affiliated with the Army were nobility with usually long and prestigious family histories in Punjab's history.

End of Empire

After Maharaja Ranjit Singh's death in 1839, the empire was severely weakened by internal divisions and political mismanagement. This opportunity was used by the British Empire to launch the Anglo-Sikh Wars. The Battle of Ferozeshah in 1845 marked many turning points, the British encountered the Punjabi Army, opening with a gun-duel in which the Sikhs "had the better of the British artillery". But as the British made advancements, Europeans in their army were especially targeted, as the Sikhs believed if the army "became demoralised, the backbone of the enemy's position would be broken". The fighting continued throughout the night earning the nickname "night of terrors". The British position "grew graver as the night wore on", and "suffered terrible casualties with every single member of the Governor General's staff either killed or wounded".

British General Sire James Hope Grant recorded: "Truly the night was one of gloom and forbidding and perhaps never in the annals of warfare has a British Army on such a large scale been nearer to a defeat which would have involved annihilation" The Punjabi ended up recovering their camp, and the British were exhausted. Lord Hardinge sent his son to Mudki with a sword from his Napoleonic campaigns. A note in Robert Needham Cust's diary revealed that the "British generals decided to lay down arms: News came from the Governor General that our attack of yesterday had failed, that affairs were disparate, all state papers were to be destroyed, and that if the morning attack failed all would be over, this was kept secret by Mr.Currie and we were considering measures to make a unconditional surrender to save the wounded...".

However, a series of events of the Sikhs being betrayed by some prominent leaders in the army led to its downfall. Maharaja Gulab Singh and Dhian Singh, were Hindu Dogras from Jammu, and top Generals of the army. Tej Singh and Lal Singh were secretly allied to the British. They supplied important war plans of the Army, and provided the British with updated vital intelligence on the Army dealings, which ended up changing the scope of the war and benefiting the British positions.

The Punjab Empire was finally dissolved after a series of wars with the British at the end of the Second Anglo-Sikh War in 1849 into separate princely states, and the British province of Punjab that where granted a statehood, and eventually a lieutenant governorship stationed in Lahore as a direct representative of the Royal Crown in London.

Modern

The months leading up to the partition of India in 1947, saw heavy conflict in the Punjab between Sikh and Muslims, which saw the effective religious migration of Punjabi Sikhs and Hindus from West Punjab which mirrored a similar religious migration of Punjabi Muslims in East Punjab. The 1960s saw growing animosity and rioting between Punjabi Sikhs and Hindus in India, as the Punjabi Sikhs agitated for the creation of a Punjabi Sikh majority state, an undertaking which was promised to the Sikh leader Master Tara Singh by Nehru in return for Sikh political support during the negotiations for Indian Independence. Sikhs obtained the Sikh majority state of Punjab on November 1, 1966.

Communal tensions arose again in the late 1970s, fueled by Sikh claims of discrimination and marginalization by the secularist dominated Indian National Congress ruling party and the "dictatorial" tactics adopted the then Indian Prime Minister, Indira Gandhi. Frank argues that Gandhi's assumption of emergency powers in 1975 resulted in the weakening of the "legitimate and impartial machinery of government" and her increasing "paranoia" of opposing political groups led her to instigate a "despotic policy of playing castes, religions and political groups against each other for political advantage". As a reaction against these actions came the emergence of the Sikh leader Sant Jarnail Singh Bhindranwale who vocalized Sikh sentiment for justice and advocated the creation of a Sikh homeland, Khalistan. This accelerated Punjab into a state of communal violence. Gandhi's 1984 action to defeat Sant Jarnail Singh Bhindranwale led to desecration of the Golden Temple in Operation Bluestar and ultimately led to Gandhi's assassination by her Sikh bodyguards. This resulted in an explosion of violence against the Sikh community in the Anti Sikh Riots which resulted in the massacre of thousands of Sikhs throughout India; Khushwant Singh described the actions as being a Sikh pogrom in which he "felt like a refugee in my country. In fact, I felt like a Jew in Nazi Germany". Since 1984, relations between Sikhs and Hindus have reached a rapprochement helped by growing economic prosperity; however in 2002 the claims of the popular right-wing Hindu organisation the RSS, that "Sikhs are Hindus" angered Sikh sensibilities. Many Sikhs still are campaigning for justice for victims of the violence and the political and economic needs of the Punjab espoused in the Khalistan movement. In 1996 the Special Rapporteur for the Commission on Human Rights on freedom of religion or belief, Abdelfattah Amor (Tunisia, 1993–2004), visited India in order to compose a report on religious discrimination. In 1997, Amor concluded, "it appears that the situation of the Sikhs in the religious field is satisfactory, but that difficulties are arising in the political (foreign interference, terrorism, etc.), economic (in particular with regard to sharing of water supplies) and even occupational fields. Information received from nongovernment (sic) sources indicates that discrimination does exist in certain sectors of the public administration; examples include the decline in the number of Sikhs in the police force and the absence of Sikhs in personal bodyguard units since the murder of Indira Gandhi". In May 22, 2004 Manmohan Singh became the first Sikh to become the Prime Minister of India.

●●

7

Hinduism and Sikhism

Hinduism and Sikhism, both religions from India, have had a complex relationship. Sikhism is among the newer world religions, while Hinduism is often considered one of the oldest. There are examples of Hindu and Sikh shrines being located in close proximity, and Hindus seem to hold the Sikh Golden Temple site in high regard.

Hinduism in Punjab is usually held by *Sants* who claim to incorporate a personal and private path of spiritual development in the common tradition of mystics past and present. They discuss the irrelevance of rituals, priestly class, mandatory contributions, and compulsory gatherings of Hindus and Sikhs, they are regarded as the real Hindu/Sikh who follow teachings from both Sikhism and Hinduism.

These movements are more present in Punjab. However in Sikhism, the tenth Guru stated that as a Sikh, one must not follow any other religion. Sikhism is traditionally seen as a religion of warriors who were protectors of those who could not defend themselves.

In the days of Mughal oppression, which intensified in the 18th century as the Sikhs openly defied Mughal leadership both local and upward, many non-Sikhs would offer their firstborn sons to join the Khalsa Army to aid in this cause.

History of Similarities and Differences

Nanak, was born in a Hindu Khatri family. However, he declared that all are equal in the eyes of God in his famous proclamation "I am not a Hindu, nor am I a Muslim." A unity between Hindus and Muslims under the teachings and revelations of the Guru. The Guru had some familiar and common beliefs as in Hindu concepts like Karma, Dharma, Reincarnation, and meditating on God's name to break the cycle of birth

Before Guru Nanak's death, he instructed his disciple Guru Angad Dev to carry on the teachings of his religion as Guru Angad had shown selflessness, compassion and endless service and was in tuned with the teachings of his Master, Guru Nanak. Sri Chand, one of his sons, founded the Udasi order. Various orders have arisen since the beginning of Sikhism, such as the Radhasoamis and the Nirankaris. It is debatable whether these religions constitute offshoots of Sikhism or merely differing Sikh philosophies. The Khalsa, ordained by Guru Gobind Singh, is regarded by many Sikhs as being the completion of the development of the Sikh religion.

Guru Tegh Bahadur

In 1675 Aurangzeb caused the martyrdom of Guru Tegh Bahadur. He had gone to Aurangzeb on behalf of Kashmiri Pandits, who requested him to plead against their forceful conversion. Aurangzeb asked Guru Tegh Bahadur to convert and had him executed after he refused to convert to Islam. According to Kushwant Singh, when "Guru Tegh Bahadur was summoned to Delhi, he went as a protector of the Kashmiri Hindu community and encourage them to stand against the increasing oppression of the Mughals. He was executed in the year 1675. His son who succeeded him as Guru later described his father's martyrdom as in the cause of the humanity. Guru Tegh Bahadar undertook the supreme sacrifice for the protection of the most fundamental of human rights - the right of a person to freely practice his or her religion without interference or hindrance. This is why Guru Tegh Bahadur is also known as (Tegh Bahadur, Hind Di Chadar" (Tegh Bahadur, Protector of Hindus).

Guru Tegh Bahadur is also honored by Hindus and the Guru Tegh Bahadur Martyrdom Day is also observed by many Hindus.

Maharaja Ranjit Singh

Also called "Sher-e-Punjab" ("The Lion of the Punjab") (1780–1839) was a Sikh emperor and the founder of Sikh Empire.Ranjit Singh crowned himself as the ruler of Punjab and willed the Koh-i-noor back to its original location at Jagannath Temple in Orissa while on his deathbed in 1839.

19th century

The Sikh scholar Harjot Oberoi has argued that in the nineteenth century, the Singh Sabha movement, began to view the non-monolithic world view of Sikhism with suspicion and hostility, and tried to redefine a more limited Sikh identity.

Similarities

Here are some of the similarities between Hinduism and Sikhism:

- At the time of the Gurus, most North Indian families would remain "Hindu" while the eldest son was a "Sikh." Hindus enlisting their eldest sons in the Khalsa was done for protection against the Mughals.
- Many Hindus visit Sikh temples.. For instance, the Hemkhund Sahib is a high-altitude lake in the Indian State of Uttarakhand is regarded as a pilgrimage site by the adherents of Hindus and a Lakshman Temple and Sikh Gurudwaara exist close together on the banks of the same lake there.
- When a Sikh dies, cremation is the preferred method. This is the same in Hinduism, although this is a cultural similarity between many cultures.

- Sikhs may also do the 'immersion of corpse remains' in a river after cremation, as Hindus do, although this is not a requirement; ashes may be deposited anywhere sentimental.

Mutual Views

In the Hindu and Sikh traditions, there is a distinction between religion and culture, and ethical decisions are grounded in both religious beliefs and cultural values. Both Hindu and Sikh ethics are primarily duty based. Traditional teachings deal with the duties of individuals and families to maintain a lifestyle conducive to physical, mental and spiritual health. These traditions share a culture and world view that includes ideas of karma and rebirth, collective versus individual identity, and a strong emphasis on spiritual purity.

The notion of dharma, karma, prasad, moksha and a belief in rebirth are very important for many Hindus and Sikhs as they make ethical decisions surrounding birth and death. Unlike the linear view of life taken in Abrahamic religions, for Hindus and Sikhs life, birth and death are repeated, for each person, in a continuous cycle. What a person does in each life influences the circumstances and predispositions experienced in future lives. In essence, every action or thought, whether noble or sinful, has consequences that are carried forward into the next life. When a similar situation is encountered, memories of past lives arise in the consciousness as an impulse to perform actions or think thoughts similar to the earlier ones. This impulse does not necessarily compel the person to repeat the act or thought. As proclaimed in the Guru Granth Sahib:

Common Sikh views of Hinduism

The references to Hindu deities in the Guru Granth Sahib are for the most part metaphorical, not literal. This is illustrated in a quote on page 1374, among others:

Kabeer, it does make a difference, how you chant the Lord's Name, 'Raam'. This is something to consider. Everyone uses the same word for the son of Dasrath and the Wondrous Lord. Kabeer, use the word 'Raam', only to speak of the All-pervading Lord. You must make that distinction. One 'Raam' is pervading everywhere, while the other is contained only in himself. (1374)

References to Vedas

The Guru Granth Sahib refers to Hindu scripture frequently, not as an endorsement but often referring to their lack of scope regarding God. However, they are not explicitly denounced, either; the Granth encourages openmindedness of all belief systems:

Do not say that the Vedas, the Bible and the Koran are false. Those who do not contemplate them are false.(1350)

Sikhism does not have belief in Heaven/Hell system, inequality of caste and gender and held the Vedas responsible for these fallacies in the contemporary society, the quote below from second Sikh Guru mentions the same view:

"The Vedas bring forth stories and legends, and thoughts of vice and virtue.What is given, they receive, and what is received, they give. They are reincarnated in heaven and hell"

- Page 463 - Wonderful is the sound current of the Naad, wonderful is the knowledge of the Vedas.
- Page 791 - Reading the Vedas, sinful intellect is destroyed.
- Page 941 - The Gurmukh is pleasing to the True Guru; this is contemplation on the Vedas.
- Page 942 - The Gurmukh understands the Simritees, the Shaastras and the Vedas.

- Page 1188 - The Vedas say that we should chant the Name of the One Lord.

In regards to their shortcomings:

- Page 148 - The Vedas speak and expound on the Lord, but they do not know His limits.
- Page 355 - The eighteen Puraanas and the four Vedas do not know His mystery.
- Guru Nanak, on page 1021 - Neither the Vedas (four Hindu texts) nor the four Katebas [Semitic texts: the Torah, the Zabur (Psalms), the Injil (Gospel), and the Quran] know the mystery (of the Creator of the Cosmos).
- Page 1126 - The Shaastras and the Vedas keep the mortal bound to the three modes of Maya, and so he performs his deeds blindly. ||3||
- Page 1237 - You may study the nine grammars, the six Shaastras and the six divisions of the Vedas. You may recite the Mahaabhaarata. Even these cannot find the limits of the Lord.

The references above to not knowing the limits of God are a reference to the Sikh perception that the existence of demigods or devas puts a limit on the absolute power of God.

The Guru Granth Sahib

—Bhairao, Fifth Mehl - *I do not perform Hindu worship services, nor do I offer the Muslim prayers...* Guru Arjan Dev Page 1078 - *Even the Vedas do not know the Guru's Glory. They narrate only a tiny bit of what is heard*

Differences

Since Hinduism is itself an umbrella term encompassing a wide range of sects and religious philosophies, it isn't possible to list differences that would divide Sikhism from all Hindu sects taken together. From the Hindu point of view, however, Sikhism would be considered a nastika or "heterodox" sect as it does not assert the primacy of the Vedas.

Guru Nanak and other Sikh Gurus rejected many tenets of Brahmanical Hinduism, such as:

- Sikhism is a monotheistic religion; Sikhs believe there is only one God, who has infinite qualities and names. Hinduism is a diverse system of thought with beliefs spanning monotheism, polytheism, panentheism, pantheism, monism and atheism (see Hindu views on monotheism)
- The Janeo (Hindu sacred thread), or 'confirmation' ritual of Hinduism.
- The Guru Granth Sahib describes many Hindu deities like Shiva and Durga, as false illusions. Sikhs prefer not to worship in Hindu temples or go on Hindu pilgrimages.
- The caste system–Untouchability - Hindu's believe in the caste system which is linked to ones past Karma,(in modern India, caste discrimination is outlawed). Sikhism believes ones previous lives Karma do not matter, but what does in this life determines ones status .
- Sikhs do not believe in going on pilgrimages or bathing at holy rivers.

— Page 747, Line 18 - *One may read all the books of the Vedas, the Simritees and the Shaastras, but they alone will not bring liberation.*

The majority accept that the two belief systems have been separate from the beginning of Sikhism. Sikhs believe that the Gurus were receiving the beliefs and practices from God as the Gurus constantly stated that they were not part of the Hindu or Muslim religions. One belief in Sikhism that is commonly cited in support of this is the belief in equality between men and women, regardless of background or race.

Sikh writers, like Khushwant Singh, have written that despite innovations, "this new community, the [Sikh] Khalsa Panth, remained an integral part of the Hindu social and religious system. It is significant that when Tegh Bahadur was summoned to Delhi, he went as a representative of the Hindus. He was executed in the year 1675. His son who succeeded him as guru later described his father's martyrdom as in the cause of the Hindu faith, 'to preserve their caste marks and their sacred thread did he perform the supreme sacrifice'. The guru himself looked upon his community as an integral part of the Hindu social system."

Cultural Differences

Many social anthropologists have historically categorized Sikhs as a separate ethno-religious group, with its own distinct identity shaped by Mughal conflict, communalism, and a worldview including the events of 1984. In the Sikh diaspora, Sikhs see themselves completely distinct from Hindus (but this is not an issue per se with Punjabi Hindus who share a cultural and ethnic bond with Punjabi Sikhs), and have an ethnic identity of 'Punjabi Sikh,' which is often their most salient identity, even for those who are first-generation immigrant. Hindu-Sikh intermarriage is rare.

Foundation of Sikh Panth

- 1478: Guru Nanak Dev stated that he wanted nothing to do with a religion that only allowed the highest classes in society to be regarded as religious.
- 1480: Guru Nanak refused to wear *Janeu* (sacred thread of Hindus) at the age of eleven years.

- 1509: Guru Nanak's Declaration "I am not a Hindu, nor am I a Muslim" Alah râm kë pind parân. ||4||

  My body and breath of life belong to Allah - to Ram, God . ||4|| .
- 1509-1539: Guru Nanak preached against idol worship. He did not attach any importance to penance and fasting.
- 1539: The followers of Guru Nanak are called Sikhs
- 1699: Guru Gobind Singh, the tenth Guru, established the Khalsa order and the five Ks to ensure that Khalsa kept a distinct identity and were able to defend themselves in war.
- 1873: The first Tat Khalsa Singh Sabha was founded in Amritsar. They worked towards spreading the essence of Sikh scriptures against, what they considered as attempts to subvert Sikhism from within. In a short span of time the number of *Singh Sabhas* rose to 117 in Punjab.
- 1879: Another Tat Khalsa Singh Sabha; popularly known as Lahore Singh Sabha.
- 1909: Max Arthur Macauliffe published "Sikh Religion:Its Gurus, Sacred Writings, and Authors." He is widely accredited for the translation of the Guru Granth Sahib from Gurmukhi to English.
- 1920: Shiromani Gurdwara Prabhandak Committee (SGPC) formed.
- 1920s: Nankana Sahib, Punja Sahib, Harimandir Complex (Golden Temple), TarnTaran Sahib taken over from the mahants. The mahants had maintained the shrines since the time of the Gurus themselves.
- 1915, 1931: New Reht Maryada compiled to replace existing Rahits after consultations with distinguished Sikh scholars.
- 1950: Sikh Reht Maryada was approved.

Differences between Sikhism and Specific Hindu Traditions

Idol Worship

The worship of *murtis* (idols) is an important part of several Hindu traditions, such as Vaishnavism and Shaivism, although some Hindu denominations like Arya Samaj and Satya Mahima Dharma have rejected idol worship. Sikhs do not believe in worship of any sort of physical idol, symbol, picture, or statue. Pictures of Gurus and the book itself are not directly prayed to or revered in place of Sikhism's formless God. Pictures of Gurus are not a requirement in the Gurdwara, and they are often not even displayed in the Darbar Sahib (prayer hall), but by the eating areas and the shoe-removing areas. This shows the low level of spiritual reverence for physical representions of the Gurus, as opposed to prayer (Prayer is not a "verbal idol"). Fanning of the Guru Granth Sahib is a tradition carried over from Punjab to protect the Granth and its reader from airborne debris, as outside worship was common. Only recital of prayers and listening to hymns make up Sikh prayer.

Vegetarianism

Some Hindu traditions, such as Vaishnavism, emphasize strict vegetarianism.The tenets of Sikhism do not advocate a particular stance on either vegetarianism or the consumption of meat, but rather leave the decision of diet to the individual. Sikhs who follow sects and groups that have a "Vashnavite" influence (AKJ, GNNSJ, 3HO, Namdhari's etc.) believe that there is to be strict vegetarianism while the majority, that follow the Official Sikh Code of Conduct (Rehat Maryada) state the fact that, the only meat that is expressly forbidden for Sikhs to consume is Halal/Kosher (Kutha meat, the meat of animals slowly and ceremoniously killed in sacrificing rituals). Several Gurus such as Guru Hargobind Sahib and

Guru Gobind Singh hunted frequently and consumed non-Halal.. The Guru Granth Sahib states:

The Guru Granth Sahib

—*First Mehl:*

The fools argue about flesh and meat, but they know nothing about meditation and spiritual wisdom.

What is called meat, and what is called green vegetables? What leads to sin?

It was the habit of the gods to kill the rhinoceros, and make a feast of the burnt offering.

Those who renounce meat, and hold their noses when sitting near it, devour men at night.

They practice hypocrisy, and make a show before other people, but they do not understand anything about meditation or spiritual wisdom.

O Nanak, what can be said to the blind people? They cannot answer, or even understand what is said.

They alone are blind, who act blindly. They have no eyes in their hearts.

They are produced from the blood of their mothers and fathers, but they do not eat fish or meat.

On the views that eating vegetation would be eating flesh, first Sikh Guru Nanak states:

AGGS, M 1, p 1290.

— *First Mehl:*

O Pandit, you do not know where did flesh originate! It is water where life originated and it is water that sustains all life. It is water that produces grains, sugarcane, cotton and all forms of life.

On Vegetation, the Guru described it as living and experiencing pain:

Page 143 of the Sri Guru Granth Sahib Ji

— First Mehl:

Look, and see how the sugar-cane is cut down. After cutting away its branches, its feet are bound together into bundles,

and then, it is placed between the wooden rollers and crushed.

What punishment is inflicted upon it! Its juice is extracted and placed in the cauldron; as it is heated, it groans and cries out.

●●

8

Jainism, Islam and Sikhism

Both Jainism and Sikhism have originated in South Asia and are Eastern philosophical faiths. Jainism, like Sikhism, rejected the authority of the Vedas and created independent textual traditions based on the words and examples of their early teachers, eventually evolving entirely new ways for interacting with the lay community.

Jainism is the oldest living Shramana tradition in India. In its current form, the Jain tradition is traced to Vardhamana Mahavira (The Great Hero; ca. 599-527 B.C.), the twenty-fourth and last of the Tirthankaras (Sanskrit for fordmakers). Mahavira was born to a ruling family in the town of Vaishali, located in the modern state of Bihar. The first Tirthankara was Lord Rishabha, who lived long before Mahavira. That makes Jainism one of the oldest religions.

Next to the Baha'i Faith, Sikhism is the youngest of the world's major monotheistic religions. Sikhism was established in 15th century in the state of Punjab in North India. Guru Nanak, although born into a Hindu household in 1469 in the Punjab region, he challenged the existing practices and is considered the founder of the new faith.

The Guru loved to travel and observe concepts and ideas regarding spiritual practices of various faiths. At the heart of his message was a philosophy of universal love, devotion to God. By the time he had left this world he had founded a new religion of "disciples" (shiksha or sikh) that followed his example.

Lineage of Teachers

The 24th Tirthankara of the Jain community was Vardhamana, the last in a series of 24 who lived in East India. Jains have 24 Tirthankaras, the Sikhs have 10 Gurus with the final Sovereign Authority of living Guru conferred upon Guru Granth Sahib by the tenth Master, Guru Gobind Singh.

Mutual Cooperation

Noted author Khushwant Singh notes that many eminent Jains admired the Sikh Gurus and came to their help in difficult times. When the ninth Sikh Guru, Tegh Bahadur, was on his preaching mission in east India, he and his family were invited by Salis Rai Johri to stay in his haveli in Patna. In his hukamnamas sent from Assam, the Guru Sahib referred to Patna as guru-ka-ghar, meaning, home of the Guru. Salis Rai donated half of his haveli to build a gurdwara, Janam Sthaan, because Guru Gobind Singh was born there. On the other half, he built a Svetambara Jain Temple — both have a common wall. Diwan Todar Mal was an Oswal Jain who rose to become the diwan in the court of Nawab Wazir Khan of Sirhind. When the Nawab had Guru Gobind Singh's two younger sons put to death, Todar Mal conveyed the sad news to their grand mother — who died of shock — and had the three bodies cremated. He had built Gurdwara Jyoti Sarup on the site of the cremation at Fatehgarh Sahib. A large hall of this gurdwara honours the builder by being named after him — Diwan Todar Mal Jain Yadagiri Hall.

Practices and Differences

Diwali

Diwali is celebrated by both. Although Sikhs celebrate the day as Bandhi Chhor Diwas, the homecoming to Amritsar of the sixth Sikh Guru, Guru HarGobind Sahib from Gwalior. The release of 52 Rajas from the fort of Gwalior is attributed to this Guru.

For Jains, Diwali is the celebrarion of the 24th Thirthankar, Mahavir, reaching Nirvana or Moksha on this day at Pavapuri on Oct. 15, 527 BC, on Chaturdashi of Karti.

Ahimsa and Vegetarianism

The Jains are strictly vegetarian. Sikhs are not vegetarian. There are, however,some group/sects/cults of Sikhism (Akhand Kirtani Jatha, Guru Nanak Nishkam Sewak Jatha, Namdhari's, Damdami Taksal etc) who encourage vegetarianism. The majority of Sikhs believe, eating meat is left up to the individual's conscience in Sikhism, as it will not affect spirituality.Khushwant Singh also notes that most Sikhs are meat-eaters and decry vegetarians as daal khorey (lentil-eaters). The food served in the Sikh temples (Gurudwaras) is invariably vegetarian in order to accommodate all sections of society.

Asceticism

Sikhism rejects asceticism - The Gurus lived as householders. On asceticism Guru Nanak stated :

> Asceticism doesn't lie in ascetic robes, or in walking staff, nor in the ashes. Asceticism doesn't lie in the earring, nor in the shaven head, nor blowing a conch. Asceticism lies in remaining pure amidst impurities. Asceticism doesn't lie in mere words; He is an ascetic who treats everyone alike. Asceticism doesn't lie in visiting burial places, It lies not in wandering about, nor in bathing at places of pilgrimage. Asceticism is to remain pure amidst impurities. (Suhi)

Jains have an organised ascetic order of monks and nuns. The lay people are householders.

Other Practices

A Sikh is bound to the Truth at all times and practices god Consciousness through Nam Simran and selfless service (Sewa). Jains too place high regard in prayers and meditation.

Sikhs reject the caste system and promote social and gender equality as the soul is the same for both men and women. All are equal in the eyes of God. God is accessible without priests or a middle person. Sikhs and Jains, like Hindus, are expected to be tolerant of all faiths and do not believe that any one path has a monopoly on the Truth. There are many paths to seek out the Love of God and incur Divine Grace. In fact to call another's path inferior is sign of ignorance and intolerance. Both, personal devotion and communal prayers are a part of Sikh's way of life.

Customs

During the 18th century, there were a number of attempts to prepare an accurate portrayal of Sikh customs. Sikh scholars and theologians started in 1931 to prepare the Reht Maryada – the Sikh code of conduct and conventions. This has successfully achieved a high level of uniformity in the religious and social practices of Sikhism throughout the world. It contains 27 articles. Article 1 defines who is a Sikh:

Any human being who faithfully believes in:

- One Immortal Being,
- Ten Gurus, from Guru Nanak Dev to Guru Gobind Singh,
- The Guru Granth Sahib,
- The utterances and teachings of the ten Gurus and the baptism bequeathed by the tenth Guru, and who does not owe allegiance to any other religion, is a Sikh.

Fasting is an accepted practice for the Jains. A Sikh will eat to partially satisfy the hunger at all times.

Where the Guru Granth Sahib is present, that place becomes a Gurdwara. The focal point of worship in a Gurdwara (the gateway to God) is the eternal teachings of Guru Granth Sahib -the Shabad (Word) Guru.

Jains exhibit the statues of their Tirathankars in their temples. Special shrines in residences or in public temples include images of the Tirthankaras, who are not worshiped but remembered and revered; other shrines house images of deities who are more properly invoked to intercede with worldly problems. Daily rituals may include meditation and bathing; bathing the images; offering food, flowers, and lighted lamps for the images; and reciting mantras in Ardhamagadhi, an ancient language of northeast India related to Sanskrit.

Jainism express non violence in thought, word and action. Sikhism seeks peace; when all other means have been exhausted then they find it justifiable to draw the sword against oppression and injustice. Jains believe a peaceful way can always be found, perhaps sometimes after tremendous effort. War or violence against humans or animals is never justified.

Concept of God

Jains do not believe in the concept of a Godhead responsible for the manifestation of the Creation. They believe the universe is eternal, without beginning or end, and that all happens in an autonomous fashion with no necessity of a co-ordinator/God.

Sikhism is a monotheistic religion, believing in the singular power of the Formless Creator God, Ik Onkaar, without a parallel. In the Guru Granth Sahib, God is called by all the Hindu names and as Allah as well.

Karma and Salvation

Both Jains and Sikhs believe in the Karma Theory and re-incarnation of the soul. Salvation for a Sikh is attained through the Divine Grace and Will of Waheguru (God) and through good deeds in one's life and the selfless service of Sewa and charity. Jains too believe in personal effort and aims and do not depend on a heavenly being for assistance. Both believe in the conquest of the mind through control of the passions through the five senses as the path to ending the cycle of sufferance of birth and death.

ISLAM AND SIKHISM

In **Islam**, Muhammad is the 'Seal of the Prophets'. Islam views Jews, Christians and Muslims as "People of the Book" as all three major faiths are part of the Abrahamic religions. Muslims also believe Adam, Noah, Abraham, Moses, David and Jesus were prophets. However, Muslims do not consider any Sikh guru as a prophet.

Sikhism recognizes all humans as equal before Waheguru, regardless of colour, caste or lineage.

The book of the Muslims is known as the Holy Qu'ran, Islam further believes the angel Gabriel was the medium through whom God revealed the Qur'an to Muhammad, and that he sent a message to most prophets. The Sikh holy book is known as the Sri Guru Granth Sahib, it was compiled by the 10 Sikh Gurus and includes passages from both Hindus and Sufis.

Many Islamic dynasties ruled parts of the Indian subcontinent starting from the 12th century. The prominent ones include the Delhi Sultanate (1206–1526) and the Mughal Empire (1526–1857), with which the Sikh gurus frequently came into direct confrontation, however these empires helped in the spread of Islam in South Asia, but by the mid-18th century, the British Empire had ended the Mughal dynasty.

Guru Nanak Dev was the founder of Sikhism. The Guru Granth Sahib was first compiled by the fifth Sikh guru, Guru Arjan Dev, from the writings of the first five Sikh gurus and others, including those of the Hindu and Muslim faith. After the death of Guru Gobind Singh copies were distributed by Baba Deep Singh.

The Gurus and their Muslim Contemporaries

Guru Nanak's preachings were directed with equal force to all humans regardless of their religion. As such he freely borrowed and redefined religious terminology from the lexicons of other faiths.

Guru Nanak defines the transformation of man to a permanent union with God as part of his preaching against communalism summarized by the famous phrase, "There is no Hindu and no Muslim," Guru Nanak defined a Muslim as follows:

> SHALOK, FIRST MEHL:
>
> It is difficult to be called a Muslim; if one is truly a Muslim, then he may be called one.
>
> First, let him savor the religion of the Prophet as sweet; then, let his pride of his possessions be scraped away.
>
> Becoming a true Muslim, a disciple of the faith of Mohammed, let him put aside the delusion of death and life.
>
> As he submits to God's Will, and surrenders to the Creator, he is rid of selfishness and conceit.
>
> And when, O Nanak, he is merciful to all beings, only then shall he be called a Muslim.
>
> Allah is hidden in every heart; reflect upon this in your mind. The One Lord is within both Hindu and Muslim; Kabir proclaims this out loud.
>
> Be kind and compassionate to me, O Creator Lord. Bless me with devotion and meditation, O Lord Creator. Says

Nanak, the Guru has rid me of doubt.

The Muslim God Allah and the Hindu God Paarbrahman are one and the same.

To be Muslim is to be kind-hearted, and wash away pollution from within the heart. He does not even approach worldly pleasures; he is pure, like flowers, silk, ghee and the deer-skin.

One who is blessed with the mercy and compassion of the Merciful Lord, is the manliest man among men. He alone is a Shaykh, a preacher, a Haji, and he alone is God's slave, who is blessed with God's Grace.

The Creator Lord has Creative Power; the Merciful Lord has Mercy. The Praises and the Love of the Merciful Lord are unfathomable.

Realize the True Hukam, the Command of the Lord, O Nanak; you shall be released from bondage, and carried across.

I am not a Hindu, nor am I a Muslim. My body and breath of life belong to Allah — to Raam — the God of both.

Says Kabir, this is what I say: meeting with the Guru, my Spiritual Teacher, I realize God, my Lord and Master.

—Sri Guru Granth Sahib

According to Sikh tradition, while in Baghdad as part of his journey to Mecca and Medina, Guru Nanak had extensive dialogue with Muslim scholars there. In one discourse with a pir.

At Mecca, Guru Nanak was found sleeping with his feet towards the Kaaba Kazi Rukan-ud-din, who observed this, angrily objected. Nanak replied with a request to turn his feet in a direction in which God or the House of God is not." The Qadi took hold of the Guru's feet. Then he lifted his eyes seeing the Kaaba standing in the direction of the Guru's feet, wherever he turned them Muslims remain unconvinced about this story as no records from Arabic sources have ever existed to back these claims.

Guru Nanak was pointing out that if he moves his feet elsewhere God is still in that direction as God is Omnipresent i.e. not confined by space (or time).

The Muslim rulers of the Lodhi dynasty and the first Mughals were too concerned with consolidating their respective rules, and Akbar's liberalism led him to establish cordial relations with India's religions. The influence of Sheikh Ahmad Sirhindi and the Sufi Naqshbandi order on Jahangir led to the subsequent execution of Guru Arjan Dev in 1606.

Sikh Rebellion against Mughal Rule

Early in Aurangzeb's reign, various insurgent groups of Sikhs engaged Mughal troops in increasingly bloody battles. In 1670, the ninth Sikh Guru, Guru Tegh Bahadur encamped in Delhi, receiving large numbers of followers, was said to have attracted the wrath of Emperor Aurangzeb.

The execution of Guru Tegh Bahadur infuriated the Sikhs. In response, his son and successor, the tenth Guru of Sikhism Guru Gobind Singh further militarized his followers.

In a temporary alliance, both groups Hindu Kings and Muslim Governors attacked Gobind Singh and his followers. The united Mughal-Rajput Imperial alliance laid siege to the fort at Anandpur Sahib. In an attempt to dislodge the Sikhs, Aurangzeb vowed that the Guru and his Sikhs would be allowed to leave Anandpur safely. Aurangzeb is said to have validated this promise in writing. However Aurangzeb deliberately failed to keep his promise and when the remaining few Sikhs were leaving the fort under the cover of darkness, the Mughals were alerted and enagaged them in battle once again; where two of the younger sons of Guru Gobind Singh [Zoravar Singh and Fateh Singh] of 9 and 7 yrs respectively were bricked up alive within a wall by Wazir Khan in Sirhand (Punjab). The other two elder sons [Ajit Singh and Jujhar Singh] as well as many other Singhs fought with giant Mughal force achieving martyrdom and proved words of tenth guru "Sava Lakh se Ek Laraun Tabhe Gobind Singh Naam Kahaun" [That each brave Khalsa must fight with more than a million oppressor]. The events of which Guru Gobind Singh wrote a letter to Aurangzeb, called a [Zafarnamah :- epistle of Victory]. The Emperor died shortly after on March 3, 1707. Eventually the Guru was attacked and wounded by two of Aurangzeb's soldiers, Jamshed Khan and Wazir Khan who was the Mughal Governor of the Punjab at Sirhind before. The Guru would later die because the inflicted wounds.

Differences between Islam and Sikhism

Sikhs are prohibited from eating halal (and kosher) food or any other ritually slaughtered (known as Kutha meat) meat/fish. Most Sikhs eat non-halal meat (Jhatka), although Gurudwara Langar is largely lacto-vegetarian, though this is understood to be a result of efforts to present a meal that is respectful of the diets of any person who would wish to dine, rather than out of dogma. Sikhs do not believe in pilgrimages; Muslims, in contrast, consider Hajj (pilgrimage to Mecca) a crucial part of the faith. Male Sikhs do not circumcise unlike Muslim males.

The **Five Pillars of Islam** is the term given to the five duties incumbent on every Muslim. These duties are Shahada (Profession of Faith), Salat (prayers), Zakat (Giving of Alms), Sawm (Fasting during Ramadan) and Hajj (pilgrimage to Mecca). These five practices are essential to Sunni Islam; Shi'a

Muslims subscribe to eight ritual practices which substantially overlap with the five Pillars.

The **Three Pillars of Sikhism** are set of instructions from Guru Nanak formalized as *Naam Japna* (meditation on Waheguru), *Kirat karô* (honest labour), and *Vand chakkô* (Charity to the community)

In Islam and Abrahamic faiths, when a Muslim dies, he or she is buried. In Sikhism when a person dies he or she is Cremated

Islamic Predestination

In accordance with the Islamic belief in predestination, or divine preordainment (*al-qadâ wa l-qadar*), God has full knowledge and control over all that occurs. This is explained in Qur'anic verses such as "Say: 'Nothing will happen to us except what God has decreed for us: He is our protector'..." For Muslims, everything in the world that occurs, good or evil, has been preordained and nothing can happen unless permitted by God. In Islamic theology, divine preordainment does not suggest an absence of God's indignation against evil, because any evils that do occur are thought to result in future benefits men may not be able to see. According to Muslim theologians, although events are pre-ordained, man possesses free will in that he has the faculty to choose between right and wrong, and is thus responsible for his actions. According to Islamic tradition, all that has been decreed by God is written in *al-Lawh al-Mahfûz,* the "Preserved Tablet".

Islamic predestination concerns in reality less the life after the current life but the regulation of cases within the current life, like for instance the life of a warrior in Jihad or struggle in the way of God, which renders him a place in Paradise. Concerning eternal life, it is positively acquired through the absolute declaration of faith in Allah and Muhammed. The key concepts mentioned in the Qu'ran are Jabar (determination) and qadar (predestination).

The Shia understanding of predestination is called "divine justice" (*adalah*). This doctrine, developed in Sunnism as well by the Mu'tazili, stresses the importance of man's responsibility for his own actions. In contrast, the Sunni de-emphasizes the role of individual free will in the context of God's creation and foreknowledge of all things.

Sufism as a whole is primarily concerned with a direct personal experience and is considered one of the mystical dimensions of Islam, and as such may be compared to various forms of mysticism such as Bhakti form of Hinduism, Hesychasm form of Greek Orthodox, Zen form of Buddhism, Kabbalah from Judaism and Gnosticism from Christian mysticism.

The concept of a Last Judgment is found in all of the Abrahamic religions whereas the Sikh Gurus taught reincarnation and karma, which are also Hindu beliefs, and Muhammad preached of a Qiyamah. Muslims, as do Christians, accept from their scriptures, the concepts of Heaven or Jannah and Hell or Jahannam, whereas in the Dharmic faiths one reaps the fruit of his/own own Karma to attain Nirvana. Sikhs are instructed to transcend and merge one's soul directly with God. The Sikh has to rise above ego in order to escape repetitive reincarnation and attain permanent union with the creative immanence of God. Having done so, the soul retains its identity; man and God are never ontologically identical.

Sufi saints in Holy Guru Granth Sahib Ji

- Bhagat Beni
- Bhagat Bhikhan
- Fariduddin Ganjshakar (Baba Farid)
- Bhagat Sadhana

Sufi saint: Hazrat Mian Mir Construction of Golden Temple

In December 1588, the Sufi saint of Lahore, Mian Mir, who was a close friend of Guru Arjan Dev, initiated the construction of the Harmandir Sahib (Golden Temple) by laying the first foundation stone.

Bhai Mardana Ji: Muslim Follower of Guru Nanak

Bhai Mardana Ji (1459–1534) was a Muslim and one of the first followers alongside Bhai Bala, who travelled with Nanak in his early journeys across India and Asia. On his later journeys, Nanak was accompanied by Saido and Greho, and Mardana remained with his family. Mardana was born a Muslim to a Mirasi couple, Badra and Lakkho, of Rai Bhoi di Talwandi (modern Nankana Sahib, capital of Nankana Sahib District of Pakistan).

Shah Bhikhan

Pir Bhikhan Shah, a 17th century Sufi saint, was born the son of Sayyid Muhammad Yusaf of Siana Sayyidari, a village 5 km (3.1 mi) from Pehowa (in modern Kurukshetra district of Haryana). For a time, he lived at Ghuram in present day Patiala district of the Punjab and finally settled at Thaska, again in Kurukshetra district. He was the disciple of Abu l-Muali Shah, a Sufi divine residing at Ambhita, near Saharanpur in Uttar Pradesh, and soon became a saint of much repute and piety in his own right.

According to a tradition preserved in Bhai Santokh Singh, Sri Gur Pratap Suraj Granth, Pir Bhikhan Shah, as he learnt through intuition of the birth of Guru Gobind Singh (1666–1708) at Patna, made obeisance that day to the east instead of to the west. At this, his disciples demurred, for no Muslim should make such respectful gestures except towards the Kaaba in Mecca.

The pir explained that in a city in the east, God had revealed Himself through a newborn baby, to whom he had bowed and to no ordinary mortal. Bhikhan Shah with his disciples then traveled all the way to Patna to have a glimpse of the infant Gobind Rai, barely three months old. Desiring to know what would be his attitude to the two major religious peoples of India, he placed two small pots in front of the child, one representing in his own mind Hindus and the other Muslims. As the child covered both the pots simultaneously with his tiny hands, Bhikhan Shah felt happy concluding that the new seer would treat both Hindus and Muslims alike and show equal respect to both.

Sikh chronicles record another meeting between Guru Gobind Singh and Pir Bhikhan Shah, which took place in 1672 when the latter went to see him at Lakhnaur, near Ambala, where he was halting for some time on his way from Patna to Kiratpur.

Relations between Sikhs and Muslims

During the partition of India in 1947, there was much bloodshed between Sikhs, Hindus and Muslims, there was mass migration of people from all walks of life to leave their homes and belongings and travel by foot across the new border, on trains and on land people were killed in what was felt to be revenge attacks.

Today in the Indian subcontinent, relations between Indians and Pakistanis are very positive since relations between India and Pakistan have improved overall in the last 10 years, both countries have experienced increased levels of tourism by Pakistani Muslims wishing to visit Indian Islamic shrines or sport events in India, or Sikhs wishing to visit the few historical gurudwaras in neighboring Punjab in Pakistan.

There are, however, tensions that remain in UK between Sikhs and Muslims regarding some allegations that some Sikhs have been forced to convert to Islam.

In 2009, the Taliban in Pakistan demanded that Sikhs in the region pay them the "Jizya" poll tax levied by Muslims on non-Muslim minorities. In 2010 the Taliban attacked many minorities including Sikhs resulting in two beheadings.

●●

9
Guru Granth Sahib

The Guru Granth Sahib, or Adi Granth, is the final Guru of the Sikhs. It is a voluminous text of 1430 angs, compiled and composed during the period of Sikh Gurus, from 1469 to 1708. It is a collection of hymns or shabad, which describe the qualities of God and why one should meditate on God's name. Guru Gobind Singh (1666–1708), the tenth of the Sikh Gurus, affirmed the sacred text Dasam Granth as his successor, and elevating the book to *Guru Granth Sahib*. Thenceforward the text remained the holy scripture of the Sikhs, regarded as the teachings of the Ten Gurus. The role of Adi Granth, as a source or guide of prayer, is pivotal in worship in Sikhism.

The Adi Granth was first compiled by the fifth Sikh guru, Guru Arjan Dev (1563–1606), from hymns of the first five Sikh gurus and other great saints, including those of the Hindu and Muslim faith. After the demise of the tenth Sikh guru many edited copies were prepared for distribution by Baba Deep Singh.

Written in the Gurmukhi script, predominantly in archaic Punjabi with occasional use of other languages including Braj, Punjabi, Khariboli (Hindi), Sanskrit, regional dialects, and Persian, often coalesced under the generic title of Sant Bhasha.

Sikhs consider the Adi Granth a spiritual guide for all mankind for all generations to come, and it plays a central role in "guiding" the Sikhs' way of life. Its place in Sikh devotional life is based on two fundamental principles; that the text is divine revelation, and that all answers regarding religion and morality can be discovered within it. Its hymns and teachings are called *Gurbani* or "Word of the guru" and sometimes *Dhur ki bani* or "Word of God". Truthfully, the revealed divine word is written by the past Gurus.

The numerous holy men other than the Sikh Gurus whose writing were included in the Adi Granth are collectively referred to as *Bhagats* "devotees" and their writings are referred to as *Bhagat bani*"Word of Devotees". These saints belonged to different social and religious backgrounds, including Hindus and Muslims, cobblers and untouchables. Though Sri Guru Granth Sahib Ji contains the compositions of both Sikh Gurus as well the other great saints (Bhagats)—including those of the Hindu and Muslim faith—no distinction whatsoever is made between the works of Sikh Gurus and the works of the Bhagats contained within the Siri Guru Granth Sahib; the titles "Guru" and "Bhagat" should not be misleading. Although, sikhs do not consider any of these castes or cultures to be a part of their religion. Guru Granth Sahib is said to be the the sole and final successor of the line of gurus.

The work of transcribing the teachings of Guru Nanak Dev, the first guru and founder of Sikhism, began in his lifetime. Guru Angad, the second guru of Sikhs, received Guru Nanak Dev's collection of songs and words in manuscript form: he added sixty-three of his own compositions. The third guru, Guru Amar Das, prepared a number of manuscripts, supplemented with 974 of his own compositions as well as the works of various Bhagats. These manuscripts, known as *Goindwal pothis*, mention the message of Guru Amar Das as to why the *Bhagat Bani* was included and how the Bhagats were influenced by Guru Nanak.

The fourth Guru also composed hymns. The fifth guru, Guru Arjan Dev, in order to consolidate the *Bani* (Divine word) of earlier Gurus and to prevent spurious compositions creeping in, began early in 1599 to compile the *Adi Granth* according to the plan laid out by Guru Nanak Dev. The *Tawarikh Guru Khalsa* mentions that he issued a *Hukamnama* (official order), asking anyone who could contribute to do so. All of the sourcing and content was reviewed in order to ensure the authenticity of the existing revelation.

The final prepared volume, written by Bhai Gurdas, under the direct supervision of Guru Arjan Dev, included the compositions of the first five Sikh Gurus and of fifteen Bhagats, seventeen Bhatts ("bards", or traditional composers) and four others such as Bhai Mardana, a lifelong companion of Guru Nanak. The Adi Granth took five years to complete and was installed in Harmandir Sahib ("the abode of God"), popularly known as the Golden Temple, on September 1, 1604, with Baba Buddha as the first Granthi. This original volume is presently in Kartarpur and bears the signature of Guru Arjan Dev.

This master copy was initially in the possession of Guru Hargobind, the sixth guru but was stolen by one of his grandsons, Dhir Mal, who wanted to lay claim to the title of Guru. The Sikhs, about 30 years later, recovered it forcibly and were made to return it on the order of the ninth Guru, Tegh Bahadur. Even though this master copy was improperly wrested from the community, its return underscored the message that no particular copy of the Adi Granth was more divine than another. This master copy of the Adi Granth (known as the "Kartarpur Pothi") which is of significant historical value, is displayed every year on the occasion of Vaisakhi by the descendants of Dhir Mal in Kartarpur.

The final redaction of the Adi Granth was prepared by Guru Gobind Singh with Bhai Mani Singh as the scribe at *Talwandi Sabo* (renamed as Damdama Sahib). Guru Gobind

Singh added the hymns composed by Guru Tegh Bahadur but excluded his own. There is mention of Guru Gobind Singh's holding an "Akhand Path" (continued recital of Guru Granth Sahib).

From Talwandi Sabo, Guru Gobind Singh went to Deccan. While at Nanded, Guru Gobind Singh installed the final version prepared by him as the perpetual Guru of Sikhs in 1708.

The hymns in Guru Granth Sahib are grouped under ragas or classical musical compositions. The chronological arrangement is on the basis of ragas and not on the order of succession of the ten Gurus. As with the Adi Granth, Sikhs do not lay emphasis on any particular copy of the Siri Guru Granth Sahib as the Guru.

The Supreme Court of India holds that the Guru Granth Sahib should be, for historic and legal reasons, considered a 'Juristic person': "The Granth replaces the Guru after the tenth Guru. We unhesitatingly hold Guru Granth Sahib to be a juristic person." The court articulated this finding in the context of a case pertaining to a property dispute.

Elevation of Adi Granth to Guru Granth Sahib

The Adi Granth was conferred the title of "Guru of the Sikhs" by the tenth Guru, Guru Gobind Singh, 1708. The event, when Guru Gobind Singh installed Adi Granth as the Guru of Sikhism, was recorded in a *Bhatt Vahi* (a bard's scroll) by an eyewitness, Narbud Singh, who was a bard at the Guru's court. There are a variety of other documents attesting to this proclamation by the tenth Guru.

Thus, despite some aberrations, the Sikhs overwhelmingly accept that the Guru Granth is their eternal Guru. This has been the understanding and conviction of the Sikhs, since that October day of 1708.

Guru's Commandment

Transliteration: "Sab sikhan kô hukam hai gurû mânyô granth"

English: *"All Sikhs are commanded to take the Granth as Guru."*

- Guru Gobind Singh, October, 1708, Nanded

A close associate of Guru Gobind Singh and author of *Rehit-nama,* Prahlad Singh, recorded the Guru's commandment saying "With the order of the Eternal Lord has been established [Sikh] Panth: all the Sikhs hereby are commanded to obey the Granth as their Guru".(*Rehat-nama, Bhai Prahlad Singh*) Similarly Chaupa Singh, another associate of Guru Gobind Singh, has mentioned this commandment in his *Rehat-nama.*

Composition

The Sikh Gurus developed a new writing system, Gurmukhî, for writing their sacred literature. Although the exact origins of the script are unknown, it is believed to have existed in an elementary form during the time of Guru Nanak. According to Sikh tradition, Guru Angad is said to have invented the script, and popularised its use among the Sikhs. It is stated in *Mahman Prakash*, an early Sikh manuscript, that the script was invented by Guru Angad at the suggestion of Guru Nanak during the lifetime of the founder. The word Gurmukhî translates as "from the mouth of the Guru". The script was used, from the onset, for compiling Sikh scriptures. The Sikhs assign high degree of sanctity to Gurmukhî language script. The Gurmukhî language Script is also the official script for the Indian State of Punjab.

The *Guru Granth Sahib* is divided into fourteen hundred and thirty pages known as *Angs* (limbs) in Sikh tradition. It can be divided into three different sections:

1. Introductory section consisting of the Mul Mantra, Japji and Sohila composed by Guru Nanak
2. Compositions of Sikh Gurus followed by those of Sikh Bhagats, collected according to chronology of *Ragas* or musical notes.
3. Compositions of Guru Tegh Bahadur.

The poems are divided on the basis of their musical setting in different ragas. A raga is a series of melodic motifs, based upon a definite scale or mode, that provide a basic structure around which the musician performs. The *ragas* are associated with different moods and times of the day and year. The total number of ragas in the Sikh system is thirty one, divided into fourteen ragas and seventeen *raginis* (less important or less definite ragas). Within the raga division, the songs are arranged in order of the Sikh gurus and Sikh bhagats with whom they are associated.

The various ragas are, in order: Raga Sri, Manjh, Gauri, Asa, Gujri, Devagandhari, Bihagara, Wadahans, Sorath, Dhanasri, Jaitsri, Todi, Bairari, Tilang, Suhi, Bilaval, Gond (Gaund), Ramkali, Nut-Narayan, Mali-Gaura, Maru, Tukhari, Kedara, Bhairav (Bhairo), Basant, Sarang, Malar, Kanra, Kalyan, Prabhati and Jaijawanti. In addition there are twenty-two compositions of *Vars* (Traditional ballads). Nine of these have specific tunes and the rest can be sung to any tune.

Sanctity among Sikhs

Sikhs observe total sanctity of the text in the Guru Granth Sahib. No one can change or alter any of the writings of the Sikh Gurus written in Adi Granth, except for the committee at Golden Temple. This includes sentences, words, structure, grammar, meanings etc. This total sanctity was observed by the Gurus themselves, but not by current extreme sikhs. Guru Har Rai had disowned his elder son, Ram Rai, because he had altered the wording of one of Guru Nanak's hymn. Ram Rai had been sent to Delhi, by Guru Har Rai, to explain *Gurbani* to Mughal Emperor Aurangzeb. In order to please the Emperor he altered the wording of hymns of Guru Nanak. The matter was reported to the Guru, who was displeased with his son and disowned him. Later when aged, Ram Rai was forgiven by Guru Gobind Singh.

Translations

Edited translations of the Guru Granth Sahib are available. However, Sikhs believe that it is necessary to learn Gurmukhî, designed and used by the Sikh Gurus, to fully understand and appreciate the message. Translations only give a preliminary understanding of the Guru Granth Sahib. A Sikh is encouraged to learn Gurmukhi to fully experience and understand the Guru Granth Sahib.

Printing

The editing of Guru Granth Sahib is done by the official religious body of Sikhs based in Amritsar. It is the sole worldwide publisher of Guru Granth Sahib. Great care is taken while making edited copies and strict code of conduct is observed during the task of editing.

Before the twentieth century, only hand written copies of Guru Granth Sahib were prepared. The first printed copy of Guru Granth Sahib was made in 1864. Since the early 20th century Guru Granth Sahib has been edited to a standard 1430 pages.

The Sri Guru Granth Sahib ji is currently printed in an authorized printing press in the basement of the Gurdwara Ramsar in Amritsar; any resulting printer's "waste" that has any of the sacred text on, is cremated at Goindval . However, unauthorised copies of Sri Guru Granth Sahib ji have also been edited.

Recitation

The Adi Granth is always placed in the centre of a Gurudwara and placed on a raised platform, known as *Takht* (throne). The Guru Granth is given the greatest respect and honour. Sikhs cover their heads and remove their shoes while in the presence of Guru Granth. Before coming into its presence, they bow before the Granth. The Guru Granth is normally carried on the head and as a sign of respect not touched with unwashed hands or put on the floor.

The Guru Granth Sahib is always the focal point in any Gurudwara. It is attended with all signs of royalty, as was the custom with Sikh Gurus, and is placed upon a throne, and the congregation sits on the floor. It is waved upon by a *chaur* (sort of fan) which is made of fine material and a canopy is always placed over it. The devotees bow before the Guru as a sign of respect.

The Guru Granth Sahib is taken care of by a Granthi. He is responsible for reciting from Guru Granth and leading the Sikh prayer. The Granthi also acts as the caretaker of Guru Granth and collector of the devotees money. This function may not be performed by any other person. It is kept covered in silken cloths, known as *Rumala,* to protect from heat, dust, pollution etc. It rests on a *manji sahib* under a *rumala* until brought out again.

Treatment of Damaged Copies

Any copies of their sacred book Guru Granth Sahib which are too badly damaged to be used, and any printer's waste which has any of its text on, are cremated with a similar ceremony as cremating a deceased person. Such burning is called Agan Bhet. (For similar reasons, observant Jews bury damaged Torah scrolls and hold for them a funeral similar to that for a human being. Muslims also bury pages of the Quran that are deemed unreadable.)

- : A copy damaged in a fire
- A copy damaged in a fire
- : 4 copies damaged in New Orleans by the flood caused by Hurricane Katrina
- Printer's waste: see above.
- : on the Nicobar Islands after the 2004 tsunami (end of page).
- MrSikhNet.com Blog query about an accumulation of download printouts of Sikh sacred text

Digitization of Guru Granth Sahib Manuscripts

Panjab Digital Library (PDL) in collaboration with the Nanakshahi Trust has taken up digitization of centuries old manuscripts in year 2003.

Comments on Sri Guru Granth Sahib by Non-Sikhs

This is what Max Arthur Macauliffe writes about the authenticity of the Guru's teaching:

The Sikh religion differs as regards the authenticity of its dogmas from most other theological systems. Many of the great teachers the world has known, have not left a line of their own composition and we only know what they taught through tradition or second-hand information. If Pythagoras wrote of his tenets, his writings have not descended to us. We know the teachings of Socrates only through the writings of Plato and Xenophon. Buddha has left no written memorial of his teaching. Kungfu-tze, known to Europeans as Confucius, left no documents in which he detailed the principles of his moral and social system. The founder of Christianity did not reduce his doctrines to writing and for them we are obliged to trust to the gospels according to Matthew, Mark, Luke and John. The Arabian Prophet did not himself reduce to writing the chapters of the Quran. They were written or compiled by his adherents and followers. But the compositions of Sikh Gurus are preserved and we know at first hand what they taught.

Pearl Buck, a Nobel laureate, gives the following comment on receiving the First English translation of the Guru Granth Sahib:

> .... I have studied the scriptures of the great religions, but I do not find elsewhere the same power of appeal to the heart and mind as I find here in these volumes. They are compact in spite of their length, and are a revelation of the vast reach of the human heart, varying from the most noble concept of God, to the recognition and indeed the insistence upon the practical needs of the human body. There is something strangely modern about these scriptures and this puzzles me until I learned that they are in fact comparatively modern, compiled as late as the 16th century, when explorers were beginning to discover that the globe upon which we all live is a single entity divided only by arbitrary lines of our own making. Perhaps this sense of unity is the source of power I find in these volumes. **They speak to a person of any religion or of none**. They speak for the human heart and the searching mind. ...

Message of Guru Granth Sahib

Some of the major messages can be summarized as follows: -

1. All people of the world are equal
2. Women are equal to men
3. One God for all
4. Speak and live truthfully
5. Control the five vices

6. Live in God's hukam (The Will of the One GOD)
7. Practice Humility, Kindness, Compassion, Love, etc.

Care and Protocol

Personal Behaviour

Any person carrying out any *Service or Sewa* must observe the following:

- Head must be covered at all times.
- Shoes and socks must be removed outside the Guru's room.
- Basic standards of personal hygiene are to be observed especially relating to cleanliness
- Eating or drinking while in service is strictly avoided.
- Complete silence is observed while in Guru's service.
- Respectful attitude towards others who are present.No Discrimination while doing Sewa

Environment

- The room should be kept clean
- The clothes that are used to cover Guru Granth are kept clean and changed daily. Some people choose to use decorated cloth, but this is not necessary.
- Guru Granth is always placed on a Manji Sahib (small handmade bed like throne).
- A canopy is always placed over Guru Granth.
- A Chaur Sahib (artificial hairs bundled together to fan over the Guru Granth Sahib) is be provided besides Guru Granth with a small platform to house the Karah Parshad (sacramental food) and other offerings.

On the Move

While Guru Granth Sahib is on the move the following is observed:

- Five initiated Sikhs accompany Guru Granth Sahib at all times when traveling
- Another Sikh does Chaur Sahib seva
- The Main Sikh carrying Guru Granth Sahib must put a clean rumâl on his or her head before carefully and respectfully placing Guru Granth Sahib on this rumâl. At all times, Guru Granth Sahib should be covered with a small rumâl so that Guru Granth Sahib's form is always fully "covered". Also the Sikh carrying Guru Granth Sahib should have "Keshi Ishnaan" or washed hair to show respect.
- There should be recitation of "Waheguru" at all times.

Other Considerations

- No one sits on a higher platform than the Guru.

Guru Granth Sahib World University

Guru Sahib World University would be formally launched in July 2009. A decision to this effect was taken at a meeting of Sri Guru Granth Sahib Fourth Centenary Memorial Trust. The meeting was chaired by the Punjab Chief Minister Paraksh Singh Badal. Disclosing this, Mr. Harcharan Bains, Media Advisor to the Chief Minister said that apart from intensive work on Guru Granth Sahib studies, the University would focus on imparting education in post modern technologies such as Nano-technology, Bio-technology, Information Technology and Business Management besides comparative study of different religions. These courses would be introduced in the inaugural academic session next year.

Later, the University would also house the faculties in Emerging Technologies, Basic Sciences, Management, Social Sciences, Arts, Languages, Engineering, Architecture, Law and Social Justice. Work will soon commence on the construction of the Complex.

Other Universities

Punjabi University, Patiala, has established a department which provides a number of academic courses on Guru Granth Sahib. The department was established in 1962. Sikhism is a revealed religion and as such the department was established to do research in Sikhism and Sikh scriptures.

The aim of the department is to study Sikhism as an academic discpline and to produce source material for students working in the field of Sikh studies. The thrust areas of the departmental research are Sikh theology and Sikh Philosophy

The university has started work on an online academic course in advanced studies of the Guru Granth sahib. This academic course would be available internationally, to any student who wants academic training in the Sikh scripture. The academic exam papers would be designed by

"The Advanced Centre for Development of Punjabi Language, Literature and Culture".

Dasven Padshah Da Granth

The ***Dasven Patshah Da Granth, Dasam Granth, (Book of the Tenth Emperor)*** also referred as *Dasam Granth,* is a scripture of Sikhism, containing some of the texts composed by 10th Sikh Guru, Guru Gobind Singh. Some compositions of the Dasam Granth like Jaap Sahib, Tvai Prasad Sawaiye (Amrit Savaiye), and Benti Chaupai are part of daily prayers Nitnem of the Sikhs. These compositions are also part of Sikh baptism (Khande di Pahul).

Structure

Overview

The Dasam Granth contains 1428 pages and contains the writings of the 10th Sikh Guru, Guru Gobind Singh. It contains Jaap Sahib, the Akal Ustat or praise of the Creator, the Bachitar Natak or Wonderful Drama, in which gives an account of his parentage, his divine mission, and the battles in which he had been engaged.

Then come three abridged compositions of the wars of Durga with demons, (Chandi Chritras: Chandi Chritra I, Chandi Chritra II, Chandi di Var). These were written to instill the spirit of war among Sikhs. The first stanza of the Sikh ardaas, an invocation to God and the 9 Guru's preceding Guru Gobind Singh Ji, is from Chandi di Var.

Then follow the Gyan Parbodh, or awakening of knowledge; the Shabad Hazare; quatrains called Sawaiyas, which are religious hymns in praise of God and reprobation of idolatry and hypocrisy; the Shastar Nam Mala, a list of offensive and defensive weapons used in the Guru's time, with special reference to the attributes of the Creator; the Kabiovach Bainti Chaupai will "absolve the suffering, pain or fear of the person, who will even once recite this Bani"; the Zafarnamah, containing the tenth Guru's epistle to the emperor Aurangzeb; and Hikayats, several metrical tales in the Persian language.

The Dasam Granth is said to have been compiled by Bhai Mani Singh a companion and disciple of the Guru, after the tenth Guru's death.

Contents

The Contents of the Dasam Granth are:

- Jaap (Meditation)
- Akal Ustat (praises of God)

- Bachitar Natak (autobiography of the Guru)
- Chandi Charitar I & II (the character of Goddess Chandi)
- Chandi di Var (a ballad to describe Goddess Chandi)
- Gyan Prabod (The Awakening of Knowledge)
- Chaubis Avtar (Narrative of 24 incarnations of Vishnu as ordered by God Almighty)
- Shabad Hazare (Ten Shabads)
- Swayyae (33 stanzas)
- Khalsa Mehma (the praises of the Khalsa)
- Shastar Nam Mala (a list of weapons)
- Charitropakhyan (various character of men and women [details both negative and positive])
- Zafarnamah (epistle of victory, a letter written to Emperor Aurangzeb)

Language and Literary Quality

The Dasam Granth is all rhymed poetry. It was designed to be heard, so there is considerable repetition, and a variety of meters to hold the attention. The language of most of the Dasam Granth is largely Braj Bhasha veering towards Sanskrit at one extreme and simple colloquial Hindi at the other, although conventional Hindi is used marginally. The Braj dialect is a variety of medieval Hindi with a mixture of Sanskrit and Arabic words. The Zafarnamah and the Hikayats are in Persian using Gurmukhi characters and several passages in other works are in Punjabi. The 'author(s)' not only used this melange of languages but also coined words half Arabic half Sanskrit (and sometimes words without any meaning just to create a musical effect). Some of this kind of writing has great power and beauty.

From *A Short History of the Sikhs,* Ganda Singh & Teja Singh:

"In Hindi he developed a style, which for martial cadence, variety of form and richness of imagination...has remained unsurpassed since his times. In lines ranging from monosyllabic verse to long and multiplied swayyas and kabits, we seem to hear the torrential flow of hill streams or the galloping sweep of cavalry on the march. His intellect quivers in emotion and breaks out against superstition and hypocrisy into humour, irony or banter. His emotion...is raised to the highest pitch of ecstasy when he communes with God."

From *Sikhan de Raj di Vithya* (History of the Sikh Rule):

"This Granth is very difficult, and is composed in the Gurmukhi dialect in several kinds of verses. In it there is the description of several weapons of warfare, the rules of warfare, the shortcomings in the character of men and women, and some information on worship and religious knowledge. The descriptions of scenes of battle are couched in extremely vigorous staccato rhyme often reduced to lines of one word each. The battles waged by Chandi encounters with the hill chiefs at Bhangani and Nadaun are among the most stirring that exist.

Quotes from Dasam Granth

Internal evidence to the dates of compilation of different portions of various compositions

- (This work has been completed) in the year 1745 of the Vikrami era in the Sudi aspect of the moon in the month of Sawan, (July 1688 A.D.) in the town of Paonta at the auspicious hour, on banks of the flowing Yamuna. (Sri Guru Gobind Singh Sahib in 'Krishnavtar')

- In Samvat 1745 (1688 A.D.), this 'katha' (composition) was improved and if there is any error and omission in it, then the poets may still improve it.755. (Sri Guru Gobind Singh Sahib in 'Krishnavtar')
- The Granth was completed on Sunday, the 18th day of month of Bhadon, in 1753 Bikrami Sammat (September 14, 1696 A.D.) on the banks of river Satluj.(Sri Guru Gobind Singh Sahib in 'Charitropakhyan')
- This Granth has been completed (and improved) in Vadi first in the month of Haar in the year 1755 Bikrami (July 1698); if there has remained any error in it, then kindly correct it.(Sri Guru Gobind Singh Sahib in 'Ramavtaar')
- This (part of the) Granth has been prepared after revision in Paonta city on Wednesday in Sawan Sudi Samvat 1744 (August 1687 AD). 983.(Sri Guru Gobind Singh Sahib in 'Krishnavtar')

Condemnation of the concept in Hindu theology that God takes various incarnations

- He hath Created millions of Krishnas like worms. He Created them, annihilated them, again created them, again destroyed them.
- Somewhere He hath created millions of servants like Krishna. Somewhere He hath effaced and then created (many) like Rama. (pg.98)
- Ram and Rahim whose names you are uttering cant save you. Brahma, Vishnu Shiva, Sun and Moon, all are subject to the power of Death.1. .(pg.1349)
- O God ! the day when I caught hold of your feet, I do not bring anyone else under my sight; none other is liked by me now; the Puranas and the Quran try to

know Thee by the names of Ram and Rahim and talk about you through several stories, but I do not accept these

- He, whose form and colour are not, how can he be called Shyaam (black)? .(p1349)
- Brahma came into being under the control of time and taking his staff and pot his hand, he wandered on the earth; Shiva was also under the control of time and wandered in various countries far and near;
- Someone calls Him Ram or Krishna and someone believes in His incarnations, but my mind has forsaken all useless actions and has accepted only One Creator.12. (p. 1352)
- Thou hast meditated on millions of Krishnas, Vishnus, Ramas and Rahims. Thou hast recited the name of Brahma and established Shivalingam, even then none could save thee.......They cannot save themselves from the blow of death, how can they protect thee? They are all hanging in the blazing fire of anger, therefore they will cause thy hanging similarly. (pg111)
- He, whom Shiva etc. had been searching, but could not know His Mystery; O Shukdev ! relate to me the story of that Lord.2403.
- I do not adore Ganesha in the beginning and also do not meditate on Krishna and Vishnu; I have only heard about them with my ears and I do not recognize them; my consciousness is absorbed at the feet of the Supreme Lord.434.
- If you consider Ram, the Lord as Unborn, then how did he take birth from the womb of Kaushalya? He, who is said to be the destroyer of death, then why did he become subjugated himself before death?

- If he (Krishna) is called the Truth-incarnate, beyond enmity and opposition, then why did he become the charioteer of Arjuna? O mind! you only consider him the Lord God, whose Mysetry could not be known to anyone.13.

- If he (Krishna) is said to be unborn and without a beginning, then how did he come into the womb of Devaki? He, who is considered without any father or mother, then why did he cause Vasudev to be called his father? 14.

- Krishna himself is considered the treasure of Grace, then why did the hunter shot his arrow at him? He has been described as redeeming the clans of others then he caused the destruction of his own clan;

- Why do you consider Shiva or Brahma as the Lord? There is none amongst Ram, Krishna and Vishnu, who may be considered as the Lord of the Universe by you;

- Someone calls Brahma as the Lord-God and someone tells the same thing about Shiva; someone considers Vishnu as the hero of the universe and says that only by remembering him, all the sins will be destroyed;

- O fool ! think about it a thousand times, all of them will leave you at the time of death. Therefore, you should only meditate on Him, who was in the past, is there in the present and will also be there in the future.16.

- Relinquishing One Lord, you worship many. Likewise Sukhdev, Prashar and Vyas were proven false due to pantheism. All have established hollow religions. I believe in One God who reveals Himself in multifarious modes.(15)

- He, who created millions of Indras and Upendras and then destroyed them; He, who created innumerable gods, demons, Sheshnaga, tortoises, birds, animals etc.,
- And for knowing whose Mystery, Shiva and Brahma are performing austerities even till today, but could not know His end; He is such a Guru, whose Mystery could not be comprehended also by Vedas and Katebs and my Guru has told me the same thing.17.
- How can He be said to come in human form? The Siddha (adept) in deep meditation became tired of the discipline on not seeing Him in any way.....Pause. (p. 1348)
- The Vedas and Ketebs could not comprehend His Mystery and the adepts have been defeated in practicing contemplation; Different kinds of thoughts have been mentioned about God in Vedas, Shastras, Puranas and smrities; (p1351)
- Sheshnaga, Indra, Ganesha, Shiva and also the Shrutis (Vedas) could not know Thy Mystery; O my foolish mind! why have you forgotten such a Lord. 4.

Condemnation of Idol Worship

- Someone worships stone and places it on his head. Someone hangs the phallus (lingam) from his neck. .(pg.42)
- O fool! Fall at the feet of Lord-God, the Lord is not within the stone-idols.99.(pg.111)
- Some fools worship the idols and some go to worship the dead. (pg.42)
- They also were overpowered by 'mineness' and exhibited the Lord in statues.13. .(pg.134)

- Worshipping the stones, they will not meditate on One Lord; there will be prevalent the darkness of many sects; Leaving the ambrosia they will desire for poison, and they will name the evening time as early-morning; .(pg.1142)
- Rice, incense and lamps are offered, but the stones do not eat anything. (pg.1349)
- Of what use is the worship of the stones with devotion and sincerity in various ways? The hand became tired of touching the stones, because no spiritual power accrued. O fool! where is the spiritual power in them, so that they may bless you with some boon. (pg.1349)
- Why do you not pray to Him, who will be there in future and who is there in the present? You are worshipping the stones uselessly; what will you gain by that worship? (pg. 1289)
- Why do you worship stones? Because the Lord-God is not within those stones; you may only worship Him, whose adoration destroys clusters of sins; (pg.1353)
- The hollow religion became fruitless and O being! you have lost years and years by worshipping the stones; you will not get power with the worship of stones; the strength and glory will only decrease; (pg.1353)
- You may even perform the austerities for an age, but these stones will not fulfill your wishes and please you; they will not raise their hands and grant you the boon; (pg.1353)
- You had been wandering with bowed head in the temples of stones, but you realized nothing; O foolish mind! you were only entangled in your bad intellect abandoning that Effulgent Lord.26. (pg.1354)

- Someone has tied the stone-idol around his neck and someone has accepted Shiva as the Lord; someone considers the Lord within the temple or the mosque; (p1351)
- They were the idol worshippers, and me the idol destroyer

●●

10

Janamsakhis

The Janamsakhis, literally *birth stories,* are writings which profess to be biographies of the first Sikh guru, Guru Nanak. These compositions have been written at various stages after the death of the first guru.

All the Janamsakhis record miraculous acts and supernatural conversations. Many of them contradict each other on material points and some have obviously been touched up to advance the claims of one or the other branches of the Guru's family, or to exaggerate the roles of certain disciples. Macauliffe compares the manipulation of janamsakhs to the way gospels were also in early Christian Church:

> "Vast numbers of spurious writings bearing the names of apostles and their followers, and claiming more or less direct apostolic authority, were in circulation in the early Church - Gospels according to Peter, to Thomas, to James, to Judas, according to the Apostles, or according to the Twelve, to Barnabas, to Matthias, to Nicodemus, & co.; and ecclesiastical writers bear abundant testimony to the early and rapid growth of apocryphal literature. - *Supernatural Religion, vol.i, p.292.*

The falsification of old or the composition of new Janamsakhis were the result of three great schisms of the Sikh religion: The Udasis, the Minas and the Handalis.

Though from the point of view of a historian the janamsakhis may be inadequate, they cannot be wholly discarded because they were based on legend and tradition which had grown up around the Guru in the years following his demise, and furnish useful material to augment the bare but proved facts of his life. The main janamsakhis which scholars over the years have referred to are as follows:

Main Janamsakhis

Bhai Bala Janamsakhi

This is probably the most popular and well known Janamsakhi, in that most Sikhs and their Janamsakhi knowledge comes from this document. This work claims to be a contemporarry account written by one Bala Sandhu in the Sambat year 1592 at the instance of the second Guru, Guru Angad. According to the author, he was a close companion of Guru Nanak and accompanied him on many of his travels. There are good reasons to doubt this contention:

- Guru Angad, who is said to have commissioned the work and was also a close companion of the Guru in his later years, was, according to Bala's own admission, ignorant of the existence of Bala.
- Bhai Mani Singh's Bhagat Ratanwali, which contains essentially the same list as that by Bhai Gurdas, but with more detail, also does not mention Bala Sandhu.
- Bhai Gurdas, who has listed all Guru Nanak's prominent disciples whose names were handed down, does not mention the name of Bhai Bala Sandhu. (This may be an oversight, for he does not mention Rai Bular either.)
- It is only in the heretic janamsakhis of the Minas that we find first mention of Bhai Bala.
- Some of the hymns ascribed to Nanak are not his but those of the second and fifth Gurus.

- The language used in this janamsakhi was not spoken at the time of Guru Nanak or Guru Angad, but was developed at least a hundred years later.
- At several places expressions which gained currency only during the lifetime of the last Guru, Guru Gobind Singh (1666-1708), are used e.g. Waheguru ji ki Fateh. Bala's janamsakhi is certainly not a contemporary account; at best it was written in the early part of the 18th Century.

This janamsakhi has had an immense influence over determining what is generally accepted as the authoritative account of Guru Nanak Dev Ji's life. Throughout the nineteenth century the authority of the Bala version was unchallenged. An important work based on the Bahi Bala janam-sakhi is Santokh Singh's Gur Nanak Purkash commonly known as Nanak Parkash. Its lengthy sequel, Suraj Parkash carries the account up to the tenth Guru and contains a higher proportion of historical fact, this was completed in 1844.

In the first journey or udasi Guru Nanak Dev Ji left Sultanpur towards eastern India and included, in the following sequence : Panipat (Sheikh Sharaf), Delhi (Sultan Ibrahim Lodi), Hardwar, Allahbad, Banaras, Nanakmata, Kauru, Kamrup in Assam (Nur Shah), Talvandi (twelve years after leaving Sultanpur), Pak Pattan (Sheikh Ibrahim), Goindval, Lahore and Kartarpur.

The Second udasi was to the south of India with companion Bhai Mardana. Delhi, Ayodhya, Jagannath Puri, Rameswaram, Sri Lanka, Vindhya mountains, Narabad River, Ujjain, Saurashtra and Mathura

The third udasi was to the north : Kashmir, Mount Sumeru and Achal

The fourth udasi was to the west. Afghanistan, Persia, Mecca, Madina and Baghdad

Vilayat Vali Janamsakhi

In the year 1883 a copy of a janamasakhi was dispatched by the India Office Library in London for the use of Dr.Trumpp and the Sikh scholars assisting him. (It had been given to the library by an Englishman called Colebrook; it came to be known as the Vilayat Vali or the foreign janamsakhi.) This janamsakhi was the basis of the accounts written by Trumpp, Macauliffe, and most Sikh scholars. It is said to have been written in 1588 AD by one Sewa Das.

Hafizabad Vali Janamsakhi

A renowned Sikh scholar, Gurmukh Singh of the Oriental College, Lahore, found another janamsakhi at Hafizabad which was very similar to that found by Colebrook. Gurmukh Singh who was collaborating with Mr. Macauliffe in his research on Sikh religion, made it available to the Englishman, who had it published in November 1885. This biography agrees entirely with the India Office janamsakhi.

Bhai Mani Singh's Janam-sakhi

The fourth and eveidently the latest is the Gyan-ratanavali attributed to Bhai Mani Singh who wrote it with the express intention of correcting heretical accounts of Guru Nanak Dev Ji. Bhai Mani Singh was a Sikh of Guru Gobind Singh Ji. He was approached by some Sikhs with a request that he should prepare an authentic account of Guru Nanak Dev Ji's life. This they assured him was essential as the Minas were circulating objectionable things in their version. Bhai Mani Singh referred them to the Var of Bhai Gurdas Ji, but this, they maintained was to brief and a longer more fuller account was needed. Bhai Mani Singh writes :

Just as swimmers fix reeds in the river so that those who do not know the way may also cross, so I shall take Bhai Gurdas's var as my basis and in accordance with it, and with the accounts that I have heard at the court of the tenth

Master, I shall relate to you whatever commentary issues from my humble mind. At the end of the Janam-sakhi there is an epilogue in which it is stated that the completed work was taken to Guru Gobind Singh Ji for his seal of approval. Guru Sahib Ji duly signed it and commended it as a means of acquiring knowledge of Sikh belief.

Other Janamsakhis

Many other janamsakhis have since been discovered. They follow the above two in all material points. The famous historian, Karam Singh, mentions half a dozen he came across in his travels.

The term Puratan janamsakhis means ancient janamsakhis and is generally used with reference to the composite work which was compiled by Bhai Vir Singh and first published in 1926. Of the still existing copies of the Puratan Janam-sakhis the two most important were the Colebrooke and Hafizabad versions. The first of these was discovered in 1872, the manuscript had been donated to the library of the east India company by H.T. Colebrooke and is accordingly known as the Colebrooke or Vailaitwali Janamsakhi. Although there is no date on it the manuscript points to around 1635.

According to the Puratan Janamsakhi, Guru Nanak Dev Ji was born in the month of Vaisakh, 1469. The date is given as the third day of the light half of the month and the birth is said it have taken place during the last watch before dawn. His father Kalu, was a khatri of the Bedi sub-cast and lived in a village Rai Bhoi di talwandi, his mothers name is not given. When Guru Ji turned seven he was taken to a pundit to learn how to read. After only one day he gave up reading and when the pundit asked him why Guru Ji lapsed into silence and instructed him at length in the vanity of worldly learning and the contrasting value of the Divine Name of God. The child began to show disturbing signs of withdrawal from the world. He was sent to learn Persian at the age of nine but returned home and continued to sit in silence. Locals advised his father that Nanak should be married. This advice was taken and at the age of twelve a betrothal was arranged at the house of Mula of the Chona sub-caste. Sometime later Nanak moved to Sultanpur where his sister Nanaki was married. Here he took up employment with Daulat Khan. One day Nanak went to the river and while bathing messengers of God came and he was transported to the divine court. There he was given a cup of nectar (amrit) and with it came the command " Nanak, this is the cup of My Name (Naam). Drink it." This he did and was charged to go into the world and preach the divine Name.

The Miharban Janam-Sakhi

Of all the manuscripts this is probably the most neglected as it has acquired a disagreeable reputation. Sodhi Miharban who gives his name to the janam-sakhi was closely associated to the Mina sect and the Minas were very hostile towards the Gurus around the period of Guru Arjan Dev Ji. The Minas were the followers of Prithi Chand the eldest son of Guru Ram Das Ji. Prithi Chand's behaviour was evidently unsatisfactory as he was passed over in favour of his younger brother, (Guru) Arjan Dev, when his father chose a successor. The Minas were a robber tribe and in Punjabi the word has come to mean someone who conceals his true evil intent. The Minas were subsequently execrated by Guru Gobind Singh Ji and Sikhs were instructed to have no dealings with them. The sect is now extinct. It is said that it was due to this janam-sakhi and its hostility towards the Gurus that prompted Bhai Gurdas Ji's account and the commission of the Gyan-ratanavali.

The first three sakhis recount the greatness of Raja Janak and describes an interview with God wherein Raja Janak is instructed that he is to return to the world once again to propagate His Name. Details of Guru Nanak's birth are given in the fourth sakhi and his father was Kalu, a Bedi and his mother Mata Tripta. The account of Guru Ji learning to read from the pundit is also recounted here. After the interlude at Sultanpur Guru Nanak Dev Ji set out to Mount Sumeru. Climbing the mountain Guru Ji found all nine Siddhus seated there – Gorakhnath, Mechhendranath, Isarnath, Charapatnath, Barangnath, Ghoracholi, Balgundai, Bharathari and Gopichand. Gorakhnath asked the identity of the visitor and his disciple replied, " This is Nanak Bedi, a pir and a bhagat who is a housholder."

●●

11

Sikh and Teachings

A Sikh is a follower of Sikhism. Sikhism (Sikhi in Punjabi) primarily originated in 15th century Punjab region of South Asia and now constitutes one of the major religions with adherents throughout the world. The term "Sikh" has its origin in the Sanskrit term *[isya,* meaning "disciple, learner" or *[iksa,* meaning "instruction".

According to Article I of the "Rehat Maryada" (the Sikh code of conduct and conventions), a Sikh is defined as "any human being who faithfully believes in One Immortal Being; ten Gurus, from Guru Nanak Dev to Sri Guru Gobind Singh; the Sri Guru Granth Sahib; the utterances and teachings of the ten Gurus and the baptism bequeathed by the tenth Guru; and who does not owe allegiance to any other religion". The most common symbol of all Sikhs, because of its simplicity, is uncut hair (including beards for men) and turbans.

The greater Punjab region is the historic homeland of Sikhism. Most Sikhs are Punjabis and come from the Punjab region, although significant communities exist around the world. Punjabis and the Punjab region's history has been tremendously important in the formation of Sikhism as a religion. One of the most important and very often forgotten beliefs of Sikhism is the non-belief in any caste, group, distinction of any sort within all the human race, which their Gurus (teachers) had left behind. The Punjabi influence is the main reason why Sikhs have, sometimes, been described as an ethnoreligious group outside of India.

Philosophy

The core philosophy of the Sikh religion can be understood in the beginning hymn of the holy Guru Granth Sahib

> "There is one supreme eternal reality; the truth; immanent in all things; creator of all things; immanent in creation. Without fear and without hatred; not subject to time; beyond birth and death; self-revealing. Known by the Guru's grace."

Guru Nanak, the founder of the faith, summed up the basis of Sikh lifestyle in three requirements: Naam Japo, Kirat Karni and Wand kay Shako, which means meditate on the holy name (Waheguru), work diligently and honestly, and share one's fruits.

The Sikhs revere Guru Granth Sahib as their supreme teacher, as it is a literal transcript of the teachings of the Sikh Gurus. The tenth Guru appointed Guru Granth Sahib as his successor. Compiled by the Sikh Gurus, and maintained in its original form, Sikhs revere Guru Granth Sahib as their supreme guide. Non-Sikhs can partake fully in Sikh prayer meetings and social functions. Their daily prayers include the well being of all of mankind.

The martyrdom of Shri Guru Teg Bahadur Ji 9th Guru to protect Hindus from religious persecution, in Delhi, on 11 November 1675 AD, is an example to be followed.

Sikhs are required not to renounce the world, and aspire to live a modest life. Seva (service) is an integral part of Sikh worship, very easily observed in the Gurdwara. Visitors of any religious or socio-economic background are welcomed, where langar, (food for all) is always served.

The Sikhs also revere *Bhaghats* or Saints belonging to different social backgrounds. The work of these Bhagats is collected in Guru Granth Sahib, and is known as Bhagat-Bani (sacred word of bhagat) as against work of Sikh Gurus being known as Gur-Bani (sacred word of guru).

People revered by Sikhs also include:

- Bhai Mardana: *(One of the first followers and lifelong companion of Guru Nanak)*
- Bhai Bala: *(One of the first followers and lifelong companion of Guru Nanak)*
- Baba Buddha: *(Sikh saint, held the position of high Granthi in the Sikh religion)*
- Baba Banda Singh Bahadur: *(Fought and Defeated Mughal Governor of Punjab Wazir Khan and established Sikh force in Punjab)*
- Baba Deep Singh: *(Sikh saint, defended Golden Temple with his head in his hand)*
- Bhai Mani Singh *(Sikh Scholar, compiled the Dasam Granth)*
- Bhai Taru Singh *(Was a great patron of the poor)*
- Bhai Gurdas *(Known for his interpretation of bani)*
- Bhai Kanhaiya *(Known for starting the first action of Red Cross)*
- Bhai Mati Das *(Known for sacrificing their life for the right of faith)*
- Bhai Sati Das *(Known for sacrificing their life for the right of faith)*
- Bhai Dayala *(Known for sacrificing their life for the right of faith)*
- Bhai Bachittar Singh *(Known for sacrificing their life in battle in bravery, by putting a spear through an intoxicated elephant which was covered in armour)*

Early Sikh Scholars included Bhai Santokh Singh, Bhai Vir Singh and Bhai Kahn Singh Nabha.

Teachings

Sikhism believes in one supreme God. The Sikh school of thought started by Guru Nanak teaches gender and race equality, sharing, working hard and honestly, being honest, contentment, selfless service, talking sweetly, worshiping naam, good etiquette, tradition, prayer, meditation, the concept of miri-piri, the concept of the saint-soldier/warrior, remembering God all the time in all actions, keeping in good company, proper sexual conduct, the life of a house person instead of becoming a celibate monk and rejecting the world, compassion, faith, justice, mastery, righteous actions, bravery, courage, love for God, humility, salvation, the afterlife, the law of karma (karam) which is counteracted by dharma (dharam), charity, and good will to humanity. It also teaches God's omnipresence, transcendence, omnipotence, and omniscience.

The Sikh school of thought believes in reincarnation as well as the concept of many hells and heavens. Besides ethics, morals and values the Sikh faith accepts miracles. Sikhs believe in the angel of death (yam, yamraj, Azrael (see also farishta/ jinn/angels/dieties/demons/Genie), yama, yamraj, jamdoot. dharamraj, jaam) reaping the soul after death from the body for its next life.

Sikhs have to pray 5 prayers in morning (japji, Anand Sahib, Jaap Sahib, Tav-Prasad Savaiye, Chaupai (Sikhism) and Ardas.) (between 1am-6am), 1 prayer in evening Rehras and Ardas (5-7 pm) and 1 before sleeping Kirtan Sohila and Ardas (8-10 pm).

Sikh scriptures teach to the concept of moderation from the teachings of eat little, sleep little, talk little, consume as less as possible (not to extremes, but in the middle way) and to live pious saintly lives as well as that of a warrior (understanding the greatest battle is within). Sikhism teaches a person to remove (the Five Evils); (kaam (kam)), krodh, lobh, moh and hankar) ego (see also Ego (spirituality)), pride, raging anger, sexual lust, worldly attachment, greed and oppose hedonism as well as materialism and indulgences.

Sikhism teaches the Hierarchy of the master and the student as one and the same, a great student is the master's master an idea which was in place in the western world after the French Revolution.

Sikhism teaches all of humanity was created by the same one God who has many names and many forms. Sikhism teaches to respect all other religions (tolerant) and that one should defend the rights of not just one's own religion, but the religion and faith of others, as a human right. The end of every Sikh prayer is a prayer to help all of humanity.

Sikhism believes in the Human Soul (Self (spirituality) or consciousness or spirit or astral body). Sikhs believe they can unite and become one with God in this life, as the consciousness merges with with God (Supreme Consciousness).

Sikh doctrines teach of macroism and microism relation, cosmological principles such as many planets and the exact distance of the Earth to the moon being revelled by Guru Nanak (approx. 500 years ago), ideas of life in rocks, Sikhism also brings ideas which are not proven in modern science such as the number of life forms being 8.4 million and the existence of Aliens.

Sikhs do not cut their uncut hair kesh (this being covered with a turban, every human hair follicle has a nerve attached, non-removal of an organ for which the functionality is not fully understood i.e. to be believed it is a spiritual organ, the idea of humans being made in the image of God, to honour God, the direct command and compulsory mandate of the Gurus, a symbol of honour, warrior hood, saintliness and radiance/aura, to work as an antenna for the third eye, dasamdwar, heaven eye, Dasam Dwaar, 10th doorway, brahmdwar, 7th chakra (chakra, yoga), pineal gland, pituitary gland, crown chakra, inner eye, minds eye). This practice was further enhanced in the west by Sikhs within 3ho who teach Kundalini yoga (see also Kundalini yoga.

The Sikh movement started during turbalent periods in the history of empires of India, one of such was the Mughal empire who presented Law and order from Islamic viewpoint into a majorily Hindu Society where the existence of Buddhism had been wiped out, Sikhism has paralels with the Bhagati (Bhakti) movement, mysticism and Sufism.

Sikhism strictly forbids the use of intoxicants, drugs, alcohol, cigarettes, Narcotics and any other foreign substance which disrupts the body.

The Sikh religion also teaches human life is very valuable, which is described to be more precious then a diamond which comes after great spiritual deeds and merits are done, to have gone through 8.4 million life cycle of sansara before human life was attained. Therefore the meaning of life from Sikh teachings is to meet God. Sikhs refrain from maya (illusion), false perception of reality where utter truth is only God and everything else is a lie.

Five Ks

The Five Ks, or *panj kakaar/kakke,* are five articles of faith that all *baptized Sikhs* (also called Khalsa Sikhs) are typically obliged to wear at all times, as commanded by the tenth Sikh Guru, who so ordered on the day of Baisakhi Amrit Sanskar in 1699. The symbols are worn for identification and representation of the ideals of Sikhism, such as honesty, equality, fidelity, militarism, meditating on God, and never bowing to tyranny.

The five symbols are:-

- Kesh (uncut hair, usually tied and wrapped in the Sikh Turban, Dastar.)
- Kanga (wooden comb, usually worn under the Dastar.)
- Kachchhera (characteristic shorts, usually white in color.)
- Kara (iron bracelet, which is a symbol of eternity.)
- Kirpan (curved sword, comes in different sizes, for example in the UK Sikhs would wear a small sharp dagger whereas in the Punjab Sikhs would wear the traditional curved sword, from one to three feet in length.)

History

Essentially Sikh history, with respect to Sikhism as a distinct political body, can be said to have begun with the martyrdom of the fifth Sikh Guru, Guru Arjan Dev in 1606. Sikh distinction was further enhanced by the establishment of the Khalsa, by Guru Gobind Singh in 1699. The evolution of Sikhism began with the emergence of Guru Nanak as a religious leader and a social reformer during the fifteenth century in Punjab. The religious practice was formalized by Guru Gobind Singh on March 30, 1699. The latter baptised five people from different social backgrounds to form Khalsa. The first five, Pure Ones, then baptized Gobind Singh into the Khalsa fold. This gives Sikhism, as an organised grouping, a religious history of around 400 years.

Generally Sikhism has had amicable relations with other religions. However, during the Mughal rule of India (1556–1707), emerging religion had strained relation with the ruling Mughals. Prominent Sikh Gurus were martyred by Mughals for opposing some Mughal emperors' persecution of minority religious communities. Subsequently, Sikhism militarized to oppose Mughal hegemony. The emergence of the Sikh Empire under reign of the Maharajah Ranjit Singh was characterized by religious tolerance and pluralism with Christians, Muslims and Hindus in positions of power. The establishment of the Sikh Empire is commonly considered the zenith of Sikhism at political level, during this time the Sikh Empire came to include Kashmir, Ladakh, and Peshawar. Hari Singh Nalwa, the Commander-in-chief of the Sikh army along the North West Frontier, took the boundary of the Sikh Empire to the very mouth of the Khyber Pass. The Empire's secular administration integrated innovative military, economic and governmental reforms.

The months leading up to the partition of India in 1947, saw heavy conflict in the Punjab between Sikh and Muslims, which saw the effective religious migration of Punjabi Sikhs and Hindus from West Punjab which mirrored a similar religious migration of Punjabi Muslims in East Punjab.

The 1960s saw growing animosity and rioting between Punjabi Sikhs and Hindus in India, as the Punjabi Sikhs agitated for the creation of a Punjabi Sikh majority state, an undertaking which was promised to the Sikh leader Master Tara Singh by Nehru in return for Sikh political support during the negotiations for Indian Independence. Sikhs obtained the Sikh majority state of Punjab on November 1, 1966.

Communal tensions arose again in the late 1970s, fueled by Sikh claims of discrimination and marginalization by the secularist dominated Indian National Congress ruling party and the "dictatorial" tactics adopted the then Indian Prime Minister, Indira Gandhi. Frank argues that Gandhi's assumption of emergency powers in 1975 resulted in the weakening of the "legitimate and impartial machinery of government" and her increasing "paranoia" of opposing political groups led her to instigate a "despotic policy of playing castes, religions and political groups against each other for political advantage". As a reaction against these actions came the emergence of the Sikh leader Sant Jarnail Singh Bhindranwale who vocalized Sikh sentiment for justice and advocated the creation of a Sikh homeland, Khalistan. This accelerated Punjab into a state of communal violence. Gandhi's 1984 action to defeat Sant Jarnail Singh Bhindranwale led to the attack of the Golden Temple in Operation Bluestar and ultimately led to Gandhi's assassination by her Sikh bodyguards. This resulted in an explosion of violence against the Sikh community in the Anti Sikh Riots which resulted in the massacre of thousands of Sikhs throughout India; Khushwant Singh described the actions as being a Sikh pogrom in which he "felt like a refugee in my country. In fact, I felt like a Jew in Nazi Germany". Since 1984, relations between Sikhs and Hindus have reached a rapprochement helped by growing economic prosperity; however in 2002 the claims of the popular right-wing Hindu organisation the RSS, that "Sikhs are Hindus" angered Sikh sensibilities. Many Sikhs still are campaigning for justice for victims of the violence and the political and economic needs of the Punjab espoused in the Khalistan movement.

In 1996 the Special Rapporteur for the Commission on Human Rights on freedom of religion or belief, Abdelfattah Amor (Tunisia, 1993–2004), visited India in order to compose a report on religious discrimination. In 1997, Amor concluded, "it appears that the situation of the Sikhs in the religious field is satisfactory, but that difficulties are arising in the political (foreign interference, terrorism, etc.), economic (in particular with regard to sharing of water supplies) and even occupational fields. Information received from nongovernment (sic) sources indicates that discrimination does exist in certain sectors of the public administration; examples include the decline in the number of Sikhs in the police force and the absence of Sikhs in personal bodyguard units since the murder of Indira Gandhi".

Sikh Music and Instruments

Sikhs have developed their own instruments: Rabab, Dilruba, Taus, Jori and the Sarinda. The Sarangi was also encouraged by Guru Har Gobind. The Rabaab was first used by Bhai Mardana, as he accompanied Guru Nanak Dev on his journeys. Jori and Sarinda were both designed by Guru Arjan Dev. The Taus was made by Guru Har Gobind, it is said that he heard a peacock singing and wished to create such an instrument that could mimic it sounds, Taus is the Persian word for peacock. The Dilruba was made by Guru Gobind Singh at the request of his Sikhs. They wished for a smaller instrument as the Taus was hard to carry and maintain, due to constant battles. After Japji Sahib all of the shabd in the Guru Granth Sahib are written in raag. The shabd is typically played in accordance with that particular raag. This style of singing is known as Gurmat Sangeet.

When marching into battle, the Sikhs would boost their morale and become psyched. This was called the Ranjit Nagara (Drum of Victory). Nagaras are huge war drums, making a thundering sound. These are huge, about 2 to 3 feet in diameter, and played with two sticks. The special or original Ranjit Nagara, used in past battles, are up to 5 feet across. The thundering beat of the huge drums usually meant that the army was marching into battle. It was also taken into the battle sometimes, the Singhs would raise the Nishan Sahib high, the opposing forces would know the Singhs were coming. While the Singhs spirit was boosting, the opposing forces would be losing morale.

Distribution

Numbering approximately 27 million worldwide, Sikhs make up 0.39% of the world population of which approximately 83% live in India. Of the Indian Sikh community 19.2 million, i.e. 76% of all Indian Sikhs, live in the northern Indian State of Punjab, where they form a majority 70.9% of the population. Substantial communities of Sikhs, i.e. greater than 200,000, live in the Indian States/Union territories of Haryana, Rajasthan, Uttar Pradesh, Delhi, Maharashtra, Uttaranchal and Jammu and Kashmir.

Sikh migration from the then British India began in earnest from the 2nd half of the 19th century when the British had completed their annexation of the Punjab. The British Raj preferentially recruited Sikhs in the Indian Civil Service and, in particular, the British Indian Army, which led to migration of Sikhs to different parts of British India and the British Empire. During the era of the British Raj, semiskilled Sikh artisans were also transported from the Punjab to British East Africa to help in the building of railways. After World War II, Sikhs emigrated from both India and Pakistan, most going to the United Kingdom but many also headed for North America. Some of the Sikhs who had settled in eastern Africa were expelled by Ugandan dictator Idi Amin in 1972. Subsequently the main 'push' factor for Sikh migration has been economic with significant Sikh communities now being found in the United Kingdom, Canada, the United States, Malaysia, East Africa, Australia and Thailand.

Whilst the rate of Sikh migration from the Punjab has remained high, traditional patterns of Sikh migration, that favored English speaking countries, particularly the United Kingdom has changed in the past decade due to factors such as stricter immigration procedures. Moliner (2006) states that as a consequence of the 'fact' that Sikh migration to the UK had "become virtually impossible since the late 1970s", Sikh migration patterns altered to continental Europe. Italy has now emerged as a fast growing area for Sikh migration, with Reggio Emilia and the Vicenza province being areas of significant Sikh population clusters. The Italian Sikhs are generally involved in areas of agriculture, agro-processing, machine tools and horticulture.

Due primarily to socio-economic reasons, Indian Sikhs have the lowest adjusted decadal growth rate of any major religious group in India, at 16.9% per decade (est. 1991–2001). Johnson and Barrett(2004) estimate that the global Sikh population increases annually by 392,633 Sikhs, i.e. by 1.7% p.a. on 2004 figures, this growth rate takes into account factors such as births, deaths and conversions.

Representation

Sikhs are represented in Indian politics, with the current Indian Prime Minister Manmohan Singh who is the de facto head of the government and wields the supreme authority , including the nuclear button, and the Deputy Chairman of the Indian Planning Commission Montek Singh Ahluwalia, both hailing from the community. The current Chief-minister of Punjab, Parkash Singh Badal, is a Sikh. Past Sikh politicians in India have included Giani Zail Singh, the former President of India, Dr. Gurdial Singh Dhillon, Speaker of the Parliament of India. Pratap Singh Kairon, Union minister, famous Sikh Indian independence movement leader and former Chief-minister of Punjab (India).

Prominent politicians of the Sikh Diaspora include the first Asian American to be elected as a Member of United States Congress Dalip Singh Saund, the former mayoress of Dunedin Sukhi Turner, the current UK Parliamentary Under Secretary of State Parmjit Dhanda MP and the famous first couple to ever sit together in any parliament in the history of commonwealth countries Gurmant Grewal and Nina Grewal, who sought apology by the Canadian Government for the historical Kamagatamaru incident, and the Canadian Shadow Social Development Minister Ruby Dhalla MP. Vic Dhillon, is a famous Sikh Canadian politician and current member of the

Legislative Assembly of Ontario. Ujjal Dosanjh was the New Democratic Party Premier of British Columbia from July 2004 through February 2005, and currently serves as a Liberal frontbench MP in Ottawa. In Malaysia, two Sikhs were elected as MPs during the 2008 general elections. The two are Karpal Singh (Bukit Gelugor) and his son Gobind Singh Deo (Puchong). Whereas, two other Sikhs were elected as assemblymen; Jagdeep Singh Deo (Datuk Keramat) and Keshvinder Singh (Malim Nawar).

Sikhs make up 10–15% of all ranks in the Indian Army and 20% of its officers, whilst Sikhs only forming 1.87% of the Indian population, which makes them over 10 times more likely to be a soldier and officer in the Indian Army than the average Indian. The Sikh Regiment is one of the highest decorated and believed to be the most courageous, powerful and skilled regiment of the Indian Army, with 73 Battle Honours, 14 Victoria Crosses, 21 *first class* Indian Order of Merit *(equivalent to the Victoria Cross)*, 15 Theatre Honours and 5 COAS Unit Citations besides 2 Param Vir Chakras, 14 Maha Vir Chakras, 5 Kirti Chakras, 67 Vir Chakras and 1596 other gallantry awards. The highest-ranking General in the history of the Indian Air Force is a Punjabi Sikh Marshal of the Air Force Arjan Singh. Advanced plans by the MOD to raise an Infantry UK Sikh Regiment were scrapped in June 2007 to the disappointment of the UK Sikh community and Prince Charles of Britain.

Historically, most Indians have been farmers and even today 66% *(two-thirds)* of Indians are farmers. Indian Sikhs are no different and have been predominately employed in the agro-business, India's 2001 census found that 39% of the working population of Punjab were employed in this sector *(less than the Indian average)*. The success, in the 1960s, of the Green Revolution, in which India went from "famine to plenty, from humiliation to dignity", was based in the Sikh majority state of Punjab which became known as "the breadbasket of India". The Sikh majority state of Punjab is also statistically the wealthiest *(per capita)* with the average Punjabi enjoying the highest income in India, 3 times the national Indian average. The Green Revolution centered upon Indian farmers adapting their farming methods to more intensive and mechanized techniques; note this was aided by the electrification of Punjab, cooperative credit, consolidation of small holdings and the existing British Raj developed canal system. Swedish political scientist, Ishtiaq Ahmad, states that a factor in the success of the Indian green revolution transformation was the "Sikh cultivator, often the Jat, whose courage, perseverance, spirit of enterprise and muscle prowess proved crucial". However not all aspects of the green revolution were beneficial, Indian physicist Vandana Shiva argues that the green revolution essentially rendered the "negative and destructive impacts of science [i.e. the green revolution] on nature and society" invisible; thus having been separated from their material and political roots in the science system, when new forms of scarcity and social conflict arose they were linked not to traditional causes but to other social systems e.g. religion. Hence Shiva argues that the green revolution was a catalyst for communal Punjabi Sikh and Hindu tensions; despite the growth in material affluence.

Punjabi Sikhs feature in varied professions such as scientists, engineers and doctors; notable Punjabi Sikhs include nuclear scientist Professor Piara Singh Gill who worked on the Manhattan project; optics scientist *("the father of fibre optics")* Dr. Narinder Singh Kapany; physicist and science writer/broadcaster Simon Singh and agricultural scientist Professor Baldev Singh Dhillon.

In the sphere of business, the clothing retailers/brands of UK based New Look and Thai based JASPAL were started by Sikhs. India's largest pharmaceutical company Ranbaxy

Laboratories is headed by Sikhs. UK Sikhs have the highest percentage of home ownership, at 82%, out of all UK religious communities. UK Sikhs are the 2nd wealthiest (after the Jews) religious community in the UK, with a median total household wealth of £229, 000. In Singapore, Kartar Singh Thakral has built up his family's trading business, Thakral Holdings/ Corp, into a commercial concern with total assets of close to $1.4 billion. Thakral is Singapore's 25th richest person. Bob Singh Dhillon is the first Indo-Canadian billionaire and a Sikh. Perhaps no Sikh diaspora group has had as much success as those who have migrated to North America; especially the Sikhs who have migrated to California's fertile Central Valley. The farming skills of the Sikhs and their willingness to work hard, ensured that they rose from humble migrant labourers to become landowners who control much of agriculture in California. Today American Sikh agriculturists such as Harbhajan Singh Samra and Didar Singh Bains dominate Californian agriculture and are known colloquially as the "Okra" and "Peach" kings respectively.

Prominent Sikh intellectuals, sportsmen and artists include the veteran writer Khushwant Singh, England cricketer Monty Panesar, former 400 m world record holder Milkha Singh, and Harbhajan Singh, India's most successful off spin Cricket bowler, actors Parminder Nagra, Namrata Singh Gujral, Archie Panjabi and director Gurinder Chadha.

The Sikhs have migrated to most parts of the world and their vocations are as varied as their appearances. The Sikh community of the Indian subcontinent comprises many diverse sets of peoples as the Sikh Gurus preached for ethnic and social harmony. These include different ethnic peoples, tribal and socio-economic groups. Main groupings (i.e. over 1,000 members) include:Ahluwalia, Arain, Arora, Bhatra Sikhs(Roudh), Bairagi, Bania, Basith, Bawaria, Bazigar, Bhabra, Brahman, Chamar, Chhimba, Darzi, Dhobi, Gujar,

Jatt, Jhinwar, Kahar, Kamboj, Khatri, Kumhar, Labana, Lohar, Mahtam, Mazhabi, Megh, Mirasi, Mochi, Nai, Rajput, Ramgharia, Saini, Sarera, Sikligar, Sunar, Sudh, Tarkhan and Zargar. In India, the Jatt and Khatri ethnic grouping is by far the largest at a population of 11,855,000 followed by the Mazhabi at 2,701,000 with the Tarkhans totaling 1,091,000 the Sikh Rajputs 769,000 and the khatris 290,000 . The Ahluwalia, Khatris, Jatts, Lohars, Kambojas, Gujjars, Rajputs and Ramgarhias are related to each other and are of Indo-Scythian origin as well as mythological Aryan race origin.

There has also emerged a specialized group of Punjabi Sikhs calling themselves Akalis, which have existed since Maharaja Ranjit Singh's time. Under their leader General Akali Phula Singh, in the early 1800s, they won many battles for the Sikh Empire.

Sikhs in the Indian and British Armies

By the advent of World War I, Sikhs in the British Indian Army totaled over 100,000; i.e. 20% of the British Indian Army. In the years to 1945, 14 Victoria Crosses were awarded to the Sikhs, a per capita record given the size of the Sikh Regiments. In 2002, the names of all Sikh VC and George Cross winners were commemorated by being inscribed on the pavilion monument of the Memorial Gates on Constitution Hill next to Buckingham palace, London. Lieutenant Colonel Chanan Singh Dhillon (rtd.), Punjabi Indian World War II hero & Veteran, and president of the ex-services league (Punjab & Chandigarh) was instrumental in campaigning for the memorials building.

During World War I, Sikh battalions fought in Egypt, Palestine, Mesopotamia, Gallipoli and France. Six battalions of the Sikh Regiment were raised in the World War II, and served at El Alamein and in Burma, Italy and Iraq, winning 27 battle honours.

Across the world Sikhs are commemorated in Commonwealth cemeteries.

General Sir Frank Messervy

—"In the last two world wars 83,005 turban wearing Sikh soldiers were killed and 109,045 were wounded. They all died or were wounded for the freedom of Britain and the world, and during shell fire, with no other protection but the turban, the symbol of their faith."

Sir Winston Churchill

—"British people are highly indebted and obliged to Sikhs for a long time. I know that within this century we needed their help twice [in two world wars] and they did help us very well. As a result of their timely help, we are today able to live with honour, dignity, and independence. In the war, they fought and died for us, wearing the turbans."

The Battle of Saragarhi

The Battle of Saragarhi is considered one of the greatest battles in Sikh military history. On 12 September 1897 a contingent of twenty-one soldiers from the 36th Sikhs led by Havildar Ishar Singh held off an Afghan attack of 10,000 men for several hours. All 21 Sikh soldiers chose to fight to the death instead of surrendering. In recognition of their sacrifice, the British Parliament payed them respect, and each one of them was awarded the Indian Order of Merit *(equivalent to the Victoria Cross)*. The battle is commemorated by Sikhs worldwide on 12 September every year, Saragarhi Day.

Pre-Independence : Sikhs Contribution to Freedom & Promises Made

The Sikhs played a pioneering role in India's struggle for independence from the British. They made sacrifices wholly out of proportion to their demographic strength (the Sikhs make up less than 2% of the Indian population).

(Figures below provided by Maulana Abul Azad, President of the Congress Party at the time of Indepedence.)

Out of 2125 Indians killed in the atrocities by the British, 1550 (73%) were Sikhs.

Out of 2646 Indians deported for life to the Andaman Islands (where the British exiled political and hardened criminals) 2147 (80%) were Sikhs.

Out of 127 Indians sent to the gallows, 92 (80%) were Sikhs.

At Jalliawalla Bagh out of the 1302 men, women and children slaughtered, 799 (61%) were Sikhs.

In the Indian Liberation Army, out of the 20,000 ranks and officers, 12,000 (60%) were Sikhs.

Out of 121 persons executed during the freedom struggle, 73 (60%) were Sikhs.

The Sikhs were the third party with whom the British negotiated for the transfer of power. However, due to inadaquency of Sikh leadership, misplaced trust, and false promises, the Sikhs lost their claim to power.

In 1929, following a huge peaceful Independence rally was held by Sikhs in Lahore; in the words of The Times, the 500,000 strong procession "put the Congress show into shame and shadow," Gandhi and Nehru met the Sikh leaders and put forward the notion of Sikh-Hindu unity, a unified India where all Sikh sentiments (social, economical and religious) would be catered for.

The following solemn assurances were made:

"Let God be the witness of the bond that binds me and the Congress to you. Our Sikhs friends have no reason to fear that it would betray them. For, the moment it does so, the Congress would not only thereby seal its own doom but that of the country too. Moreover, the Sikhs are brave people. They know how to safeguard their rights, by the exercise of arms, with perfect justification before God and man, if it should ever come to that" (Young India 19 March 1931)

"No Constitution would be acceptable to the Congress which did not satisfy the sikhs." (Collected works of M K Gandhi Vol.58. p. 192)

"The brave Sikhs of Panjab are entitled to special consideration. I see nothing wrong in an area and a set up in the North wherein the Sikhs can also experience the glow of freedom. (Jawaharlal Nehru, Congress meeting: Calcutta – July, 1944)

The Sikh homeland Panjab was divided and the Sikhs suffered great loss. Sikh shrines such as Nankana Sahib, Panja Sahib and many more along with the capital city of Lahore was given to Pakistan, over 75% of the most fertile land owned by sikhs was taken by Pakistan and over 500,000 men, women and children lost their lives during the partition.

Sikhism in the Western World

As Sikhs wear turbans (although different from Middle Eastern turbans) and due to the relatively small number of Sikhs, there have been incidents of Sikhs in Western countries being mistaken for Middle Eastern Muslim men. This has led to mistaken attitudes and acts against Sikhs living in the west especially with respect to the 9/11 terrorist attack and recent Iraq War conflict.

After the September 11, 2001 attacks, some people associated Sikhs with terrorists or members of the Taliban. A few days after the attack Balbir Singh Sodhi, a Sikh man, was gunned down by Frank Roque, who thought that the victim had ties to Al-Qaeda. CNN suggests that there has been an increase in hate crimes against Sikh men in the United States and the UK.

Sikhism has never actively sought converts, thus the Sikhs have remained a relatively ethnically homogeneous group. However, mainly due to the activities of Harbhajan Singh Yogi via his Kundalini Yoga focused 3HO (Happy, Healthy, Holy) Organisation, Sikhism has witnessed a moderate growth in non-Indian adherents. In 1998 it was estimated that these 3HO Sikhs, known colloquially as 'gora' or 'white' Sikhs, totaled 7,800 and were mainly centered around Española, New Mexico and Los Angeles, California. Recently, a law in Oregon was passed banning the wearing of turbans by teachers and government officials. Sikhs and the Council on American-Islamic Relations are working together to overturn the law.

Art and Culture

Sikh art and culture is synonymous with that of the Punjab region. The Punjab itself has been called India's melting pot, due to the confluence of invading cultures, such as Greek, Mughal and Persian, that mirrors the confluence of rivers from which the region gets its name. Thus Sikh culture is to a large extent informed by this synthesis of cultures.

Sikhism has forged a unique form of architecture which Bhatti describes as being "inspired by Guru Nanak's creative mysticism" such that Sikh architecture "is a mute harbinger of holistic humanism based on pragmatic spirituality". The 'key-note' of Sikh architecture is the Gurdwara which is the personification of the "melting pot" of Punjabi cultures, showing both Islamic, Sufi and Hindu influences. The reign of the Sikh Empire was the single biggest catalyst in creating a uniquely Sikh form of expression, with Maharajah Ranjit Singh patronising the building of forts, palaces, bungas (residential places), colleges, etc that can be said to be of the *Sikh Style*. Characteristics of Sikh architecture are gilded fluted domes, cupolas, kiosks and stone lanterns with an ornate balustrade on square roofs. The "jewel in the crown" of the *Sikh Style* is the Harmindar Sahib.

Sikh culture is heavily influenced by militaristic motifs, with Khanda being the most obvious; thus it is no surprise that the majority of Sikh artifacts, independent of the relics of the Gurus, have a military theme. This motif is again evident in the Sikh festivals of Hola Mohalla and Vaisakhi which feature marching and practicing displays of valor respectively.

The art and culture of the Sikh diaspora has been merged with that of other Indo-immigrant groups into categories such as 'British Asian', 'Indo-Canadian' and 'Desi-Culture'; however there has emerged a niche cultural phenomenon that can be described as 'Political Sikh'. The art of prominent diaspora Sikhs such as Amarjeet Kaur Nandhra & Amrit and Rabindra Kaur Singh ('The Singh Twins'), is informed by their Sikhism and the current affairs of the Punjab.

Bhangra and the Gidha are two forms of indigenous Punjabi folk dancing that have been appropriated, adapted and pioneered by Punjabi Sikhs. The Punjabi Sikhs have championed these forms of expression all over the world, such that Sikh culture has become inextricably linked to Bhangra, even though "Bhangra is not a Sikh institution but a Punjabi one."

●●

12
Women in Sikhism

The role of women in Sikhism is outlined in the Sikh Scriptures, which state that the Sikh woman is to be regarded as equal to the Sikh man. In Sikhism, women are considered to have the same souls as men and an equal right to grow spiritually. They are allowed to lead religious congregations, take part in the Akhand Path (the continuous recitation of the Holy Scriptures), perform Kirtan (congregational singing of hymns), work as a Granthi, and participate in all religious, cultural, social, and secular activities.

Sikh history has prominently recorded the role of women, portraying them as equal in service, devotion, sacrifice, and bravery to men. Examples of various women's moral dignity, service, and self-sacrifice are a source of inspiration to the Sikhs.

According to Sikhism, men and women are two sides of the same coin of the human race, a system of inter-relation and inter-dependence in which man takes birth from a woman, and woman is born of a man. Also, according to Sikhism a man can never feel secure and complete during his life without a woman, and a man's success depends upon the love and support of the woman who shares her life with him, and vice-versa.

The founder of Sikhism, Sri Guru Nanak Dev Ji, reportedly said in 1499 that " is a woman who keeps the race going" and that we should not "consider woman cursed and condemned, [when] from woman are born leaders and rulers."

Sikhs, therefore, have had an obligation to treat women as equals, and gender discrimination in Sikh society has not been allowed. However, gender equality has been difficult to achieve.

Women who were used to having the same privileges as men in Vedic India were reduced to a position of subordination during the time of the Lawgivers.

Purdah and Sati

The Smrtis pressured widows to practise sati, (burning herself on the funeral pyre of her late husband). Even when widows were pregnant or had young children, she was expected to live a life of extreme self-denial.

Sikhism was a liberating force for women in Indian society. Affirmation of the dignity of the human being, both men and women, was central to Guru Nanak's teaching. He said that all creatures were equal before God, so to make distinctions among them on the grounds of birth or sex was sinful. He was also bold, at least for his time, in his praise of women. In the Asa ki Var, a long composition sung in sangat in the morning service, he expresses extreme respect and admiration for women, "of whom great men are born".

Sutak and Celibacy

In another stanza in the Asa ki Var, Guru Nanak Dev Ji rejects the prevalent superstition of *sutak*, the belief that a woman giving birth to a child is unclean for a given number of days depending upon the caste to which she belongs:

> "The impurity of the mind is greed, and the impurity of the tongue is falsehood. The impurity of the eyes is to gaze upon the beauty of another man's wife, and his wealth. The impurity of the ears is to listen to the slander of others. O Nanak, the mortal's soul goes, bound and gagged, to the city of Death. All impurity

comes from doubt and attachment to duality. Birth and death are subject to the Command of the Lord's Will; through His Will we come and go."(GG, 472)

Instead of celibacy and renunciation, Guru Nanak recommended *grhastha* – the life of a householder. Husband and wife were seen as equal partners and fidelity was enjoined upon both. In sacred verse, domestic happiness was presented as a cherished ideal and marriage provided a running metaphor for the expression of love for the Divine. Bhai Gurdas Ji, poet of early Sikhism and authoritative interpreter of Sikh doctrine, pays high tribute to women. He says:

"A woman, is the favourite in her parental home, loved dearly by her father and mother. In the home of her in-laws, she is the pillar of the family, the guarantee of its good fortune... Sharing in spiritual wisdom and enlightenment and with noble qualities endowed, a woman, the other half of man, escorts him to the door of liberation." (Varan, V.16)

Equal status for Women

To ensure equal status for women, the Gurus made no distinction between the sexes in matters of initiation, instruction or participation in sangat (holy fellowship) and pangat (eating together). According to Sarup Das Bhalla, Mahima Prakash, Guru Amar Das disfavoured the use of veil by women. He assigned women to supervise some communities of disciples, and preached against the custom of sati. Sikh history records the names of several women such as Mai Bhago, Mata Sundari, Rani Sahib Kaur, Rani Sada Kaur and Maharani Jind Kaur who played an important role in the events of their time.

Women's displays of steadfastness during the eighteenth century when Sikhs were fiercely persecuted have had a strong impact on modern-day Sikhs, who recount these stories in their ardas:

> "Our mothers and sisters they repeat every time in their prayer, who plied handmills in the jails of Mannu [the Mughal governor of Lahore (1748-53)], grinding daily a maund-and-a-quarter of corn each, who saw their children being hacked to pieces in front of their eyes, but who uttered not a moan from their lips and remained steadfast in their Sikh faith—recall their spirit of fortitude and sacrifice, and say, Vahiguru, Glory be to God!"

Praised Treatment of Enemy Women

Even in times of severe trial and suffering, Sikhs were guided in their treatment of the women prisoners of war by the highest standards of chivalry. In 1763, for instance, one of Ahmad Shah Durrani's generals, Jahan Khan, was defeated by the Sikhs at Sialkot and a number of his female relations and dependants fell into their hands. Ali ud-Din writes in his *Ibratnamah*;

> "as the Sikhs of old would not lay their hands on women, they had them escorted safely to Jammu."

Another Muslim chronicler, Ghulam Muhaiy ud-Din, vituperates against the Sikhs in his *Fatuhat Namah-i-Samadi*, but notices the esteem they had for women. He writes;

> "[The Sikhs] look upon all women in the light of mothers."

This had been how a Sikh was defined by Bhai Gurdas a century earlier;

> "A Sikh casting his eyes upon the beautiful womenfolk of families other than his own regards them as his mothers, sisters and daughters."

Monogamy, Infanticide and Widow Burning

Such being the respect for womanhood among the Sikhs, monogamy has been the rule for them, and polygamy is exceptionally rare.

Female infanticide is prohibited. The Rahitnamas, (codes of conduct) prohibit Sikhs from having any contact or relationship with those who indulge in this practice.

As for sati (widow-burning), Scripture itself rejects it.

In a shabad (hymn) in measure Suhi, Guru Amar Das says;

> "Satis are not those that burn themselves on the husband's funeral pyre; satis are they, O Nanak, who die of the pangs of separation (GG, 787)"
>
> Stanza follows:
>
> "They, too must be reckoned satis who live virtuously and contentedly in the service of the Lord, ever cherishing Him in their hearts... Some burn themselves along with their dead husbands: but they need not, for if they really loved them they would endure the pain alive."

As a practical step towards discouraging the practice of sati, Sikhism permitted remarriage of widows.

In the present-day democratic politics of India, women as a whole have been rid of many of their disadvantages. They enjoy political franchise and many new opportunities for advancement have opened up for them. Sikh women have shown enterprise in several fields and are among the most progressive in education and in the professions such as teaching and medicine. Within the Sikh system, they are the equals of men in all respects. They can lead congregational services and participate in akhand paths, uninterrupted readings of scripture to be accomplished within forty-eight hours. They vote with men to elect Sikhs' central religious body, the Shiromani Gurdwara Parbandhak Committee, which administers their places of worship.

Famous women in Sikhism

The first woman to be remembered in Sikhism is Mata Tripta Ji, the mother of the first and founding Guru, Guru Nanak Dev Ji. She is said to have meditated while carrying the child Nanak in her womb, and to have brought him up with love and tender care, while attempting to protect him from his father Mehta Kalu's undue wrath.

Another famous woman is Bebe Nanaki Ji, the elder and only sister of Guru Nanak Dev Ji. She is a highly intelligent, spiritually awake, and pious lady who recognised the divine light in her brother and envisaged his mission of life before anyone else could perceive it; she did not treat him just as a brother but also respected him as she would a Guru, supporting him throughout her life. Her brother would become known as a revolutionary who had come to redeem people from misconception and superstition.

Quotes

Equality of Women, in Sikh Ideology and Practice

A real distinction between the roles of the male and female exists in all historic and modern human societies. In the 15th century, Guru Nanak established Sikhism, the first religion to advocate emphatically the equality of all people, especially women. However, gender (and class) inequalities still exist.

CHANGES BY GURU NANAK

At the time of Guru Nanak, Indian women were severely degraded and oppressed by their society. Given no education or freedom to make decisions, their presence in religious, political, social, cultural, and economic affairs was virtually non-existent. Woman was referred to as "man's shoe, the root of all evil, a snare, a temptress." Her function was only to perpetuate the race, do household work, and serve the male members of society. Female infanticide was common, and the practice of sati, the immolation of the wife on her husband's funeral pyre, was encouraged, sometimes even forced.

Guru Nanak condemned these notions of the inferiority of women, and protested against the subjugation of women. According to Sikh doctrine, The Ultimate Truth was revealed to Guru Nanak through a mystical experience, in direct communion with God. Guru Nanak conveyed this Truth through the bani, Sikh Scripture. It argues against sexist notions as follows:

> *"In a woman man is conceived,* From a woman he is born, With a woman he is betrothed and married, With a woman he contracts friendship. Why denounce her, the one from whom even kings are born ? From a woman a woman is born, None may exist without a woman."

The fundamental analogy used in the bani depicts the relationship between God and man, and proves that the physical body does not matter. The bani parallels all human beings (men and women) to the woman or wife, and God to the man or husband. This means that every person is a *sohagan* - a woman who is the beloved of the Lord - whether they have the body of a man or woman. Because the human body is transitory, the difference between man and woman is only transitory, and as such superficial. Thus, according to Sikh ideology, all men and women possess equal status. All human beings, regardless of gender, caste, race, or birth, are judged only by their deeds.

With this assertion, the Sikh Gurus invited women to join the sangat (congregation), work with men in the langar (common kitchen), and participate in all other religious, social, and cultural activities of the gurdwaras (Sikh places of worship). The Gurus redefined celibacy as marriage to one wife and taught that male and female alike need to practice conjugal fidelity. They advocated marriage of two equal partners. Guru Amar Das, the third guru, wrote :

"Only they are truly wedded who have one spirit in two bodies."

Guru Amar Das also condemned purdah, the wearing of the veil, and female infanticide. He spoke against the custom of sati, thus permitting the remarriage of widows. Out of 146 missionaries chosen, the Guru appointed 52 women to spread the message of Sikhism, and out of 22 Manjis established by the Guru for the preaching of Sikhism, four were women. The steps the Gurus took to advocate the equality of women, revolutionized the tradition of Indian society. As they began to partake in social, religious, and political affairs, their contribution and worth as equal partners of men became more obvious.

However, the Guru's teachings of equality have never been fully realized, which is clearly evident in the treatment of women even in Sikh society today. Either because of the influence of the majority community on the Sikh minority or the Sikh male's unwillingness to give up his dominant role, women continue to suffer prejudice. A woman has never been elected as the president of Shiromani Gurdwara Prabandhak Committee (the Central Management Committee to manage the affairs of the Gurdwaras in the Punjab)(this changed in 2005), or as the head of any of the five Takhats (the thrones of authority). Indian society discriminates against women in workplaces, and denies them the right to fight on the battlefield. People measure a woman's value as a bride by the size of her dowry, not necessarily by her character and integrity. Alice Basarke, a free-lance writer, sadly realizes, "After 500 years head start, Sikh Women are no better off than their counterparts in any other religion or nation."

Historical Background

To understand what the Gurus said of women in Gurbani one must understand the conditions prevalent in India at the time of the Gurus. In the very early Vedic period women had much of the same access to an education, participation in religious, political and social roles. They even composed some of the hymns in the Vedas. That all changed drastically with the arrival of the laws of Manu. The status of women was totally degraded at every level and women were effectively enslaved. Women in Hindu society were now bound by a series of rigid laws that defined social, occupational and religious conduct.

The women were not only relegated to their households, they were literally under the control of men from cradle to grave. They were compelled to observe Purdah. Sati was expected at the death of the spouse in some castes or permanent widowhood in others even in the case of very young widows. Widowhood meant destitution at best, social rejection and lifelong loneliness. The birth of a daughter was viewed with disdain and sorrow and female infanticide rampant. The birth of a boy was celebrated lavishly but that of a girl meant scorn and blame by the in-laws. Women and girls' health was poor due to frequent childbirth coerced by husband and in-laws till the birth of a male heir occurred for the former and sheer neglect of health care and nutrition of the latter. The Laws of Manu still maintain a powerful hold over Indian Society today in overt and covert fashions. Women are expected to dress modestly, and wear no make-up. Also they are expected to cover their head as a sign of respect. They manifest as such in present societal mores and attitudes.(article on Laws of Manu as applies to women). These affect as much the modern Punjabi as well as Hindu societies. (This article a blessing for boys and girls are killed)Many of the same conditions that plague women in Indian society described above still exist today in many villages and city centers.

Under Islamic rule women fared no better. Hindu women and children were enslaved and force-marched by their captors to be sold on the markets of Persia, Afghanistan and sent further to Arabia and Africa. Muslim women had some limited rights under Muslim law but functioned primarily in the home.

Coming of Sikhism

It is against such a backdrop that the Gurus implemented reform via their missions and tackled prevalent issues in their teachings.

This passage offers a powerful rejection of mistreatment of women:

> "We are conceived in woman, We are born to woman. It is to woman we get engaged, and then get married. Woman is our lifelong companion, And pillar of our survival. It is through woman, that we establish social relationships. Why should we denounce her, When even kings and great men are born from her?" (P. 473 SGGS Guru Nanak)

Guru Amar Das abolished the tradition of Sati and Purdah and indeed refused to have an audience with ladies that kept Purdah. He established religious centers and women alongside men were recruited to lead and teach. Women worked alongside the men in maintaining the Guru's kitchen, performing all duties and sitting side by side the men folk in Pangat.

Guru Angad strongly encouraged the education of women.

Women swelled the ranks in spreading the message of the Gurus as missionaries. By the time of Guru Gobind Singh, 40% of them were women.

With the birth of the Khalsa the last of the barriers of caste and gender oppression had been smashed. Women though continuing their roles of mothers and wives were forever changed. They were lifted up and given the same Amrit at the side of their brothers. The same rules that applied to them to follow the Khalsa way applied to them. They were granted the same 5 K's. Guru Gobind Singh's encouragement of women to keep even shastars symbolized that he did not envision her role in society as being that of a "nice, meek housewife," but rather that of a fearless, active, independent warrior, involved in the world.

Kaur - Princess

Kaur has an interesting history. Its origin can be found in the word Kanwar, literally meaning princess or lioness. Women were named Kaur to give them an identity independent of that of their husband and to uplift their spirit.

At the time of SHRI Guru Gobind Singh Ji, women who were literally and legally possessions of their husbands in Europe and in the American colonies, women who had no voice in administration in Europe, the Americas or India were now orators, teachers, warriors, and administrators and participated in the Guru's kitchen. Shri Guru Gobind Singh Ji's wife Mata Sundri Ji led the Khalsa Panth for many years after passing of the tenth Guru. Jathedar Sada Kaur along with Maharaja Ranjit Singh made possible the formation of the Sikh Empire. She gave her contribution to the Amrit, sweet Patashey so that the disposition of the Sikhs would be also sweet.

After Shri Guru Gobind Singh Ji the situation of women and lower castes, had deteriorated as people reverted to the old ways of caste and oppression of women. The old habits and attitudes, as read in the laws of Manu continue, in some form or another, to ensnare the Sikh religion.

Gurbani and Practises

Given what we know of the history then and now here are some of the quotes regarding women:

In regard to dowry:

"O my Lord, give me thy name as my wedding gift and dowry." Shri Guru Ram Das ji, Page 78, line 18 SGGSji

"Any other dowry offered is a valueless display of false pride and of no earthly use." Shri Guru Ram Das ji, Page 79, line 2

In regard to marriage:

"They are not called husband and wife who merely sit together Rather they alone are called husband and wife who have one soul in two bodies." In regard to the odious practice of Sati:

"A Sati is not she, who burns herself on the pyre of her spouse. Nanak, a Sati is she, who dies with the sheer shock of separation (from God). Yea, the Sati is one who lives contended and embellishes herself with good conduct (rather than jewels and dress) And cherishing her Lord ever calls on Him each morning. The women burn themselves on the pyres of their lords, If they love their spouses well, they suffer the pangs of separation. (moh) She who loves not her spouse, why burns she herself in fire? For, be he alive or dead she owns him not (only God does)" Page 787,13, SGGSji Guru Amar Das ji)

Shri Guru Hargobind singh ji called woman "the conscience of man" without whom moral living was impossible. Child marriage was discouraged and the practice of female infanticide, which had been strongly discouraged, was severely banned. Shri Guru Gobind Singh ji enshrined in the Khalsa code of conduct for his Khalsa, male or female not to have social conduct, relations or marriage to those who kill their daughters. This Hukam is always told in any Amrit Sanchaar.

Regarding the practice of Purdah:

> "Stay, stay, O daughter-in-law - do not cover your face with a veil. In the end, this shall not bring you even half a shell. The one before you used to veil her face; do not follow in her footsteps. The only merit in veiling your face is that for a few days, people will say, "What a noble bride has come". Your veil shall be true only if you skip, dance and sing the Glorious praises of the Lord (P. 484, SGGSji, Kabeer)

Women and indeed all souls were strongly encouraged to lead a spiritual life:

> "Come, my dear sisters and spiritual companions; hug me close in your embrace. Let's join together, and tell stories of our All-powerful Husband Lord."-Guru Nanak, pg 17, Shri Guru Granth Sahib ji.

WOMEN IN THE GURU GRANTH SAHIB

The *Guru Granth Sahib* is the holy text of Sikhs. Several of the shabads (hymns) from the *Guru Granth Sahib* address the role of women in Indian and Sikh society.

Shabads from the Guru Granth Sahib

From Woman, Man is Born

In this Shabad, the Guru expresses the importance of a woman. It begins with the line "From a woman, a man is born" which removes a doubt from the minds of man that they are all a produce of a woman. This theme then continues with the Guru highlighting in a logical sequence the various stages of life where the importance woman is noted – "within woman, man is conceived" and then " he is engaged and married" to a woman who becomes his friend, partner and the source for future generations. So throughout man's life, he is dependent on woman and every critical stage. The Shabad continues, " When his woman dies, he seeks another woman" – so if his wife dies, he may seek another woman and bound to the female gender. In the final lines, the Guru asks: "So why call her bad?" – when even kings are born from a female mother as are other women themselves. The Guru then conclude that "without woman – there would be no one at all". So this leave no doubt in the faithful person's mind that the female gender is critical for the survival of the race and that there would be no one alive without women. The Guru in very simple terms has outlined the importance, the magnitude and value of women and shown how significant a role they play in the propagation of the race.

> From woman, man is born;
>
> within woman, man is conceived; to woman he is engaged and married.
>
> Woman becomes his friend; through woman, the future generations come.
>
> When his woman dies, he seeks another woman; to woman he is bound.
>
> So why call her bad? From her, kings are born.
>
> From woman, woman is born; without woman, there would be no one at all.
>
> – Guru Nanak, Raag Aasaa Mehal 1, Page 473

Shabad against Sati

Sati is an Indian custom of immolation of a woman on her dead husband's funeral pyre either self-willingly or by societal inducement and compulsion. Guru Nanak say the following about this practice:

> Do not call them 'satee', who burn themselves along with their husbands' corpses.

O Nanak, they alone are known as 'satee', who die from the shock of separation. (1)

...Some burn themselves along with their dead husbands: [but they need not, for] if they really loved them they would endure the pain alive.

– Sri Guru Granth Sahib page 787

The Guru said that if the wife really loves her husband, then she should endure the pain of separation alive and she would rather live her life then suffer a quick death in the fire of her husband's funeral pyre. Further Guru Nanak explains that a true "Sati" is the person who cannot endure the pain of separation from their loved one.

Shabad against Dowry

The Sikh Gurus spoke against the common practice of dowry when a gift of money or valuables had to be given by the bride's family to that of the groom at the time of their marriage. Huge pressure was exerted on the bride's family for the extraction of a sizeable fortune at times of marriage. It has been regarded as contribution of her family to the married household's expenses. The Guru's called this giving of gifts an "offer for show" of the guests and a "worthless display" which only increase the "false egotism". Sikhs families were discouraged this practise and slowly this trend has diminished. The following Shabad explains the Guru's position:

Any other dowry, which the self-willed manmukhs offer for show, is only false egotism and a worthless display.

O my father, please give me the Name of the Lord God as my wedding gift and dowry. (4)

– Sri Guru Granth Sahib page 79

●●

13

Sikh Ethics

Every religion provides a code of conduct for its followers, and Sikhism is no exception to this rule. There is no formal list of commandments and prohibitions in the Sikh Scriptures. But they have been tabilized in the "Rehat Maryada." The Gurus by their words and deeds guided their followers to a holy and purposeful life. Guru Nanak declared:" Without virtuous living , there can be no devotional worship." (AG, 4) He elaborates this idea through the homily of the love of a bride for her groom. The good wife adorns herself with patience, contentment and sweet speech in order to win the love of her husband. Then gives up anger, covetousness and pride, so that she may enjoy bliss with her lord. Hence, morality is the basis of spiritual life. Holiness and altruistic action go together. The perfect man will always try to help others.

The sources of Sikh Ethics are the Guru Granth Sahib, the Dasam Granth, compositions of Bhai Gurdas, Janam-sakhis, Rahit-namas and The Sikh Rahat Maryada as issued by the Shromani Gurdwara Parbandhak Committee, Amritsar. The Sikh principles of conduct and dynamic participation in secular matters are based on the stories and poems (hymns) contained in this literature.

Concept of Virtue

It is difficult to define virtue or morality. Dictionary definitions cannot possibly cover its entire dimensions, but they all agree on "Righteous action and honorable conduct"

In the Sikh credo, virtue in its essence is love. That universal love which finds expression in the brotherhood of man and in respecting the common man. This love is the source of selfless service and charitable work. It drives Out ego, which is the root of conceit and exploitation. In its real sense, virtue means the love of God and His creation. Guru Gobind Singh declared:" Only those who love God unite with God." So basically, any action which takes one nearer to God is virtuous. Guru Nanak says: "All meditations, disciplines, happiness, repute and respect O Musan, I will sacrifice again and again, for a moment of love." (AG, 1364) Putting it in different words, all that is pleasing to God is virtuous and holy. According to the Gurus, fasting, mortification, asceticism, poverty are not virtues, for they affect the body adversely, as do an over-regard for eating, drinking, dressing and amusement. The Guru lays down a simple rule, namely, "Shun those things which cause pain or harm to the body or produce evil thought in the mind." This rule is basic to the Sikh way of life.

Sikhism believes in divine justice and the morality of the world order. Evil will ultimately fail, though it may often seem to succeed for a while. God alone is the Perfect Judge; He cannot be deceived by hypocritical acts or any cunning of man. He reads all hearts and knows every person's innermost motivation. Goodness is to be rewarded and wickedness punished. Ultimately Truth alone will prevail.

Sikhism does not regard altruistic acts or good conduct as ends in themselves. These are a means to achieve the goal. Man's divine spark is dimmed only by his ignorance or indifference to the force and suddenness of the temptations that constantly beset him; it is this inbuilt weakness that leads to his surrender to such forces and pressures. It is only by association with good and virtuous people that he will feel encouraged to "gird up his loins" and face the challenge of life.

Another important touchstone or yard-stick for man is the quest for "The Truth." The Gurus considered Truthful living to be better than only a belief in "The Truth." Many people swear by truth, knowing very well that they are following the path of falsehood or cant. Such double-conduct is found not only in political leaders, but also in men of apparent goodness and piety. The Gurus insisted on overcoming these negative forces before one attempted purity of conduct. The Guru says:

"Shun vice and run after virtue; those who commit sins wilt have to repent;

Those who cannot distinguish between right and wrong will, sink in mud repeatedly

Shun greed, give up calumny and falsehood, then you may come to "The Truth." (AG, 598)

A common human weakness is to criticize the vices of others, without trying to eradicate them in one's self. One should endeavor to correct himself, before he criticizes others. Generally he finds excuses and compulsions for his own defects and lapses: This means that he is not true to himself. Progress follows where one can see oneself objectively.

Sikhism itself enjoins positive action and moral conduct. It must originate from good motivation and tend to further the right objective. We do many traditional things, little realizing that they have no meaning or value.

Concept of Sin

The general concept of sin is that it is "action in wilful disobedience of the Will of God or the Commandments of the Scriptures." According to Dr. S. Radhakrishanan, "Sin is not the violation of a law or a convention, but of the central source of all finiteness through ignorance or an assertion of the independence of that ego, which seeks its own private gain at the expense of others." Amongst Christians there is the concept of 'Original Sin.' This refers to the disobedience of God's order by Adam and Eve in eating the fruit of Knowledge in the Garden of Eden. Sikhism has no such belief. Man is essentially of divine essence. However, on account of his self-assertion or ego, he ignores his divine source and then pretends to act in sheer ignorance. He then thinks that he is distinct from God and builds around himself, like the spider's web, a shell of the ego (haumai) which makes him forget the God in himself. Man's building up of this separate identity and his own self-conceit cause him to do things which then set in motion a chain-reaction.

Man's ego takes many forms. The most obvious is selfishness or pride due to position, power, money or knowledge. It promotes a sense of superiority within him and also a sense of a disregard for others. This alienates him from his fellow-men and leads to sin and exploitation. Egoistic actions are like chains round the neck of the individual. Egoism is the root of man's evil thought and action. The Guru says:

"The Lord has produced a play on the role of egoism.

There is one mansion and five thieves who do evil within." (AG, 1096)

The five thieves mentioned above are the five major vices in Sikhism, namely, Lust (Kam), Anger (Krodh), Greed (Lobh), Worldly attachment (Moh) and Pride (Ahankar). Some of the others sins mentioned by the and Sikh theologians are atheism, inertia, deceits, slander and ingratitude . Guru Gobind Singh further laid down four prohibitions, which are regarded as "major sins" for the Khalsa. Additionally some minor sins" are mentioned in the Rahat-namas.

Is it possible to undo or escape the consequences of one's sins? Some methods of atonement are provided by some religions by way of confession, sacrifice, austerities or fine. Generally speaking, the minor sins are said to be forgives by holy works, prayers and voluntary community-service. There is no particular penance provided by the Sikh Scriptures. Remembrance of the Holy Word or God's Name washes away the pollution of sin. Similarly association with saintly beings removes the stain of sin:

"Listen, my friends, to the benefits of attending in the company of saints:

> Filth is removed millions of sorrows vanish and the mind becomes pure!" (AG, 809)

Individual Ethics

Dutifulness

For which the world is the field of action. The Gurus called it Dharamsal—a place for the performance of one's duties and righteous deeds. Duties imply obligations—to oneself, to the family, to society, to one's country and humanity at large. Some duties are mentioned in the Scriptures and some are laid down by the State. Man has to obey both, because if he infringes them, he will reap the consequences thereof.

Man's duties as an individual: Firstly, he must look after his body and his health. He must avoid that food and drink which will impair his physical or mental well-being. Moderation is the principle which should guide one's choice in this field. Secondly, man must develop his mind through education and training and be able to earn his living. He must support his family (and his near relatives). Married life is. the normal state for an a individual, unless they are either physically or mentally retarded. One must earn his living by fair and honest means. The amassing of wealth by the exploitation of labour is forbidden in Sikhism, Thirdly, one must serve others as far as possible, share one's food and also support projects of public welfare. Voluntary service to the poor and sick are recommended by the Gurus. There are also certain dues required of an individual as the member of an organisation. For example Khalsa Sikh has to maintain the Five K's and follow the Khalsa discipline.

Man's duties to others: The basic principle is that one must so conduct oneself that he sets an example which others can follow. In any event they should behave to others as they expect others to behave towards them. The duties to others may also depend upon the holding of a particular office. As a member of the human family others must be treated with consideration. Neither slander others nor cause mischief nor harm to them. He should be kind not only to his neighbors, but to one and all. He should be ready and willing to help those who are less fortunate than himself and participate in projects of social concern like orphanages, widow's homes and institutions for the care of the sick and the handicapped. There is also a duty to one's superiors like parents, teachers and the Head of the community or the State. One must respect national leaders, obey one's parents and teachers. Seek the advice of the family elders in cases of need. Teachers should be respected for they give knowledge through precept and example. Similarly, one must show courtesy and consideration to the aged and the handicapped.

The duties to equals or peers include politeness and cordiality in one's dealings with them. Frankness and fairness will play a large part in oiling-the smooth flow of social life. The duties to one's subordinate include trying to understand their problems~ and being able to sympathize with them in their times of crisis or distress. It is one's duty to help any who seek one's help, even those who on account of shyness may no ask for aid.

Prudence

Certain religions exclude social morality and the betterment of the environment from the sphere of duty. Sikhism believes in moulding one's environment for moral goals. The Gurus paid a lot of attention to social reform, particularly in abolishing cruel practices like untouchability, infanticide and suttee.'Prudence lies in considering what is right or wrong for society or the social group as a whole. Man has the faculty of discrimination and he also has the capacity to distinguish between good and bad. There are choices or options open to man in many cases and then he must exercise his intellect to find out what is in favour of human sociability and the public good. Sometimes the choice may be difficult, as for example, traditional practice versus moral compliance. In such a case the choice should fäll on the ethical option or the one which promotes the quality of life. The Gurus protested against the tyranny of their Rulers and the corruption of bureaucracy, as well as caste prejudices and rivalries. They exposed the priestly class for their greed and hypocrisy.

It is man's duty to monitor his own environment and raise his voice against inequality and injustice. He must use his power of reason for the

betterment of society and the improvement of his surroundings. Prudence would even seem to recommend force, for a good purpose or a moral issue. Similarly, the social practices which promote inequality among men, the segregation of sexes, superstition and pollution, were condemned by the Gurus, They took steps to remove these promoters of inequality and myth. The begging mendicants pretending to holiness were dubbed as social parasites. The Gurus emphasized the use of reason in demolishing social ills and abuses.

Professional duties pertain to the relationship which a professional person has with his client, for example the duty of a doctor to his patient, of a lawyer to his client, of a merchant to his customer, or a landlord to his tenant. Besides there are also the duties of elected representatives or of holders of honorary position like the President of a mutual-benefit Society or the Secretary Trustee, of a temple or a charitable organisation.

The general duty of a professional is to discharge his functions efficiently, and with a sense of responsibility and sincerity. He must safeguard the interests of his client and give him the necessary truthful guidance and direction. A doctor's duty to his patient is very delicate, for he is dealing with a human being in trouble, therefore he must give him his undivided attention and greatest professional devotion. He cannot afford to be indifferent or negligent. Similarly it is the duty of a lawyer or attorney to offer sound advice, to his client. He must not prolong the case to make more money or do any thing to obstruct the course of justice. Many litigants get dissatisfied with their legal counsel, because the latter have adopted unfair means to gain advantage from them. Honesty and fair play are the tests of professional competence.

With regard to elected or fiduciary positions, the duties are even more onerous and sensitive. There is an element of morality in such appointments, The representative is duty bound to pay attention to the wishes of the electorate or the people he is supposed to serve. As a trustee, he must safe-guard the interest of the entire group which elected him. He must look after the assets and property of any Trust, as if these were his own. Though law regulates the nature and functions of office-bearers it is important that people in power perform their functions, impartially and with care and integrity. Office bearers must act consciously in the interest of their beneficiaries and man's duty to speak out against the malpractice

Tolerance

People belonging to different regions and faiths have different customs, habits and manners. it is therefore necessary that the individual should not be upset by them. He must accept non-conformity and diversity as an inescapable fact of life. However, this does not imply that he should change his stand because of others. He must remain firm in his own convictions and make no compromise on principles; he must control any feeling of prejudice or violence when he sees people whose manners or customs are not to his liking. Racialism is a prevalent disease among the most civilized societies today; it is in fact a form of superiority writ large. The golden principle of tolerance den ands 'live and let live.' Tolerance puts a human and charitable construction on the apparently peculiar conduct of others. The tolerant person does not feel angry or upset. He keeps his cool in times of excitement or anger. Even if he feels mentally disturbed he will not show his impatience or annoyance. Just as a sensible person tolerates the foolish behaviour of a child, in the same way, the tolerant person will be able to stand ignorance or lack of politeness in others. Why should one expect that others will always behave to us as one wants them to behave? Tolerance accepts dissent and even opposition. This quality is particularly needed by Rulers and religious teachers, because without it, they are likely to allow or condone many follies and atrocities against those who differ from them.

Justice

Justice as a virtue implies respect for the rights of others. It also stands for fairness and impartiality. The neglect or violation of the rights of others is a moral lapse. The Guru condemned the usurpation of another's right as ineligious like the eating of pork by a Muslim or beef by a Hindu. Delay and the denial of justice, is generally due to greed and selfishness. Justice must be done with a good heart, and not by shedding crocodile tears. Justice lies in apportioning correctly, what is the due of others, even if they have not the courage to ask for it.

In a wider sense, justice means the non-exploitation of others. Unfortunately in our modern competitive society, exploitation is sometimes condoned on - the grounds of the survival of the fittest. Trampling on the rights of others is justified as an ingredient of ambition and go-getting. It is generally agreed that many get rich as quickly as they can, even when this cannot be done without employing dishonest and underhand means. Making a quick buck is an art which involves cunning and trickery. Moreover, in our present-day society, the rich or the strong often get away with it. The Gurus censured the Rulers for looting the peasants and compared it to 'Devouring men at night.' Moreover, justice in its real sense connotes equity and not legalisticism. It forbids preferential treatment to any person, religious or social group. Justice in its essence manifests selflessness or the conquest of the ego, and is one of the means for self realisation.

Temperance

Self-control is necessary in desires, words and actions. It is generally agreed that man's mind runs after lower things as a matter of course. The Guru says: "The mind seeks evil things, but through the Guru's Word, it can be controlled." Such control is not to be violent or mortifying like the practices of Hath-Yoga, but mental control through a process of harmony and moderation. Thus man's faculties are rightly channelized and gently guided. This method is natural—Sahaj—and not forced or punitive. Guru Amar Das has advised in his "Anand" how to regulate the human organs of action for high and noble tasks. The eyes, the ears, the tongue, the hands and feet are to be used for good purposes to act at the right moment. Temperance is like a fence which prevents one from straying into the wilderness. It is the golden mean between self-indulgence and rigid regimentation. Temperance is just the right way for the householder. He should enjoy the normal comforts and amenities of life, but at the same time, he must keep his passion and desire under control. This self regulation would result in a balanced and harmonious existence.

Sikh Virtues

The virtues recommended by the Scriptures are many, but five of them, corresponding to the Five vices are regarded as major virtues. These five are Chastity, Patience, Contentment, Detachment and Humility.

1. Chastity

Chastity or continence, is emphasized in Sikhism, because in the human body lies the divine presence and as such, the body has to be kept clean and perfect. Those things which harm the body or cause sickness and disease have to be scrupulously avoided. Sex is to be limited to one's wife. Pre-marital or extra-marital sex is forbidden to a Sikh. He should consider females older to him as his mother, equal to him as a sister, and younger than him as a daughter. He should never entertain evil thoughts in the company of women. Marriage is a sacrament and the purpose thereof is companionship and help on the spiritual path, rather than sexual enjoyment. The marriage ideal is summed up in the maxim: 'one soul in two bodies.' Fidelity to one's married partner is the essence of continence.

Monogamy is the rule in Sikhism.

In order to avoid evil thoughts, one should keep away from obscene

books, nasty plays and films, and sexy music. Drinking of alcoholic beverages and wines or the wearing of scanty or flashy dresses and dancing of men and women together is prohibited for the Sikhs. The Guru says:

> "O Lust! You consign people to hell and to the cycle of transmigration, You cheat all minds, influence the three worlds and destroy all contemplation and culture; Your

pleasure is momentary, you make one fickle and poor and punish the high and the low; I have overcome your fear by associating with saintly persons and taking shelter with God!" (AG, 1358)

Even in married life, sex is to be mutually regulated. Those who are spiritually inclined, consider the sublimation of sex into divine love as a great virtue.

2. Patience

Patience implies forbearance in the face of provocation. Some say that it is natural to be angry, but one should think twice before giving vent to anger. Patience gives moral courage to bear the unexpected, such as sudden hardships and sorrows. Guru Amardas says:

> "There is no greater penance than patience, no greater happiness than contentment, no greater evil than greed, no greatet virtue than **mercy, and no more potent weapon than forgiveness."**

It may be noted that saints and great mens are tested through the fire of suffering, though they have not done any thing to deserve that suffering. The challenge of life are intended to evaluate the mettle of man.Even the performance of duty may involve the facing of difficulties and personal injury, but that is no excuse for shirking one's duty.One must pray for God's help and grace to overcome the difficulties.

There are people, who are in a position to injure or even to crush their opponents with the power they possess, but they control resentment and anger, because they firmly believe that if another loses his head, they should not lose theirs. Moreover patience keeps their mental faculties in balance. Their minds are tranquil. They do not cry or rail bitterly against their enemies or at God for their misfortunes or deprivation. They maintain their peace of mind and keep calm when faced by threats or tragedy:

> **"Patience is the sustenance of angelic beings!" (AG, 83)**

3. Contentment

Contentment is an attitude of mind which accepts victory or defeat in the same way. A contended man is active; he tries his best to go forward, but he does not despair if he cannot achieve what he wants. Contentment has no place for fear, fatalism, inertia or sloth. Guru Nanak tells us of a contented person in the following lines:

> "They (the contented ones) do not tread the path of evil, but do good and practise righteousness;
>
> They loosen worldly attachments and eat and drink in moderation." (AG, 467)

The contented man is free from envy, jealousy and greed. He is frugal and thrifty. He may have his ambitions, but he knows that every one does not get every thing. The Guru says:

> "No one feels satisfied without contentment." (AG, 275)

Contentment does not mean a compromise with poverty and privation. In the modern world, the common man has opportunities for self-advancement and affluence. He must develop his own potentialities and work hard to move forward; at the same time, he should not become proud through his achievement or feel frustrated in case of failure. God is the ultimate arbiter of man's destiny, and He will not leave 'an iota of a man's effort uncompensated.' Unfortunately, in this modem competitive world, one seems to keep multiplying one's needs and commitments, in order to keep up with the Jones, thus only adding to one's tensions and difficulties. The contented man knows the limits of his own needs and so does not feel frustrated if he is unable to get what his neighbor or friend has, in spite of his best efforts.

Truly conceited people realise the distinctions between means and ends. Wealth and position are the means and not the ends of life. If one has a large amount of wealth, then some must be devoted to the benefit of the community and for altruistic purposes. The hoarding of wealth and the prestige of office are not to be used as means for self-aggrandisement or inflation of the ego.

4. Detachment

Detachment implies an ever increasing non-attachment to all things of a material nature. It does not imply renunciation or asceticism or indifference to the world in which we live. It implies devotion to duty and the performance of the chores of daily life. The Sikh serves the family and the community, but he does not get deeply involved in their problems. His attitude is that of a nurse attending a patient. She ministers to their care and comfort, but maintains her distance. Similarly, a Sikh has to live the life of a family~man* at the same time, he ought to adopt an attitude as that of a trustee in reference to his near and dear ones. Bhai Gurdas explains this attitude thus:

> **"Thue Sikh is the living yogi, for he lives unattached in the midst of Maya." (Var, 29-15)**

Guru Nanak has given the example of the lotus in the pond which is unaffected by the mud or the movement of the water. In the same way, the 'detached' individual keeps him self away from worldly things. They live in the world, but are not involved in worldliness. They keep their heads high and look to a more spiritual goal.

Here is a story which reveals how detachment is possible in normal life. A Ruler once asked a saint to tell him how he could practice detachment. The holy man told the king that he had just one week more to live, that his death would occur after that. period. The king believed the holy man, and fearing death, led a good life, doing his duty, avoiding evil things and constantly thinking of his coming death. After the week when he did not die as forecast, the holy man returned to the King's pàlace and asked him how he has passed the seven days. The king replied that he had spent that period like a traveller in an inn. He had done his duties as usual, but his mind was not involved in the routine. He had avoided doing any thing wrong, fearing that God would call him to account after his end. He had also prayed as much as he could during this period. The holy man told the king that this was what was meant "practising detachment in life."

5. Humility

The individual alone, must overcome his own ego and pride. This is most easily done on the path of humility, regarding oneself as the lowest of the low and considering all others as being superior. The humble man, will serve others without material motive or the expectation of reward. He does this through his love of God and man. God is present in every living soul, and therefore to injure the feelings of another person is to hurt the God in him. Those who are vain and the haughty have an inflated ego and as such do not mind exploiting their fellow-men. Even some holy men are not free from pride and prejudice. Guru Tegh Bahadur warned pious people of that pride, which is subtle and unobstrusive.

Modesty is generally appreciated as a virtue. A tree laden with fruit bends downward. Humility is not depreciation of oneself, but rather a recognition of one's own faults and of how much one falls short of the ideal. It was a practice among the Sikhs before Guru Gobind Singh, to greet each other by touching the other's feel This was an expression of the Sikh's humility. In the Sikh religion, the opportunity to touch the feet of saintly beings or even the dust of the feet of the congregation, is regarded as a great blessing. The Gurus in their compositions have called themselves 'unworthy and without merit.' This reflects their own sense of humility.

SIKH CODE OF CONDUCT AND CONVENTIONS

CHAPTER 1

SECTION ONE

The Definition of Sikh :

Article I

Any human being who faithfully believes in

(i) One Immortal Being,

(ii) Ten Gurus, from Guru Nanak Sahib to Guru Gobind Singh Sahib,

(iii) The Guru Granth Sahib,

(iv)The utterances and teachings of the ten Gurus and

(v) The baptism bequeathed by the tenth Guru, and who does not owe allegiance to any other religion, is a Sikh

CHAPTER II

SECTION TWO

Sikh Living :

Articles II

A Sikh's life has two aspects :

individual or personal and corporate or Panthic.

CHAPTER III

A Sikh's Personal Life :

Article III

A Sikh's personal life should comprehend:-

(i) Meditation on Nam (Divine Substance, also translated as the God's attributed self) and the scriptures,

(ii) Leading life according to the Guru's teachings and

(iii) Altruistic voluntary service.

Meditating on Nam (Divine Substance) and Scriptures

Article IV

1. A Sikh should wake up in the ambrosial hours (three hours before the dawn), take bath and, concentrating his/her thoughts on One Immortal Being, repeat the name Waheguru (Wondrous Destroyer of darkness).
2. He/she should recite the following scriptural compositions every day :

   (a) The Japu, the Jaapu and the Ten Sawayyas (Quartets) - beginning "Sarwag sudh" — in the morning.

   (b) Sodar Rehras comprising the following compositions:-

      (i) Nine hymns of the Guru Granth Sahib, *occuring in the holy book after the Japuji Sahib,* (The Phrase in Italic has been interpolated by the translator to help locate the hymns more conveniently.) the first of which begins with "Sodar" and the last of which ends with "saran pare ki rakho sarma",

(ii) The Benti Chaupai of the tenth Guru (beginning "hamri karo hath dai rachha" and ending with "dusht dokh te leho bachai",

(iii) The Sawayya beginning with the words "pae gahe jab te tumre",

(iv) The Dohira beginning with the words "sagal duar kau chhad kai".

(v) The first five and the last pauris (stanzas) of Anand Sahib (The object of reciting the Anand as part of Sodar Rehras or at the conclusion of the congregational gathering is just to express joy and gratitude for the communion with the Guru) and.

(vi) The Mundawani and the slok Mahla 5 beginning "tera kita jato nahi"- in the evening after sunset.

(c) The Sohila - to be recited at night before going to bed. The morning and evening recitations should be concluded with the Ardas (formal supplication litany).

3. (a) The text (This is a model of the Ardas. It may be adapted to different occasions and for different purposes. However, the initial composition with "Pritham Bhagauti......" and the concluding phrases commencing "Nanak Nam" must not be altered.) of the Ardas : (LIT. Supplication or prayer. in reality, It is a litany comprehending very briefly the whole gamut of Sikh History and enumerating all that Sikhism holds sacred. Portions of it are invocations and prayer for the grant of strength and virtue. It concludes with : O Nanak, may the Nam (Holy) be ever in ascendance : in Thy will, may the good of all prevail !

One absolute Manifest; victory belongeth to the Wondrous Destroyer of darkness. May the might of the All-powerful help!

Ode to his might by the tenth lord.

Having first thought of the Almighty's prowess, let us think of Guru Nanak. Then of Guru Angad, Amardas and Ramdas - may they be our rescuers! Remember, then, Arjan, Hargobind and Har Rai. Meditate then on revered Har Krishan on seeing whom all suffering vanishes. Think then of Teg Bahadar, remembrance of whom brings all nine treasures. He comes to rescue every where. Then of the tenth Lord, revered Guru Gobind Singh, who comes to rescue every where. The embodiment of the light of all ten sovereign lordships, the Guru Granth - think of the view and reading of it and say, "Waheguru (Wondrous Destroyer of Darkness)".

Meditating on the achievement of the dear and truthful ones, including the five beloved ones, the four sons of the tenth Guru, forty liberated ones, steadfast ones, constant repeaters of the Divine Name, those given to assiduous devotion, those who repeated the Nam, shared their fare with others, ran free kitchen, wielded the sword and everlooked faults and shortcomings, say "Waheguru", O Khalsa.

Meditating on the achievement of the male and female members of the Khalsa who laid down their lives in the cause of Dharma (religion and righteousness), got their bodies dismembered bit by bit, got their skulls sawn off, got mounted on spiked wheels, got their bodies sawn, made sacrifices in the service of the shrines (Gurdwaras), did not betray their faith, sustained their adherence to the Sikh faith with unshorn hair uptill their last breath, say "Wondrous Destroyer of darkness", O Khalsa.

Thinking of the five thrones (of sikh religious authority) and all Gurdwaras, say "Wondrous Destroyer of darkness", O Khalsa.

Now it is the prayer of the whole Khalsa, May the conscience of the whole Khalsa be informed by Waheguru, Waheguru, Waheguru and, in consequence of such remembrance, may total well-being obtain. Wherever there are communities of the Khalsa, may there be Divine protection and grace, the ascendance of the supply of needs and of the holy sword, Protection of the tradition of grace, victory of the Panth, the succour of the holy sword, ascendance of the Khalsa. Say, O Khalsa, "Wondrous Destroyrer of darkness."

Unto the Sikhs the gift of the Sikh faith, the gift of the untrimmed hair, the gift of the discipline of their faith, the gift of sense of discrimination, the gift of trust, the gift of confidence, above all, the gift of meditation on the Divine and bath in Amritsar (holy tank of Harmander Sahib, Amritsar). May hymns-singing missionary parties, the flags, the hostels, abide from age to age. May righteousness reign supreme. Say, "Wondrous Destroyer of darkness."

May the Khalsa be imbued with humility and high wisdom! May Waheguru guard its understanding!

O Immortal Being, eternal helper of Thy panth, benevolent Lord, bestow on the Khalsa the beneficence of unobstructed visit to and free management of Nankana Sahib (Pakistan) and other shrines and places of the Guru from which the Panth has been separated.

O Thou, the honour of the humble, the strength of the weak, aid unto those who have none to rely on, True Father, Wondrous Destroyer of darkness, we humbly render to you .... (Mention here the name of the scriptural composition that has been recited or, in appropriate terms, the object for which the congregation has been held.) Pardon any impermissible accretions, omissions, errors, mistakes. Fulfil the purposes of all.

Grant us the association of those dear ones, on meeting whom one is reminded of Your name. O Nanak, may the Nam (Holy) be ever in ascendance! in Thy will may the good of all prevail!

(b) On the conclusion of the Ardas, the entire congregation participating in the Ardas should respectfully genuflect before the revered Guru Granth Sahib, then stand up and call out, "The Khalsa is of the Wondrous Destroyer of darkness: victory also is His." The Congregation should, thereafter, raise the loud spirited chant of Sat Sri Akal (True is the timeless Being).

(c) While the Ardas is being performed, all men and women in congregation should stand with hands folded. The person in attendance of Guru Granth Sahib should keep waving the whisk standing.

(d) The person who performs the Ardas should stand facing the Guru Granth Sahib with hands folded. If Guru Granth Sahib is not there, performing the Ardas facing any direction is acceptable.

(e) When any special Ardas for and on behalf of one or more persons is offered, it is not necessary for persons in the congregation other than that person or those persons to stand up.

CHAPTER IV

SECTION THREE

Joining the congregation for understanding of and reflecting on Gurbani

Article V

(a) One is more easily and deeply affected by *Gurbani* (the holy *Bani* bequeathed by the Gurus) participating in congregational gatherings. For this reason, it is necessary for a Sikh that he visits the places where the Sikhs congregate for worship and prayer (the Gurdwaras), and joining the congregation, partake of the benefits that the study of the holy scriptures bestows.

(b) The ***Guru Granth Sahib*** should be ceremonially opened in the Gurdwara every day without fail. Except for special exigencies, when there is need to keep the *Guru Granth Sahib* open during the night, The Holy Book should not be kept open during the night. It should, generally, be closed ceremonially after the conclusion of the *Rehras* (evening scriptural recitation). The Holy Book should remain open so long as a granthi or attendant can remain in attendance, persons seeking *darshan* (seeking a view of or making obeisance to it) keep coming, or there is no risk of commission of irreverence towards it. Thereafter, it is advisable to close it ceremonially to avoid any disrespect to it.

(c) The *Guru Granth Sahib* should be opened, read and closed ceremonially with reverence. The place where it is installed should be absolutely clean. An awning should be erected above. The *Guru Granth Sahib* should be placed on a cot measuring up to its size and overlaid with absolutely clean mattress and sheets. For proper installation and opening of the *Guru Granth Sahib* , there should be cushions/pillows appropriate kind etc. and, for covering it, *romalas* (sheet covers of appropriate size). When the *Guru Granth Sahib* is not being read, it should remain covered with a *romala*. A whisk too, should be there.

(d) Anything except the afore-mentioned reverential ceremonies, for instance, such practices as the arti (Waving of a platter with burning lamps and incense set in it in vertical circular motion) with burning incense and lamps, offerings of eatables to *Guru Granth Sahib* , burning of lights, beating of gongs, etc., is contrary to *gurmat* (the Guru's way). However, for the perfuming of the place, the use of flowers, incense and scent is not barred. For light inside the room, oil or butter-oil lamps, candles, electric lamps, kerosene oil lamps, etc., may he lighted.

(e) No book should he installed like and at par with the *Guru Granth Sahib* . Worship of any idol or any ritual or activity should not be allowed to be conducted inside the Gurdwara. Nor should the festival of any other faith be allowed to be celebrated inside the Gurdwara. However, it will not be improper to use any occasion or gathering for the propagation of the *gurmat* (The Guru's way).

(f) Pressing the legs of the cot on which the *Guru Granth Sahib* is installed, rubbing nose against walls and on platforms, held sacred, or massaging these, placing water below the *Guru Granth Sahib's* seat, making or installing statues, or idols inside the Gurdwaras, bowing before the picture of the Sikh Gurus or elders - all these are irreligious self-willed egotism, contrary to *gurmat* (the Guru's way).

(g) When the *Guru Granth Sahib* has to be taken from one place to another, the *Ardas* should be performed. He/she who carries the *Guru Granth Sahib* on his/her head should walk barefoot; but when the wearing of shoes is a necessity, no superstitions need be entertained.

(h) The *Guru Granth Sahib* should be ceremonially opened after performing the *Ardas*. After the ceremonial opening, a hymn should be read from the *Guru Granth Sahib*.

(i) Whenever the *Guru Granth Sahib* is brought, irrespective of whether or not another copy of the *Guru Granth Sahib* had already been installed at the concerned place, every Sikh should stand up to show respect.

(j) While going into the *Gurdwara*, one should take off the shoes and clean oneself up. If the feet are dirty or soiled, they should be washed with water.

One should circumambulate with the *Guru Granth Sahib* or the Gurdwara on one's right.

(k) No person, no matter which country, religion or caste he/she belongs to, is debarred from entering the *Gurdwara* for *darshan* (seeing the holy shrine). However, he/she should not have on his/her person anything, such as tobacco or other intoxicants, which are tabooed by the Sikh religion.

(l) The first thing a Sikh should do on entering the Gurdwara is to do obeisance before the *Guru Granth Sahib*. He/she should, thereafter, have a glimpse of the congregation and bid in a low, quiet voice, "Waheguru ji ka Khalsa, Waheguru ji ki Fateh."

(m)In the congregation, there should be no differentiation or discrimination between Sikh and non-Sikh, persons traditionally regarded as touchable and untouchable, the so-called high and low caste persons, the high and the low.

(n) Sitting on a cushion, a distinctive seat, a chair, a stool, a cot, etc. or in any distinctive position in the presence of the *Guru Granth Sahib* or within the congregation is contrary to *Gurmat*(Guru's way).

(o) No Sikh should sit bare-headed in the presence of the *Guru Granth Sahib* or in the congregation. For Sikh women joining the congregation with their persons uncomfortably draped and with veils drawn over their faces is contrary to *Gurmat* (Guru's way).

(p) There are five takhts (lit., thrones, fig., seats of high authority) : namely-

I. The Holy Akal Takht Sahib, Amritsar,

II. The Holy Takht Patna Sahib,

III. The Holy Takht Kesgarh Sahib, Anandpur,

IV. The Holy Takht Hazur Sahib, Nanded,

V. The Holy Takht Damdama Sahib, Talwandi Sabo.

(q) Only an *Amritdhari* (baptized) Sikh man or woman, who faithfully observes the discipline ordained for the batptized Sikhs, can enter the hallowed enclosures of the Takhts (Ardas for and on behalf of any Sikh or non-Sikh, except a fallen or punished (tankhahia) Sikh, can be offered at the takhts.

(r) At a high-level site in every Gurdwara should be installed the nishan sahib (Sikh flag). The cloth of the flag should be either of xanthic or of greyish blue colour and on top of the flag post, there should either be a spearhead or a Khanda (*a straight dagger with convex side edges leading to slanting top edges ending in a vertex*).

(s) There should be a drum (nagara) in the Gurdwara for beating on appropriate occasions.

CHAPTER V

Kirtan (Devotional Hymns Singing by a Group or an Indvidual)

Article VI

(a) Only a Sikh may perform Kirtan in a congregation.

(b) Kirtan means singing the scriptural compositions in traditional musical measures.

(c) In the congragation, Kirtan only of Gurbani (Guru Granth's or Guru Gobind Singh's hymns) and, for its elaboration, of the compositions of Bhai Gurdas and Bhai Nand Lal, may be performed.

(d) It is improper, while singing hymns to rhythmic folk tunes or to traditional musical measures, or in team singing, to induct into them improvised and extraneous refrains. Only a line from the hymn should be made a refrain.

CHAPTER-VI

Taking Hukam* (Command)

Article VII

(*Hukam:- Reading or Reading out to others, including the congregation, of a Shabad (hymns) or a unit of one or more slokas (short scriptural compositions normally of two to four lines) and a pauri (short stanza of four or more lines) from the Guru Granth Sahib after, or even without performing, Ardas is an important Sikh ritual.

It is called Hukam laina (Taking the order or command), Vak laina (taking the word), Awaz laina (taking the voice). The hymn or unit goes by the name of Hukam (order, command) Vak (uttered Word) or Awaz (voice).

(a) Doing obeisance to the Guru Granth Sahib, respectfully, taking a glimpse of the congregation, an embodiment of the Guru's person, and taking the command : these together constitute the view of the Satguru (Immortal destroyer of darkness, the true guru). Raising the drapery covering the Guru Granth Sahib and merely taking a look or making others take a look at the exposed page, without taking command (reading the prescribed hymn) is contrary to Gurmat (Guru's way).

(b) In the course of the congregational sessions, only one thing should be done at a time : performing of kirtan, delivering of discourse, interpretative elaboration of the scriptures, or reading of the scriptures.

(c) Only a Sikh, man or woman, is entitled to be in attendance of the Guru Granth Sahib during the congregational session.

(d) Only a Sikh may read out from the Guru Granth Sahib for others. However, even a non- Sikh may read from it for himself/herself.

(e) For taking the command (Hukam), the hymn that is continuing on the top of the left hand page must be read from the beginning. If the hymn begins on the previous page, turn over the page and read the whole hymn from the beginning to the end. If the scriptural composition that is continuing on the top of the left hand page is a var (ode) then start from the first of the slokas preceding the pauri and read upto the end of the pauri. Conclude the reading at the end of the

Hymn with the line in which the name 'Nanak' occurs.

(f) Hukam must also be taken at the conclusion of the congregational session or after the Ardas.

CHAPTER - VII

Sadharan Path (Completion of Normal Intermittent Reading of the Guru Granth Sahib)

Article VIII

(a) Every Sikh should, as far as possible, maintain a separate and exclusive place for the installation of Guru Granth Sahib, in his home.

(b) Every Sikh, man, woman, boy or girl, should learn Gurmukhi to be able to read the Guru Granth Sahib.

(c) Every Sikh should take the Hukam (Command) of the Guru Granth Sahib in the ambrosial (early)hours of the morning before taking meal. If he/she fails to do that, he/she should read or listen to reading from the Guru Granth Sahib some time during the day. If he/she cannot do that either, during travel etc., or owing to any other impediment, he/she should not give in to a feeling of guilt.

(d) It is desirable that every Sikh should carry on a continuous reading of the Guru Granth Sahib and complete a full reading in one or two months or over a longer period.

(e) While undertaking a full reading of the Guru Granth Sahib, one should recite the Anand Sahib (the first five and the last stanzas) and perform the Ardas. One should, thereafter, read the Japuji. Akhand Path (Uninterrupted-Non-stop-Completion of the reading of the Guru Granth Sahib)

Article IX

(a) The non-stop reading of the Guru Granth Sahib is carried on at hard times or on occasions of elation or joy. It takes approximately fortyeight hours. The non-stop reading implies continuous, uninterrupted reading. The reading must be clear and correct. Reading too fast, so that the person listening in to it cannot follow the contents, amounts to irreverence to the Scriptures. The reading should be correct and clear, due care being bestowed on consonant and vowel even though that takes a little longer to complete.

(b) Whichever family or congregation undertakes the non-stop reading should carry it out itself through its members, relatives, friends, etc., all together. The number of reciters is not prescribed.

If a person, himself, cannot read, he should listen in to the reading by some competent reader. However, it should never be allowed to happen that the reader carries on the reading all by himself/herself and no member of the congregation or the family is listening in to the reading. The reader should be served with food and clothing to the best of the host's means.

(c) Placing a pitcher, ceremonial clarified-butter-fed lamp, coconut, etc. around, during the course of the uninterrupted or any other reading of Guru Granth Sahib, or reading of other Scriptural texts side by side with or in the course of such reading is contrary to the gurmat (Guru's way).

Commencing the Non-Stop Reading (Akhandpath)

Article X

While undertaking the intermittent reading of the whole Guru Granth Sahib, the sacred pudding (Karhah Prashad) for offering should be brought and after reciting the Anand Sahib (six stanzas) and offering Ardas, Hukam should be taken.

While beginning the unbroken reading, the sacred pudding should first be laid. Thereafter, after reciting the Anand Sahib(six stanzas), offering the Ardas and taking the Hukam, the reading should he commenced. Concluding the Reading

Article XI

(a) The reading of the whole Guru Granth Sahib (intermittent or non-stop) may be concluded with the reading of Mundawani or the Rag Mala according to the convention traditionally observed at the concerned place. (Since there is a difference of opinion within the Panth on this issue, nobody should dare to write or print a copy of the Guru Granth Sahib excluding the Rag Mala). Thereafter, after reciting the Anand Sahib, the Ardas of the conclusion of the reading should be offered and the sacred pudding (Karhah Prashad) distributed.

(b) On the conclusion of the reading, offering of draperies, fly-whisk and awning, having regard to the requirements of the Guru Granth Sahib, and of other things, for Panthic causes, should be made to the best of means.

CHAPTER-VIII

Karhah Prashad (Sacred Pudding)

Article XII

(a) Only the sacred pudding which has been prepared or got prepared according to the prescribed method shall be acceptable in the congregation.

(b) The method of preparing the Karhah Prashad is this : In a clean vessel, the three contents (wheat flour, pure sugar and clarified butter, in equal quantities) should he put and it should be made reciting the Scriptures. Then covered with a clean piece of cloth, it should be placed on a clean stool in front of the Guru Granth Sahib. Thereafter, in the holy presence of the Guru Granth Sahib , the first five and the last stanza of the Anand Sahib should be recited aloud (so that the congregation can hear) (If another vessel of the sacred pudding is brought in after the recitation of the Anand, it is not necessary to repeat the recitation of the Anand Sahib. Offering of the sacred Pudding brought later to the sacred Kirpan is enough.), the Ardas, offered and the pudding tucked with the sacred Kirpan for acceptance.

(c) After this, before the distribution to the congregation of the Karhah Prashad, the share of the five beloved ones should be set apart and given away. Thereafter, while commencing the general distribution, the share of the person in attendance of the Guru Granth Sahib (Giving double share to the person in attendance constitutes improper discrimination) should be put in small bowl or vessel and handed over. The person who doles out the Karhah Prashad among the congregation should do so without any discrimination on the basis of personal regard or spite.

He should dole out the Karhah Parshad equally to the Sikh, the non-Sikh or a person of high or low caste. While doling out the Karhah Prashad, no discrimination should be made on considerations of caste or ancestry or being regarded, by some, as untouchable, of persons within the congregation.

(d) The offering of Karhah Prashad should be accompanied by at least two piece in cash.

CHAPTER IX

Exposition of Gurbani (Sikh Holi Scriptures)

Article XIII

(a) The exposition of the Gurbani in a congregational gathering should be carried out only by a Sikh.

(b) The object of the exposition should only be promoting understanding of the Guru's tenets.

(c) The exposition can only be of the ten Guru's writings or utterances, Bhai Gurdas's writings, Bhai Nand Lal's writings or of any generally accepted Panthic book or books of history (which are in agreement with the Guru's tenets) and not of a book of any other faith. However, four illustration, references to a holy person's teachings or those contained in a book may be made

Expository Discourse

Article XIV

No discourse contrary to the Guru's tenets should be delivered inside a Gurdwara.

Gurdwara Service

Article XV

In the Gurdwara the schedule of the congregational service generally is: ceremonial opening of the Guru Granth

Sahib, Kirtan, exposition of scriptures, expository discourses, recitation of Anand Sahib, the Ardas (see Article-IV (3) (a) above), the raising of Fateh slogan and then the slogan of Sat Sri Akal and taking the Hukam.

CHAPTER X

SECTION FOUR

Living in Consonance with Guru's Tenets (Gurmat Rehni)

Article XVI

A Sikh's living, earning livelihood, thinking and conduct should accord with the Guru's tenets. The Guru's tenets are:

(a) Worship should be rendered only to the One Timeless Being and to no god or goddess.

(b) Regarding the ten Gurus, the Guru Granth Sahib and the ten Gurus' word alone as saviours and holy objects of veneration.

(c) Regarding ten Gurus as the effulgence of one light and one single entity.

(d) Not believing in caste or descent untouchabililty, Magic spells, incantation, omens, auspicious times, days and occasions, influence of stars, horoscopic dispositions, Shradh (ritual serving of food to priests for the salvation of ancestor on appointed days as per the lunar calendar), Ancestor worship, khiah (ritual serving of food to priests - Brahmins - on the lunar anniversaries of death of an ancestor) (Two words, shradh and khiah, occuring in this clause connote what appears to be the same thing - the ritual serving of food to the priests (Brahmins). The difference between the connotations of the two words is implicit in the dates on which the ritual is performed. The ritual of serving of food on the lunar anniversary of the death goes by the name khiah; whereas the ritual of serving food on the lunar date corresponding to the date of death during the period of the year designated shradhs is known as sharadh.) pind (offering of funeral barley cakes to the deceased's relatives), patal (ritual donating of food in the belief that that would satisfy the hunger of a departed soul), diva (the ceremony of keeping an oil lamp lit for 360 days after the death, in the belief that that lights the path of the deceased), ritual funeral acts. hom (lighting of ritual fire and pouring intermittently clarified butter, food grains etc. into it for propitiating gods for the fulfilment of a purpose), jag (religious ceremony involving presentation of oblations), tarpan (libation), sikha-sut (keeping a tuft of hair on the head and wearing thread), bhadan (shaving of head on the death of a parent), fasting on new or full moon or other days, wearing of frontal marks on forehead, wearing of thread, wearing of a necklace of the pieces of tulsi (A plant with medicinal properties, Bot, Ocimum sanctum.), stalk, veneration of any graves, of monuments erected to honour the memory of a deceased person or of cremation sites, idolatry and such like superstitious observances (Most, though not all, rituals and ritual or religious observances listed in this clause are hindu rituals and observances. The reason is that the old rituals and practices, continues to be observed by large numbers of Sikhs even after their conversion from their old to new faith and a large bulk of the Sikhs novices were Hindu converts. Another reason for this phenomenon was the strangle hold of the Brahmin priest on Hindus' secular and religious life which the Brahmin priests managed to maintain even on those leaving the Hindu religious fold, by the his astute mental dexterity and rare capacity for compromise. That the Sikh novitiates included a sizeable number of Muslims is shown by inclusion in this clause of the taboos as to the sanctity of graves, shirni etc.)

Not owning up or regarding as hallowed any place other than the Guru's place- such, for instance, as sacred sports or places of pilgrimage of other faiths.

Not believing in or according any authority to Muslim seers, Brahmins' holiness, soothsayers, clairvoyants, oracles, promise of an offering on the fulfillment of a wish, offering of sweet loaves or rice pudding at graves on fulfillment of wishes, the Vedas, the Shastras, the Gayatri,(Hindu scriptural prayer unto the sun) the Gita, the Quaran, the Bible, etc. However, the study of the books of other faiths for general self-education is admissible.

(e) The Khalsa should maintain its distinctiveness among the professors of different religions of the world, but should not hurt the sentiments of any person professing another religion.

(f) A Sikh should pray to God before launching off any task.

(g) Learning Gurmukhi (Punjabi in Gurmukhi script) is essential for a Sikh. He should pursue other studies also.

(h) It is a Sikh's duty to get his children educated in Sikhism.

(i) A Sikh should, in no way, harbour any antipathy to the hair of the head with which his child is born. He should not temper with the hair with which the child is born. He should add the suffix "Singh" to the name of his son & "Kaur" to the name of his daughter. A

Sikh should keep the hair of his sons and daughters intact.

(j) A Sikh must not take hemp (cannabis), opium, liquor, tobacco, in short, any intoxicant. His only routine intake should be food.

(k) Piercing of nose or ears for wearing ornaments is forbidden for Sikh men and women.

(l) A Sikh should not kill his daughter; nor should he maintain any relationship with a killer of daughter.

(m)The true Sikh of the Guru shall make an honest living by lawful work.

(n) A Sikh shall regard a poor person's mouth as the Guru's cash offerings box.

(o) A Sikh shall not steal, form dubious associations or engage in gambling.

(p) He who regards another man's daughter as his own daughter, regards another man's wife as his mother, has coition with his own wife alone, he alone is a truly disciplined Sikh of the Guru. A Sikh woman shall likewise keep within the confines of conjugal rectitude.

(q) A Sikh shall observe the Sikh rules of conduct and conventions from his birth right upto the end of his life.

(r) A Sikh, when he meets another Sikh, should greet him with "Waheguru ji ka Khalsa, Waheguru ji ki Fateh" (Rendered into English:The Khalsa is Waheguru's; victory too is His !). This is ordained for Sikh men and women both.

(s) It is not proper for a Sikh woman to wear veil or keep her face hidden by veil or cover

(t) For a Sikh, there is no restriction or requirement as to dress except that he must wear Kachhehra (A drawer type garment fastened by a fitted string round the waist, very often worn as an underwear.) and turban. A Sikh woman may or may not tie turban.

CHAPTER XI

Ceremonies pertaining to Birth and Naming of Child

Article XVII

(a) In a Sikh's household, as soon after the birth of a child as the mother becomes capable of moving about and taking bath (irrespective of the number of days which that takes), the family and relatives should go to a Gurdwara with Karhah Prashad (sacred pudding) or get Karhah Prashad made in the Gurdwara and recite in the holy presence of the Guru Granth Sahib such hymns as "Parmeshar dita bana" {Sorath M. 5} (The Almighty Lord has granted support. [Sorath M. 5, Guru Granth Sahib P. 628]), "Satguru sache dia bhej" {Asa M. 5} (The true Lord has sent this gift. [Asa M. 5, Guru Granth Sahib P. 396]) that are expressive of joy and thankfulness. Thereafter if a reading of the holy Guru Granth Sahib had been taken up, that should be concluded. Then the holy Hukam (command) should be taken. A name starting with the first letter of the Shabad of the Hukam (command) should he proposed by the Granthi (man in attendance of Guru Granth Sahib) and, after its acceptance by the congregation, the name should be announced by him. The boy's name must have the suffix "Singh" and the girl's, the suffix "Kaur".

After that the Anand Sahib (short version comprising six stanzas) should be recited and the Ardas in appropriate terms expressing joy over the naming ceremony be offered and the Karhah Prashad distributed.

(b) The superstition as to the pollution of food and water in consequence of birth (There is a wide-spread belief among certain sections of Indian people that a birth in a household causes pollution (sutak) which is removed by the thorough bathing of the mother, the baby and persons attending on her as also by a thorough cleaning of the house, the utensils and the clothes, after prescribed periods of ten, twenty one and forty days.) must not be subscribed to, for the holy writ is : "The birth and death are by His ordinance; coming and going is by His will. All food and water are, in principle, clean, for these life-sustaining substances are provided by Him."

(c) Making shirts or frocks for children out of the Holy Book's draperies is a sacrilege.

Anand Sanskar (Lit. Joyful Ceremonial : Sikh Matrimonial Ceremony and Conventions)

Article XVIII

(a) A Sikh man and woman should enter wedlock without giving thought to the prospective spouse's caste and descent.

(b) A Sikh's daughter must be married to a Sikh.

(c) A Sikh's marriage should be solemnized by Anand marriage rites.

(d) Child marriage is taboo for Sikhs.

(e) When a girl becomes marriageable, physically, emotionally and by virtue of maturity of character, a suitable Sikh match should be found and she be married to him by Anand marriage rites.

(f) Marriage may not be preceded by engagement ceremony. But if an engagement ceremony is sought to he held, a congregational gathering should be held and, after offering the Ardas before the Guru Granth Sahib, a kirpan, a steel bangle and some sweets may be tendered to the boy.

(g) Consulting horoscopes for determining which day or date is auspicious or otherwise for fixing the day of the marriage is a sacrilege. Any day that the parties find suitable by mutual consultation should be fixed.

(h) Putting on floral or gilded face ornamentation, decorative headgear or red thread band round the wrist, worshipping of ancestors, dipping feet in milk mixed with water, cutting a berry or jandi (Prosopis spieigera) bushes, filling pitcher, ceremony of retirement in feigned displeasure, reciting couplets, performing havans (Sacrificial fire), installing vedi (a wooden canopy or pavilion under which Hindu marriages are performed), prostitutes' dances, drinking liquor, are all sacrileges.

(i) The marriage party should have as small a number of people as the girl's people desire. The two sides should greet each other singing sacred hymns and finally by the Sikh greetings of Waheguru ji ka Khalsa, Waheguru ji ki Fateh.

(j) For marriage, there should be a congregational gathering in the holy presence of Guru Granth Sahib. There should be hymn-singing by ragis or by the whole congregation. Then the girl and the boy should he made to sit facing the Guru Granth Sahib. The girl should sit on the left side of the boy. After soliciting the congregation's permission, the master of the marriage ceremony (who may be a man or a woman) should bid the boy and girl and their parents or guardians to stand and should offer the Ardas for the commencement of the Anand marriage ceremony.

The officiant should then apprise the boy and the girl of the duties and obligations of conjugal life according to the Guru's tenets.

He should initially give to the two an exposition of their common mutual obligations. He should tell them how to model the husband-wife relationship on the love between the individual soul and the Supreme Soul in the light of the contents of circumambulation (Lavan) hymns in the Suhi measure (rag) section (The bulk of the Guru Granth (the Sikh holy book) is divided on the basis of the ragas (measures) of the Indian classical music. Suhi is one of the ragas featuring in the Guru Granth Sahib) of the Guru Granth Sahib.

He should explain to them the notion of the state of "a single soul in two bodies" to be achieved through love and make them see how they may attain union with the Immortal Being discharging duties and obligations of the householders' life. Both of them, they should be told, have to make their conjugal union a means to the fulfillment of the purpose of the journey of human existence; both have to lead clean and Guru-oriented lives through the instrumentality of their union.

He should then explain to the boy and girl individually their respective conjugal duties as husband and wife.

The bridegroom should be told that the girl's people having chosen him as the fittest match from among a whole lot, he should regard his wife as his better half, accord to unflinching love and share with her all that he has. In all situations, he should protect her person and honour, he should be completely loyal to her and he should show much respect and consideration for her parents and relations as for his own.

The girl should be told that she has been joined in matrimony to her man in the hallowed presence of the Guru Granth Sahib and the congregation. She should ever harbour for him deferential solicitude, regard him the lord master of her love and trust; she should remain firm in her loyalty to him and serve him in joy and sorrow and in every clime (native or foreign) and should show the same regard and consideration to his parents and relatives as she would, to her own parents and relatives.

The boy and girl should bow before the Guru Granth Sahib to betoken their acceptance of these instructions. Thereafter, the girl's father or the principal relation should make the girl grasp one end of the sash which the boy is wearing over his shoulders and the person in attendance of the Guru Granth Sahib should recite the matrimonial circumambulation stanzas {Lavan of the fourth Guru in the Suhi musical measure section of the Guru Granth Sahib } (Pp. 773-4). After the conclusion of the recitation of each of the stanzas, the boy, followed by the girl holding the end of the sash, should go round the Guru Granth Sahib while the ragis or the congregation sing out the recited stanza.

The boy and girl, after every circumambulation, should bow before the Guru Granth Sahib in genuflexion, lowering their forehead to touch the ground and then stand up to listen to the recitation of the next stanza.There being four matrimonial circumambulation stanzas in the concerned hymn, the proceeding will comprise four circumambulations with the incidental singing of the stanza.After the fourth circumabulation, the boy and girl should, after bowing before the Guru Granth Sahib, sit down at the appointed place and the Ragis or the person who has conducted the ceremony should recite the first five and the last stanza of the Anand Sahib. Thereafter, the Ardas should he offered to mark the conclusion of the Anand marriage ceremony and the sacred pudding, distributed'.

(k) Persons professing faiths other than the Sikh faith cannot be joined in wedlock by the Anand Karaj ceremony.

(l) No Sikh should accept a match for his/her son or daughter for monetary consideration.

(m)If the girl's parents at any time or on any occasion visit their daughter's home and a meal is ready there, they should not hesitate to eat there. Abstaining from eating at the girl's home is a superstition. The Khalsa has been blessed with the boon of victuals and making others eat by the Guru and the Immortal Being. The girl's and boy's people should keep accepting each other's hospitality, because the Guru has joined them in relationship of equality (Prem Sumarag).

(n) If a woman's husband has died, she may, if she so wishes, finding a match suitable for her, remarry. For a Sikh man whose wife has died, similar ordinance obtains.

(o) The remarriage may be solemnized in the same manner as the Anand marriage.

(p) Generally, no Sikh should marry a second wife if the first wife is alive.

(q) A baptised ought to get his wife also baptised.

Funeral Ceremonies (Antam Sanskar)

Article XIX

(a) The body of a dying or dead person, if it is on a cot, must not be taken off the cot z and put on the floor. Nor must a lit lamp be placed beside, or a cow got bestowed in donation by, him/her or for his/her good or any other ceremony, contrary to Guru's way,performed. Only Gurbani should be recited or "Waheguru, Waheguru" repeated by his/her side.

(b) When some one shuffles the mortal coil, the survivors must not grieve or raise a hue and cry or indulge in breast beating. To induce a mood of resignation to God's will, it is desirable to recite Gurbani or repeat "Waheguru".

(c) However young the deceased may be, the body should be cremated. However, where arrangements for cremation cannot be made, there should be no qualm about the body being immersed in flowing water or disposed of in any other manner.

(d) As to the time of cremation, no consideration as to whether it should take place during day or night should weigh.

(e) The dead body should be bathed and clothed in clean clothes. While that is done, the Sikh symbols-comb, kachha, karha, kirpan-should not be taken off. Thereafter putting the body on a plank, Ardas about its being taken away for disposal be offered. The hearse should then be lifted and taken to the cremation ground. While the body is being carried to the cremation ground, hymns that induce feelings of detachment should be recited. On reaching the cremation ground, the pyre should be laid. Then the

Ardas for consigning the body to fire be offered. The dead body should then be placed on the pyre and the son or any other relation or friend of the deceased should set fire to it, The accompanying congregation should sit at a reasonable distance and listen to kirtan or carry on collective singing of hymns or recitation of detachment-inducing hymns. When the pyre is fully aflame, the Kirtan Sohila (prescribed preretirement night Scriptural prayer) be recited and the Ardas offered. (Piercing the Skull half an hour or so after the pyre has been burning with a rod or something else in the belief that will secure the release of the soul- kapal kriya-is contrary to the Guru's tenets). The congregation should then leave. Coming back home, a reading of the Guru Granth Sahib should be commenced at home or in a nearby Gurdwara, and after reciting the six stanzas of the Anand Sahib, the Ardas, offered and Karhah prashad (sacred pudding) distributed. The reading of the Guru Granth Sahib should be completed on the tenth day. If the reading cannot, or is sought not to, be completed on the tenth day, some other day may be appointed for the conclusion of the reading having regard to the convenience of the relatives. The reading of the Guru Granth Sahib should be carried out by the members of the household of the deceased and relatives in cooperation. If possible, Kirtan may be held every night. No funeral ceremony remains to be performed after the "tenth day."

(f) When the pyre is burnt out, the whole bulk of the ashes, including the burnt bones, should be gathered up and immersed in flowing water or buried at that very place and the ground levelled. Raising a monument to the memory of the deceased at the place where his dead body is cremated is taboo.

(g) Adh Marg (the ceremony of breaking the pot used for bathing the dead body amid doleful cries half way towards the cremation ground), organised lamentation by women, foorhi (sitting on a straw mat in mourning for a certain period), diva (keeping an oil lamp lit for 360 days after the death in the belief that that will light the path of the deceased), Pind (ritual donating of lumps of rice flour, oat flour, or solidified milk (khoa) for ten days after death), kirya (concluding the funeral proceedings ritualistically, serving meals and making offerings by way of Shradh, Budha marna (waving of whisk, over the hearse of an old person's dead body and decorating the hearse with festoons), etc. are contrary to the approved code. So too is the picking of the burnt bones from the ashes of the pyre for immersing in the Ganga, at Patalpuri (Kiratpur), at Kartarpur Sahib or at any other such place.

Other Rites and Conventions

Article XX

Apart from these rites and conventions, on every happy or sad occasion, such as moving into a new house, setting up a new business (shop), putting a child to school, etc., a Sikh should pray for God's help by performing the Ardas. The essential components of all rites and ceremonies in Sikhism are the recitation of the Gurbani (Sikh Scriptures) and the performing of the Ardas.

CHAPTER-XII

SECTION FIVE

Voluntary Service

Article XXI

1. Seva (Voluntry Service) is a prominent part of Sikh religion. Illustrative models of voluntary service are organised for imparting training, in the Gurdwaras. Its simple forms are : sweeping and plastering the floors (In older times, buildings, particularly in rural areas had mud and not brick paved or cement floors. To give these floors firmness and consistency, they were thinly plastered with a diluted compound of mud.) of the Gurdwara, serving water to or fanning the congregation, offering provisions to and rendering any kind of service in the common kitchen-cum-eating house, dusting the shoes of the people visiting the Gurdwara, etc.

   (a) Guru Ka Langar (Guru's Kitchen-cum-Eating House) The philosophy behind the Langar (Guru's kitchen-cum-eating-house) is two-fold : to provide training to the Sikhs in voluntary service and to help banish all distinction of high and low, touchable and untouchable from the Sikhs' minds.

   (b) All human beings, high or low, and of any caste or colour may sit and eat in the Langar. No discrimination on grounds of the country of origin, colour, caste or religion must be made while making people sit in rows for eating. However, only baptised (Amritdhari) Sikhs can eat off one plate.

CHAPPTER XIII

Panthic Rehni (Facets of Corporate Sikh Life)

Article XXII

The essential facets of Panthic life are :

1. Guru Panth (the Panth's Guru status);
2. The ceremony of ambrosial initiation.
3. The statute of chastisement for aberrations;
4. The statute of collective resolution (Gurmata).
5. The appeal against local decisions.

Panth's Status of Guruhood

Article XXIII

The concept of service is not confined to fanning the congregation, service to and in the Guru ka Langar etc. A Sikh's entire life is a life of benevolent exertion. The most fruitful service is the service that secures the optimum good by minimal endeavour. That can be achieved through organised collective action. A Sikh has, for this reason, to fulfil his/her Panthic obligations (obligations as a member of the corporate entity, the Panth), even as he/she performs his/ her individual duties. This corporate entity is the Panth. Every Sikh has also to fulfil his obligations as a unit of the corporate body, the Panth.

(a) The Guru Panth (Panth's status of Guruhood) means the whole body of committed baptised (Amritdhari) Sikhs. This body was fostered by all the ten Gurus and the tenth Guru gave it its final shape and invested it with Guruhood.

Ceremony of Baptism or Initiation

Article XXIV

(a) Ambrosial baptism should be held at an exclusive place away from common human traffic.

(b) At the place where ambrosial baptism is to be administered, the holy Guru Granth Sahib should be installed and ceremonially opened. Also present should be six committed baptised Sikhs, one of whom should sit in attendance of the Guru Granth Sahib and the other five should be there to administer the ambrosial baptism. These six may even include Sikh women. All of them must have taken bath and washed their hair

(c) The five beloved (Panj Piyare) ones who administer ambrosial baptism not include a disabled person, such as a person who is blind or blind in one eye, lame, one with a broken or disabled limb, or one suffering from some chronic disease. The number should not include anyone who has committed a breach of the Sikh discipline and principles. All of them should be committed baptised Sikhs with appealing personalities.

(d) Any man or woman of any country, religion or caste who embraces Sikhism and solemnly undertakes to abide by its principles is entitled to ambrosial baptism.The person to be baptised should not be of very young age; he or she should have attained a plausible degree of discretion. The person to be baptised must have taken bath and washed the hair and must wear all five K's-Kesh (unshorn hair), strapped Kirpan (sword),. Kachhehra (prescribed shorts), Kanga (Comb tucked in the tied up hair), Karha (Steel bracelet). He/she must not have on his/her person any token of any other faith. He/she must not have his/her head bare or be wearing a cap. He/she must not be wearing any ornaments piercing through any part of the body. The persons to be baptised must stand respectfully with hands folded facing the Guru Granth Sahib.

(e) Anyone seeking to be rebaptised, having committed an aberration, should be singled out and the five beloved ones should award chastisement to him/her in the presence of the congregation.

(f) One from amongst the five beloved ones administering ambrosial baptism to persons seeking to be baptised should explain the principles of the Sikh religion to them: The Sikh religion advocates the renunciation of the worship of any created thing, and rendering of worship and loving devotion to, and meditating on, the One Supreme Creator. For the fulfillment of such devotion and meditation, reflection on the contents of Gurbani and practising of its tenets, participation in the congregational services, rendering service to the Panth, benevolent exertion (to promote the good of others), love of God's name (loving reflection on and experience of the Divine), living within the Sikh discipline after getting Amrit etc. are the principal means. He should conclude his exposition of the principles of Sikh religion with the query : Do you accept these willingly?

(g) On an affirmative response from the seekers of baptism, one from amongst the five beloved ones should perform the Ardas for the preparation of baptism and take the holy Hukam (command) (Reading or Reading out to others, including the congregation, of a Shabad (hymn) or a unit of one or more slokas (short scriptual compositions normally of Two to Four lines) and a pauri (short stanza of of four or more lines) from the Guru Granth Sahib after, or even without performing the Ardas is an important Sikh ritual. It is called hukam laina (Taking the order or command), Vak Laina (taking the Word), Awaz laina (taking the voice). The hymn or unit goes by the name of Hukam (order, command) vak (uttered Word) or Awaz (voice)). The five beloved ones should come close to the bowl for preparing the amrit (ambrosial nectar).

(h) The bowl should be of pure steel and it should be placed on a clean steel ring or other clean support.

(i) Clean water and sugar puffs should be put in the bowl and the five beloved ones should sit around it in bir posture (Sitting in bir posture comprised sitting resting the body on the right leg, the right calf and foot gathered inward and the left leg upto the shin kept in a verticle positon.) and recite the undermentioned scriptural compositions.

(j) The scriptural composition to be recited are : The Japuji, The Jaap, The Ten Sawayyas (commencing with Sarawag Sud), The Bainti Chaupai (From "hamri karo hath dai rachha" to "dusht dokh te leho te bachai"), Anand Sahib.

(k) Each of the five beloved ones who recites the scripture should hold the edge of the bowl with his left hand and keep stirring the water with a double-edged sword held in his right hand. He should do that with full concentration. The rest of the beloved ones should keep gripping the edge of the bowl with both hands concentrating their full attention on the ambrosial nector.

(l) After the conclusion of the recitation, one from amongst the beloved ones should perform the Ardas.

(m) Only that person seeking to be baptised who has participated in the entire ceremony of ambrosial baptism can be baptised. One who has turned up while the ceremony was in progress cannot be baptised.

(n) After the Ardas as per clause (I) above, thinking of our Father, the Tenth Master, the wearer of the aigrette, every person seeking to be baptised should sit in Bir Posture putting his/her right hand cupped on the left cupped hand and be made to drink the ambrosial mix five times, as the beloved one who pours the mix into his cupped hand exclaims : say, Waheguru ji ka Khalsa, Waheguru ji ki Fateh! (The Khalsa is of the Wondrous Destroyer of darkness; victory, too, is His!) The person being baptised should after imbibing the ambrosia, repeat : Waheguru ji ka Khalsa, Waheguru ji ki Fateh. Then five handfuls of the ambrosial mix should he sprinkled into the eyes of the person being baptised and another five into his hair. Each such sprinkling should be accompanied by the beloved one administering baptism saying, "Waheguru ji ka Khalsa Waheguru ji ki Fateh", and the person being baptised repeating the chant. Whatever ambrosial mix is left over after the administration of the ambrosial Baptism to all individual seekers, should be shipped by all (men and women) baptised together.

(o) After this the five beloved ones, all together in chorus communicating the name of Waheguru to all who have been administered the ambrosial baptism, recite to them the Mul Mantar (basic creed, seminal chant) and make them repeat it aloud :

Ik aunkar satnam karta purakh nirbhau nirwair akal murat ajuni saibhang gur prasad.

(p) After this, one from amongst the five beloved ones should explain to the initiates the discipline of the order : * Today you are reborn in the true Guru's household, ending the cycle of migration, and joined the Khalsa Panth (order). *Your spiritual father is now Guru Gobind Singh and spiritual mother, Mata Sahib Kaur. *Your place of birth is Kesgarh Sahib and your native place is Anandpur Sahib. You, being the sons of one father, are, inter-se yourselves and other baptised Sikhs, spiritual brothers. You have become the pure Khalsa, having renounced your previous lineage, professional background, calling (occupation), beliefs, that is, having given up all connections with your caste, descent, birth, country, religion, etc. You are to worship none except the One Timeless Being (Waheguru) no God, Goddess, incarnation or prophet. You are not to think of anyone except the ten Gurus and anything except their gospel as your saviour. You are supposed to know Gurmukhi (Punjabi alphabet). (If you do not, you must learn it). And recite, or listen in to the recitation of, the under mentioned scriptural compositions, the daily repetition of which is ordained, every day :*(1)* The Japuji Sahib, *(2)* The Jaap Sahib, *(3)* The Ten Sawayyas (Quartrains), beginning "sarawag sudh", *(4)* The Sodar Rahiras and the Sohila. Besides, you should read from or listen in to the recitation from the Guru Granth Sahib . Have, on your person, all the time, the five K's :

I. The Keshas (unshorn hair),

II. The Kirpan {sheathed sword} (The length of the sword to be worn is not prescribed.,

III. The Kachhehra (The Kachhehra (drawers like garment) may be made from any cloth, but its legs should not reach down to below the shins.),

IV. The Kanga (comb),

V. The Karha {steel bracelet} (The Karha should be of pure steel.)

The undermentioned four transgressions (tabooed practices) must be avoided

1. Dishonouring the hair;
2. Eating the meat of an animal slaughtered the Muslim way;
3. Cohabiting with a person other than one's spouse;
4. Using tobacco.

In the event of the commission of any of these transgressions, the transgressor must get baptised again. If a transgression is committed unintentionally and unknowingly, the transgressor shall not be liable to punishment. You must not associate with a Sikh who had uncut hair earlier and has cut it or a Sikh who smokes. You must ever be ready for the service of the Panth and of the Gurdwaras (Sikh places of worship). You must tender one tenth (Daswand) of your earnings to the Guru.

In short, you must act the Guru's way in all spheres of activity.

You must remain fully aligned to the Khalsa brotherhood in accordance with the principles of the Khalsa faith. If you commit transgression of the Khalsa discipline, you must present yourself before the congregation and beg pardon, accepting whatever punishment is awarded. You must also resolve to remain watchful against defaults in the future.

(q) The following individuals shall be liable to chastisement involving automatic boycott:

1. Anyone maintaining relations or communion with elements antagonistic to the Panth including the minas (reprobates), the masands (agents once accredited to local Sikh communities as Guru's representatives, since discredited for their faults and aberrations), followers of Dhirmal or Ram Rai, et. al., or users of tobacco or killers of female infants

2. One who eats/drinks Left-overs of the unbaptised or the fallen Sikhs;

3. One who dyes his beard;

4. One who gives off son or daughter in matrimony for a price or reward;

5. Users of intoxicants (hemp, opium, liquor, narcotics, cocaine, etc.);

6. One holding, or being a party to, ceremonies or practices contrary to the Guru's way;

7. One who defaults in the maintenance of Sikh discipline.

(r) After this sermon, one from among the five beloved ones should perform the Ardas.

(s) Thereafter, the Sikh sitting in attendance of the Guru Granth Sahib should take the Hukam. If anyone from amongst those who have received the ambrosial baptism had not earlier been named in accordance with the Sikh Naming Ceremony, he should renounce his previous name and be given a new name beginning with first letter of the Hukam now taken.

(t) And finally, the karhah prashad should be distributed. All the newly launched Sikh men and women should eat the karhah prashad together off the same bowl.

Method of Imposing Chastisement (Tankah)

Article XXV

(a) Any Sikh who has committed any default in the observance of the Sikh discipline should approach the nearby Sikh congregation and make a confession of his lapse standing before the congregation.

(b) The congregation should then, in the holy presence of Guru Granth Sahib, elect from among themselves five beloved ones who should ponder over the suppliant's fault and propose the chastisement (punishment) for it.

(c) The congregation should not take an obdurate stand in granting pardon. Nor should the defaulter argue about the chastisement. The punishment that is imposed should be some kind of service, especially some service that can be performed with hands.

(d) And finally an Ardas for correction should be performed.

Method of Adopting Gurmatta

Article XXVI

(a) The Gurmatta (Holy Resolution) can only be on a subject that affects the fundamental principles of Sikh religion and for their upholding, such as the questions affecting the maintenance of the status of the Gurus or the Guru Granth Sahib or the inviolability of Guru Granth Sahib, ambrosial baptism, Sikh discipline and way of life, the identity and structural framework of the Panth. Ordinary issues of religious, educational, social or political nature can be dealt with only in a Matta. (Resolution)

(b) A Gurmatta can be adopted only by a select primary Panthic group or a representative gathering of the Panth.

Appeals against Local Decisions

Article XXVII

An appeal can be made to the **Akal Takht** against a local congregation's decision.

The above text is edited and taken from the Book **Sikh Reht Maryada** published by Dharam Parchar Committee (Shiromani Gurdwara Parbhandak Committee, Amritsar) in July, 1997.

●●

Index